LANDMARKS OF LOS ANGELES

TEXT AND PHOTOGRAPHS BY PATRICK McGREW AND ROBERT JULIAN

LANDMARKS OF

HARRY N. ABRAMS, INC., PUBLISHERS

LOS ANGELES

FOR OUR FAMILIES:
DANICE, MARCIA, RUFUS,
INEZ, AND MICKEY

EDITOR: MARK GREENBERG

DESIGNER: ELISSA ICHIYASU

Library of Congress Cataloging-in-Publication Data
McGrew, Patrick
Landmarks of Los Angeles / text and photographs
by Patrick McGrew and Robert Julian
p.   cm.
Includes bibliographical references and index.
ISBN 0–8109–3572–4
1. Historic buildings—California—Los Angeles—
Pictorial works.
2. Architecture—California—Los Angeles—
Pictorial works.
3. Los Angeles (Calif.)—Buildings, structures,
etc.—Pictorial works.
I. Julian, Robert.
II. Title
F868.L843M38   1994
979.4'94—dc20   93–21192
Copyright © 1994 Patrick McGrew
Published in 1994 by Harry N. Abrams,
Incorporated, New York
A Times Mirror Company
Printed and bound in Japan

CONTENTS

ACKNOWLEDGMENTS

One could say that every building, in every city, has a story to tell. Walking through the streets of foreign cities and admiring the architecture, we often wonder what events have occurred behind these façades. Many times there is no record of the births or deaths, of the hopes or dreams of those who came before. Part of the enduring attraction of preservation is this kind of curiosity. What happened here? How did this building come to be? Who were the players, and what were the circumstances that motivated the construction of this city, this neighborhood, this house? How would life be different without these familiar buildings?

The case files of the Los Angeles Cultural Heritage Commission often go a long way toward answering these questions for selected buildings, and certainly in more recent times—as the preservation process has matured—the information is more detailed and complete. In 1987, on the occasion of the Commission's twenty-fifth anniversary, David Cameron and Tom Owen wrote a booklet for the Commission documenting their work. Without this text, it would have been very difficult for us to determine the significance of some of the earliest listings, and we are grateful for this fine introduction to the task we were about to undertake.

Fortunately, many of the buildings listed by the Commission are famous, even legendary, so cross-checking and verifying information was often relatively easy. For the more obscure structures, verification was sought through a few key sources. An increasing familiarity with Los Angeles's famous early names made pleasurable the search through Harris Newmark's definitive *Sixty Years in Southern California*. The often updated, though occasionally flawed, *Historic Spots in California* was particularly useful for its information on early California buildings. David Gebhard and Robert Winter's *A Guide to Architecture in Southern California* and *Architecture in Los Angeles* are remarkable for the breadth of information they offer. Charles Moore's trenchant wit, as expressed in *Los Angeles: The City Observed*, cheered us when our task seemed daunting. Finally, when erudition was called for vis à vis regional architecture, we found no substitute for Harold Kirker's perspective as expressed in both *California's Architectural Frontier* and *Old Forms on a New Land*; he certainly deserves no blame if we have misinterpreted what he said. The works of San Franciscan Kevin Starr suggested an outline upon which to hang our understanding by his enumeration of the signal events in the region. Starr made our education especially enjoyable in his remarkable *Material Dreams*. To these writers, and to the others too numerous to acknowledge individually here, we offer our unlimited gratitude. They provided a solid base of good information.

We hope that *Landmarks of Los Angeles* will serve to promote an understanding of what has been accomplished up to now in preserving the city, that it will stimulate curiosity about the wonderful historic and architectural resources that remain here (protected and otherwise), and that it will provide a context for future evaluation and decision making. The next thirty years of preservation in Los Angeles will likely be as interesting and rich as the last thirty, a claim that only a city with this diversity and assembled heritage can honestly make.

We would like to thank our friends Bill Wilkinson and Tom Givin for the use of their home during our Los Angeles photo shoots; the legendary Julius Shulman, whose work often showed us how to approach our own; our late colleague Peter Snell for his love and understanding of El Pueblo and Silver Lake; Eric Wright, for his reminiscences about his father, Lloyd; Linda Dishman and Christeen Taniguchi of the Los Angeles Conservancy and Christy Johnson McEvoy for assistance in researching architects' biographical information; Karen Voight for keeping one half of this team sane with her athleticism; and, of course, the property owners at the Ollie Tract and at the Lovell, Millbank / McFee, and Ashley residences, all of whom were cordial to us in spite of our nosy cameras. We are grateful also to the members of the Cultural Heritage Commission and their staff, who, over the years, have continued to oversee this extraordinary collection.

Finally, no book happens only through the efforts of its writers. We are especially grateful to our friend Ned Bayrd; to our editor, Mark Greenberg, who saw this project through to completion; and our designer, Elissa Ichiyasu, who made it beautiful.

Patrick McGrew
Robert Julian
Spring 1993

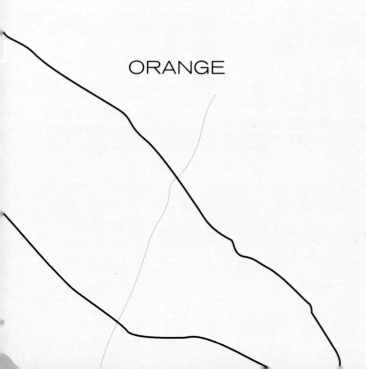

SAN BERNADINO

ANGELES

LOS ANGELES
AND VICINITY

ORANGE

RIVERSIDE

INTRODUCTION

In the preparation of this book, we spent the last year and a half examining, photographing, and documenting the historic buildings of Los Angeles, and trying to digest the mountains of written material about the city. The process included mapping and locating 576 buildings and 4 Historic Districts, and in this effort our Thomas Brothers maps were indispensable. The landmarks are grouped by neighborhood, as suggested by these maps. The most important source documents were the case files of the Los Angeles Cultural Heritage Commission; they form the basis for declaring Historic-Cultural Monuments (HCMs) and also serve as the basis for this book. Our efforts herein focus only on those landmarks officially designated by the City of Los Angeles. The designations of other county, state, or federal agencies are not the subject of this book.

To our surprise, the question we encountered most often during our research was, "Landmarks in Los Angeles?" People seem unable or unwilling to believe that anything of historic value has been retained by the city. We can only attribute this to Los Angeles's international reputation for rapid growth and change, as well as its image as a city of the future, not the past. But only in Beirut or Sarajevo are all landmarks destroyed!

LOS ANGELES: THE AREA DEFINED

The united cities of Los Angeles include many vanished historic towns, most of which are now known only as neighborhoods. People accept the idea that historic structures might remain in say, Calabasas, or Hyde Park, or even "old" Hollywood, but they are astounded when they discover how many important historic buildings are found in the city center. Yet those who visit downtown Los Angeles discover many remaining historic structures from the turn of the century through the Art Deco period. The film *Blade Runner* left an indelible impression of Los Angeles upon the American consciousness with its graphic visual speculation about Los Angeles's future. Director Ridley Scott employed real historic structures like the Bradbury Building and the as yet unprotected Million Dollar Theater as part of his vision of the future.

Understanding the preservation puzzle of Los Angeles requires a definition of the literal territory involved. The approximately 125 towns filling the Los Angeles basin do not constitute the official City of Los Angeles. While many well-known "towns" are now part of the city—such as San Pedro and Wilmington in the south, and Eagle Rock in the northeast—many neighboring towns have maintained their independence. Pasadena and Glendale are incorporated in their own right, and their rich historic architecture is protected by both privately and publicly maintained preservation programs. Santa Monica and Beverly Hills are also municipally independent from Los Angeles. Unfortunately, Beverly Hills is seeing more demolitions of architecturally significant domestic architecture than probably any place in the world. These "teardowns," as they are called, are epitomized by the near total demolition of Pickfair (a renovation carried out from 1926 through 1934 by architect Wallace Neff for Mary Pickford and Douglas Fairbanks) by entertainer Pia Zadora and her husband, Meshulam Riklis. Sadly, this famous case is but the tip of the

demolition iceberg in Beverly Hills, a town where money often speaks louder than history. Spearheaded by Jack Lemmon, the Citizens for the Preservation of Beverly Hills are beginning to make their voice heard on this issue.

To make the situation more complicated, a few landmarks protected by the city ordinance are not even in Los Angeles. Far-flung Los Angeles monuments include a carousel that was moved to San Francisco in the 1930s and the infamous and desolate Manzanar War Relocation Center in Inyo County.

GUIDEBOOKS

Guidebooks and other promotional materials about Southern California have been appearing on a regular basis since the 1884 publication of *Ramona*, a fictional account of life in early California by Helen Hunt Jackson. It became one of the most widely read American novels of its time. *Ramona*'s highly romantic images stimulated the imagination of many travelers who came to California with guidebooks in hand, seeking the locations of many of the book's fictional events.

Landmarks of Los Angeles is the next instance of a written tradition that invites the reader to visit historical sites either in person or through these pages. It is actually a hybrid combining regional history, architecture, photography, and travel. It should not be viewed as a complete history of the region (much more scholarly histories already exist), although a general sense of the evolution of Los Angeles unfolds through illustrations and written descriptions of the buildings included. By definition, the designation process reflects only a partial history of the architecture of the region; buildings are selected in an effort to prevent imminent

or potential destruction, rather than through any observable curatorial decision. By sheer numbers alone, the designation process results in a broad sampling of the important architectural styles and variations that have found expression in Los Angeles. Using our work as a guidebook, readers will find themselves directed to those sites and buildings chosen for official recognition and protection by the City of Los Angeles Cultural Heritage Commission; along the way, the rest of Los Angeles reveals itself.

As a documentary record (in both style and content) of the official preservation activities of the City of Los Angeles, with a short discussion of the origins of each building, structure, or site, this book reveals a fascinating history. To the extent possible, the statements accompanying each listing illustrate how and why these buildings came into being: the backgrounds of the original owners and architects; when the buildings were built; and other information that allows these buildings to be known to the larger community and helps bring them to life for the reader.

HISTORY OF PRESERVATION IN LOS ANGELES

Preservation increasingly is recognized not only as a valuable civic activity but as one whose roots in the United States are almost as old as the country itself. As early as 1816, Philadelphia's Old State House was saved from a threatened demolition. According to William Murtagh, the first known preservation activity in the United States took place in the early nineteenth century with the restoration of the Touro Synagogue in Newport, Rhode Island, in 1827, and many are familiar with the early—and, fortunately, unsuccessful—attempts to demolish George Washington's home, Mt. Vernon. Nonetheless, preservation is still considered a radical activity by those who remain unaware of the process that seeks to maintain our local, state, and national historical and architectural heritage. Of course, preservationists many times seek only to maintain the existing built environment, regardless of its objective value; those who feel betrayed by modern architecture often wish only to avoid change and maintain their familiar and comforting environment. These issues, and others, are reflected in the preservation choices included herein.

Sadly, the value of the Native American structures existing in this country was not recognized until most of them had already been destroyed. Environmentally sound, but delicate and somewhat temporary in nature, they vanished easily, although a few "aboriginal" settlement sites have become Los Angeles monuments. A reconstruction of a Native American village has been created and can be found alongside the de Celis (Pico) Residence in the San Fernando Valley.

As early as 1894, a movement was begun to save California's earliest remaining buildings, which had been designed or had been influenced by Mexican or European styles: the California missions. The obliteration of the Native American settlements leaves the missions as the oldest buildings in California. The Association for the Preservation of the Missions (later the California Landmarks Club) was founded by pioneer conservationist/preservationist Charles F. Lummis. He understood the human and historic value, as well as the tourist potential, of preserving these early buildings for future generations. Lummis's own home, El Alisal, which he designed and built himself in the Mission Revival style, is now a Historic-Cultural Monument.

Later, in the 1920s, a group of concerned merchants banded together, headed by an early preservation activist, Englishwoman Christine Sterling (recently arrived from San Francisco). Her group recognized the need to preserve what remained of the oldest developed area and structures in Los Angeles: Olvera Street and the adjacent plaza. While not strictly representative of the original pueblo (which by that time had already been relocated), the area nonetheless contained the city's oldest extant structures, which were falling into disrepair and were slated for demolition. Sterling interceded with the help of Otis Chandler of the *Los Angeles Times*, who donated $25,000 to get the project off the ground. The resulting protected area ultimately included most of what is now El Pueblo State Historic Park.

Beginning in the 1950s, another part of old Los Angeles, with a significant concentration of Victorian-era buildings, was readied for demolition through the redevelopment process. This was the Bunker Hill neighborhood, located on a group of low hills west of downtown, formerly the site of Fort Moore's "bunker," hence the name. Bunker Hill had been Los Angeles's first wealthy suburban enclave, home to many families whose names are well known in the development of the city. Accessed partly by the Angel's Flight funicular, this unusual hilly neighborhood, as seen in films from the late forties and fifties, strongly resembled San Francisco of the period. Its elevation and proximity to the downtown of the twenties and thirties made the area desirable for development as the city's new financial district. The hill implied a secure and elevated distance from parts of the existing city center that were becoming run-down and derelict. Demolition of the existing buildings of Bunker Hill, the dismantling of Angel's Flight, and the demolition of other historic structures in Los Angeles came to the attention of the public, and many people began to object. An organized opposition formed and many preservation organizations were founded in the city's neighborhoods, a few of which continue today.

In 1962, partly as a response to the demolitions, and also in an attempt to provide a civic forum for these issues, the Los Angeles Cultural Heritage Commission was founded by ordinance of the City of Los Angeles. Its members, who serve at the pleasure of the mayor, are charged with evaluating nominations and maintaining a list of historic-cultural resources. With the ratification of the City Council, nominated buildings are listed as Historic-Cultural Monuments (HCMs). This concept for protection is popularly known as "landmarking." HCMs are occasionally referred to herein, and are interchangeable with the term "landmark."

According to the ordinance, any listed monument must be described, along with the reasons for inclusion. Any proposed modification (including demolition) must be reviewed and approved by a majority vote of the Cultural Heritage Commission and the City Council, both of which are mandated to take "all steps necessary" to preserve such declared monuments. However, an owner of a Historic-Cultural Monument may receive permission to demolish it after observing a waiting period that can be extended up to one year. This waiting period serves as an

opportunity for interested parties to propose alternatives to demolition, although in cases like Philharmonic Auditorium, the waiting period proved meaningless and the building was demolished. As of this writing, the commission has listed 576 monuments, which are described in the body of this book. More than 43 of them have been demolished, 8 are reconstructions, and 33 more have been relocated to new sites, usually to allow new construction on the original site. Some demolitions have been by action of an owner; many have been the result of actions by others, including three monuments that were burned during the riots following the Rodney King beating trial verdict in April 1992. Of the total, more than 13 percent are either gone or located somewhere other than on their original site.

THE POLITICS OF PRESERVATION

Before proceeding, we must clarify some fundamental misconceptions about the nature of the preservation movement. Preservation and politics are often inseparable. From the beginning, preservation issues have been colored by political power plays and a persistent pandering to the constituency of elected officials. Sometimes this process helps preserve historic structures and sometimes it does not. This is no more (or less) true in Los Angeles than anywhere else. The reasons are complex and deserve some discussion.

The preservation movement triumphed with the 1978 Supreme Court ruling in *Penn Central Transportation Company* vs. *New York City*. This "landmark" decision involved New York's Grand Central Station, whose retention and preservation was deemed in "the public good." The court ruled that as long as a building retains some reasonable income potential, the preservation of that building does not constitute a "taking" of an individual's property rights. The right to introduce land-use controls to enhance the quality of life by preserving the character and desirable aesthetic features of a city was upheld by the court. Preservationists rejoiced and land-use attorneys profited.

In Los Angeles, the preservation process involves the cooperation of the City Council, which must ratify nominations presented by the Cultural Heritage Commission in order for designation to take place. There are five Cultural Heritage Commissioners and a staff of four. The staff has the responsibility of maintaining the case files and monitoring the paperwork generated by the nominating process; they also monitor the paperwork generated by changes or alterations proposed to the listed Historic-Cultural Monuments. The Commission may accept nominations from the City Council, or the public at large. Often research is prepared by the nominator, or volunteers, and forwarded to the Commission for valuation.

The commissioners are political appointees with varying degrees of expertise in the historic, cultural, and architectural traditions of the community. It is their job to visit the site, analyze the merits of the case, hold a public hearing, and return the nomination to the City Council, with or without comment. The City Council may then accept or reject the nomination with a simple majority vote, thereby deciding which buildings shall be protected by the city.

Politics may enter the process in several ways and at several points. Some feel that the commissioners are unlikely to propose landmark declaration if the mayor has a personal political stake in avoiding a designation that could adversely affect his major backers, although few actually see the process as either costly or punitive. City Council members, however, are elected by geographic district and they might feel more direct pressure to support or oppose a proposed designation. Designations are sometimes even seen as a way of honoring an individual supporter or political action group in a district. It is also true that a designation could potentially stall an important developer from constructing a new subdivision or high rise, and discussions about replacement structures often prevent a nomination from being evaluated on its own merits. In some rare cases, City Council members themselves have proposed landmarks that the Commission has found insignificant and unworthy of

designation. This can have the effect of diluting the importance of the monuments listed or calling into question the validity of the process itself. This same process, or a variation on this theme, goes on throughout the country in preservation circles.

The decision as to what should be preserved is also interwoven with the political nature of the preservation movement. In the early years of the movement, opposition to demolitions came primarily from grass-roots activists whose supporting documentation was largely subjective. Over the years, criteria were evolved to assist in evaluating potentially historic structures, and it became easier to assess significance; questions regarding the scale of significance (local, state, national, international) began to be asked and answered. But because of the inherently political nature of the process, the objective criteria may occasionally be selectively applied or even completely ignored in favor of emotional appeals from the community.

Too often, the value of a proposed architectural resource seems to be subjective. Often buildings are designated with very little information offered to substantiate the claim of importance. Insufficiently documented cases are brought into the public arena by neighborhood groups who hope to make a case for retention based solely upon neighborhood popularity. Conversely, it is not uncommon (especially in Los Angeles) to hear of cases where a building mysteriously burns to the ground following designation. Imagine the level of frustration (or greed) that brings a property owner to conclude that

such a rash, dangerous, and illegal act is an acceptable response to the landmarking process. Preservation advocates and opponents alike may be characterized as strong willed and vocal about their buildings.

EVOLUTION OF THE LOS ANGELES PRESERVATION MOVEMENT

Los Angeles's preservation ordinance was an early one, and though considered strong in its day, it is now insubstantial in comparison to those subsequently enacted in other cities. On December 3, 1991, the *Los Angeles Times* stated that the city has

one of the worst preservation records in the nation. With a tiny preservation staff, one of the weakest ordinances in the country and a history of city government caving-in to developers, Los Angeles has been left with relatively few protected structures.

A long-contemplated revision to the Cultural Heritage Ordinance is still in the works; stalled in the city bureaucracy for nearly eight years, its emergence cannot be guaranteed. Among the proposed changes to the ordinance is one mandating that some commissioners have professional qualifications relating to this work. It would also allow commissioners to nominate buildings rather than just review the nominations proposed by others.

As the importance of historic context has come to be appreciated, ordinances offering blanket protection for groups of related buildings and their sites and settings (as opposed to individual building designations) have been established. In Los Angeles, four such groupings, known as Historic Preservation Overlay Zones, are currently in place and are integrated into the text of this book. A few others—among them, Spalding Square and Highland Park—are still waiting in the wings. Other preservation tools available in Los Angeles include the designation of several National Register Historic Districts. These designations increase public awareness of historic structures; those districts that are nonresidential can offer tax incentives for rehabilitation of these structures. The listing of National Register Districts limits the federal funding that might otherwise be utilized to demolish valuable historic resources in these areas. Among the National Register Districts in Los Angeles are the Spring Street, St. James Place, and 20th Street districts, as well as El Pueblo, Little Tokyo, and the South Bonnie Brae Street districts.

In 1969, a group of preservationists who had a fondness for Victorian-era structures responded to the increasing demolitions of these buildings. They created the Cultural Heritage Foundation, which promoted relocation as a means for saving buildings that would otherwise have been demolished. Acquiring a vacant parcel alongside the historic Arroyo Seco Parkway (California's first freeway, now called the Pasadena Freeway), they created the Heritage Square Museum, now the receiver site of seven late nineteenth-century buildings.

Almost ten years later, another private, nonprofit preservation foundation was created, called the Los Angeles Conservancy. One source cites the needless demolition of Irving Gill's legendary 1916 Dodge Residence as the motivating factor in the establishment of the Conservancy. Its task is primarily educational in nature, preparing the public for a pro-active role in saving their communities' historic resources. At this writing, the organization has more than thirty buildings on its "critical issues" list, a compilation of significant buildings that it believes merit immediate protection. The Conservancy is dedicated to the recognition, preservation, and revitalization of historic architectural resources in greater Los Angeles. Once located in the historic Art Deco Eastern-Columbia Building, it has recently moved to the equally historic Roosevelt Building, which is located downtown and is part of an extraordinary grouping of early and recently restored office buildings.

In 1981, the Los Angeles Department of Engineering began to provide basic inventory information on every building within the city limits. This survey is beginning to prove valuable to the preservation community. Proposed demolitions can now be reviewed against these listings, which include such vital statistics as the building's age and architect. This information serves as a much needed early warning tool for the Cultural Heritage Commission in its evaluation of proposed nominations and demolitions. Unfortunately, the funding for the survey has run out, and it continues only on a piecemeal basis, with the work being done by volunteers. There is still no complete listing of historic buildings in Los Angeles, nor is it likely that there ever will be.

THE ORDINANCE AND ITS INTERPRETATION

The Los Angeles municipal code defines a Historic-Cultural Monument as

any site (including significant trees or other plant life located thereon), building or structure of particular historic or cultural significance to the City of Los Angeles, such as historic structures or sites in which the broad cultural, political, economic or social history of the nation, state or community is reflected or exemplified, or which are identified with historic personages or with important events in the main currents of national, state or local history, or which embody the distinguishing characteristics of an architectural-type specimen, inherently valuable for a study of a period, style or method of construction, or a notable work of a master builder, designer, or architect whose individual genius influenced his age.

As dense as this seems, it is this language that forms the foundation for the landmark-designation process. More importantly, designated buildings also receive special protection under the California Environmental Quality Act (CEQUA), which permits the demolition of protected structures only in extraordinary circumstances. In practice, the Los Angeles commissioners have utilized most of the conventional categories to document their monuments. They have also added a few of their own. In order to analyze and understand the designation process in Los Angeles, we provide the following summary of designation categories. Some buildings fall into several categories, but all have been chosen for at least one of the following four reasons:

Historic context: Preservation history is usually evaluated in reference to persons, events, or patterns of significance. To these categories the Commission has added cultural diversity as a criterion. This encourages a multicultural awareness that is often missing among the designated buildings of many communities. This is an emerging concern on the national preservation scene. Many structures associated with Native American, African-American, and Asian-American communities have been designated.

Architecture (including interiors), engineering, and transportation: Buildings are evaluated in terms of comparative quality, age, style, method of construction, and significance of the architect, engineer, designer, or builder. Occasionally a building interior is considered significant enough to be protected for its qualities alone; in other instances the interior adds to the merit of overall designation. While many communities are prohibited from designating the interiors of privately owned buildings, Los Angeles is not. Occasionally a building will be designated for its exterior only, but that is not usually the case. The engineering category has encouraged the protection of dams, bridges, fountains, and even historic street paving, which would not fall into the usual architectural category. It would have been less than consistent for such a transportation-dependent city to fail to acknowledge transportation as a protected category. Los Angeles has protected boats, a railcar, a railroad yard, and a funicular.

Physical context: To the traditional valuative categories of setting, continuity, and visual significance, Los Angeles pioneered the protection of the natural environment in its designation of trees, trails, rocks, and wells. The built environment is also protected, including archaeological sites, canals, reservoirs and pumping stations, signs, commemorative monuments, cemeteries, parks, portals, stairs, and fortifications.

Integrity: The degree to which a building remains as it was originally built is also often a factor in declaring it a Historic-Cultural Monument. If a building has retained its historicity, which can be measured in various ways, its preservation value is enhanced. In some cases, a building's integrity alone has been sufficient to warrant designation. Usually this is only one of a number of factors in conferring designation.

Based on the foregoing, the city has extended protection to approximately 400 buildings for their architectural significance and the remainder primarily for their history. These numbers result from our own analysis. Part of the challenge of our work was not just to visit 576 sites and compile information from the usual sources, but to assimilate, understand, and share what Los Angeles has accomplished in the way of preservation. The materials herein should assist readers in coming to their own conclusions regarding why certain buildings have received protection.

The discovery of protected buildings that are not available for public viewing is quite daunting for those who wish to have a deeper understanding of the designation process in Los Angeles. Imagine driving for an hour to Chatsworth, only to discover that Barbara Stanwyck's old home is inaccessible, hidden behind tall walls. The value of designating Frances Lederer's residence, or any building that cannot be seen or monitored by the public, often seems a questionable use of the public process. A visit to the site of Walt Disney's first studio, now a neighborhood shopping center, also proved disappointing. Designations such as these deflect energies away from other buildings whose preservation is of greater public benefit. Once declared, a building is never removed from the official list, even if it is gone. Original sites of relocated buildings offer little information to the historian or casual visitor. The continued listing of these inaccessible or demolished buildings needs to be addressed by the Commission.

Conceived at least partly in response to Los Angeles' growing reputation as a troubled city, Universal Studio's new shopping mall provides cartoonish replicas of some historic Los Angeles venues. Packaged in the safety of an entertainment, retail, and restaurant complex far removed from the city's more troubled neighborhoods is the $100 million CityWalk, located near historic Campo De Cahuenga. It is described by Sam Hall Kaplan in *Buzz* magazine as "a predigested Los Angeles city experience, replete with stylized, if not sterilized, fragments of Melrose Avenue, Hollywood Boulevard, Rodeo Drive and Venice Beach." Needless to say, this exercise in false-historicist architectural humor and economics, replete with its references to historic Olvera Street, allows visitors to "experience Los Angeles" without ever having to go there! While one cannot fault a development for recognizing the value of many of the city's quintessential experiences, it is unsettling to see so much of what Los Angeles is known for reduced to a nearly adult theme park. While the experience of CityWalk may be more enjoyable than walking the real streets of Los Angeles, there is much less to be learned: most of us were born knowing how to shop. We hope that the lesson of this book, which reflects the output of thousands of Angelenos who care about the city's past, will encourage a future in which the city reinvests in its real architectural heritage.

PART I / TO 1850

The monuments discussed in this section are among the oldest recognized in Los Angeles. The first six are prehistoric and archaeological sites: Rock formations such as Eagle Rock and Stoney Point are probably naturally immune to destruction, but their designation provides one of the best links to the region as it was when the first European explorers arrived. These few designations also document the Native American presence here. The remaining monuments, grouped under the heading "Settlement Architecture," are those associated with the first visitors to the region, the founding of the Pueblo of Los Angeles, the end of the Spanish period, and the establishment of Los Angeles city and county government.

GABRIELINO VILLAGE

CHATSWORTH

STONEY POINT

Topanga Canyon Boulevard
Chatsworth

Stoney Point, considered to be one of the most picturesque areas in Los Angeles, is one of the prehistoric treasures of the Chatsworth community. Preserving the aura of earlier times, these rocky outcroppings are a haven for rock climbers. They are also used as a background for motion-picture productions. *No. 132, declared 11/20/74*

CHATSWORTH KILN

Woolsey Canyon Road at Valley Circle Boulevard
Chatsworth

If you look southeast from this limestone-rich river-bottom location, you will spot the sheet-metal roof structure that signals the presence of an archaeological site. More to be experienced than photographed, a simple cylinder dug into the soil is the remnant of a kiln that was used in the production of mortar, concrete, whitewash, and brick. An artifact of Native American settlement, it was later used by the Spanish, the Mexicans, and ultimately the Americans. *No. 141, declared 4/2/75*

CULVER CITY

SA-ANGNA VILLAGE

CA. 1542

(DEMOLISHED 1991)

4231-4263 South Lincoln Boulevard
Culver City

Primarily of archaeological significance, this site became an Historic-Cultural Monument after a compromise with the owner/developers, who proposed construction that would have obliterated the archaeological remains of a Native American village and burial site. Noted anthropologist Alfred Kroeber believes that this site may have been occupied as early as 1542. It has yielded the remains of nearly a dozen human burials and other artifacts.

In exchange for development approval, the owner/developers agreed to place a marker on the site and make a substantial financial donation to a Native American museum to be constructed within five miles of the site. *No. 490, declared 3/19/90*

EAGLE ROCK

EAGLE ROCK

Northern Terminus of Figueroa Street
Eagle Rock

This rock gave the town its name. First noted by Spanish explorers, this 150-foot-tall rocky outcropping is located in what was the Rancho San Rafael. It is a natural rock formation with markings that resemble an eagle in flight. Eagle Rock is considered by some to be the most distinctive natural landmark in the City of Los Angeles, though the opinion is not unanimous. *No. 10, declared 11/16/62*

LOS FELIZ / GRIFFITH PARK

GABRIELINO VILLAGE

Fern Dell
Griffith Park

It is easy to imagine that this incredibly beautiful site would have been chosen, long ago, as a gathering place, or village, by the indigenous inhabitants of the region. It provided water, shelter, food sources, even sewage disposal, in a gentle and nurturing climate. Virtually a paradise, or at least an oasis in the dusty plain that was to become Los Angeles, here archaeologists have discovered traces of Native American villages, whose occupants were named *Gabrielinos* by the same priests who gave the Mission San Gabriel its name. Fragments recovered at the mouth of Fern Dell Canyon suggest that fairly large Native American settlements existed here on sites that received water from the canyons leading down through the Hollywood Hills. *No. 112, declared 2/21/73*

SYLMAR

MISSION WELLS AND THE SETTLING BASIN

Havana Street at Bleeker
Sylmar

The presence of *ciénagas*, or swamplands, from which water bubbled up, was one of the vital factors in the 1797 decision of the Franciscan fathers to erect the Mission San Fernando Rey de España at a site not far from these *ciénagas*. Still maintained by the Los Angeles Water and Power Department, and identified by a bronze plaque, this site is unfortunately fenced off and inaccessible to the public. *No. 50, declared 5/10/67*

SETTLEMENT ARCHITECTURE

The monuments in the following section are associated with the arrival of the first visitors, the Portolá Party (1769); the establishment of the Missions (1771 and 1797); the founding of the Pueblo of Los Angeles (1781); the end of the Spanish period (1822); the secularization of the Missions (1834-36); and the establishment of the city and county governments (1850).

BALDWIN HILLS

RANCHO CIÉNAGA O PASO DE LA TIJERA ADOBE STRUCTURES

CA. 1790

Sánchez Rancho Adobe Structures
3725 Don Felipe Drive
Baldwin Hills

The history of Southern California has been so colored with stories of romance under the bougainvillea that one forgets what a difficult life it must have been. Illustrations and descriptions of the Pueblo of Los Angeles, which was the established center of civilized life, describe the old plaza as dirty, wind-blown, and often filled with refuse. A single pepper tree contributed the only graceful note of urban living. Facing the early plaza stood a building called "El Palacio," which was the home and business of pioneer Abel Stearns. The Sánchez Adobe closely resembled El Palacio.

A plaque places construction of the Sánchez home structures between 1790 and 1795, when the ranch comprised over 4,000 acres. Today, little more than one acre remains, the rest having been sold and

developed. Sadly, the buildings have been subjected to numerous renovations and additions over time, many completed in the 1920s and some happening even today; it is difficult to feel the building's authenticity.

The land has an impeccable California pedigree, with ownership conveyed in 1843 from the last Mexican governor, Manuel Micheltorena, to Vicente Sánchez, whose family controlled Paso de la Tijera, or "the pass of the scissors," for more than a hundred years. It was ultimately sold to Comstock Lode silver baron "Lucky" Baldwin, who gave his name to the neighboring hills. Only a fraction of the original ranch remains, and the glimpse offered by the overly worked two-hundred-year-old adobes is not satisfying. An education project at this site would enable the public to gain a better appreciation of these old structures. By 1928, only sixty-five adobes remained in Los Angeles County. Today, that number has been reduced by more than half. *No. 487, declared 3/26/90*

CALABASAS

LEONIS RESIDENCE

1844

23537 Calabasas Road
Calabasas

It is fitting that the first Historic-Cultural Monument of the City of Los Angeles, built on what were then public lands adjacent to Rancho El Escorpión, should be in the indigenous and wonderfully appropriate Monterey style. Although the original form of the building (probably constructed by Native Americans) is not documented, it was extensively remodeled in the 1870s by Basque immigrant Miguel Leonis, "King of Calabasas." Leonis acquired his nickname because of the vast real-estate holdings he amassed in the San Fernando Valley. It is theorized that the broad, overhanging roofs

and balconies were a Yankee improvement designed to protect mud walls from the rain, as well to provide shade for the inhabitants. Interior wood paneling and elaborate fretwork on the balcony were among Leonis's "improvements" after he acquired the property. Now a house museum, the adobe structure is open to the public. For information call: (818) 712-0734. *No. 1, declared 8/6/62*

DOWNTOWN

PLAZA PARK

1781

(RECONSTRUCTED 1973)

LA IGLESIA DE NUESTRA SEÑORA LA REINA DE LOS ANGELES DE PORNCIÚNCULA

1822

Plaza Church
100 West Sunset Boulevard

CAMPO SANTO

1823

(DEMOLISHED)

First Cemetery

The original settlement of El Pueblo de Nuestra Señora la Reina de Los Angeles de Pornciúncula occurred in the general vicinity of these three designated properties. Strictly speaking, the actual site of the original pueblo has long since disappeared. Various descriptions locate it nearby.

The Spanish governor Felipe de Neve ordered the establishment of the settlement and is memorialized with a statue on the plaza. He directed a group of forty-four *pobladores* of various races (nine were Native Americans), led by four soldiers, to this loca-

LEONIS RESIDENCE

tion in September 1781. These pioneers endured a thousand-mile journey from Mexico to establish an agricultural community. The site was selected because of its location near the San Gabriel Mission, and its attributes of rich soil and plentiful water from the Porncíúncula (later Los Angeles) River. The choice was a good one: like many other inhabited parts of the region, the virtues of this area had already been recognized by its original settlers, the Yang-na Indians, who had established the village of Yabit here many years earlier. They spoke the Shoshonean dialect and welcomed the new settlers.

A plaza, some 200 feet wide by 300 feet long, was laid out here, with its long axis oriented northwest-southeast. The church and other public buildings were centered on the east end. The plaza was functional, not beautiful. The property surrounding the plaza was divided into building lots, and agricultural areas were laid out nearby. In 1800, the river

changed course, causing flooding of the settlement and leading to its relocation on higher ground, where remnants of it may be found in today's El Pueblo de Los Angeles State Historical Monument. The new church, Our Lady the Queen of the Angels, dates from this period (1818-22), but the building has undergone extensive alterations since that time. Despite the changes, it is still considered the oldest established church in continuing use in the city. The master builder, José Antonio Ramirez, employed native materials—adobe brick walls, timber rafters, a flat brea-covered roof, and a pounded earthen floor—all of which have subsequently been removed or covered over. The photograph shows the west elevation facing Sunset Boulevard, which is technically a second church added onto the rear of the original. The church is State Registered Landmark No. 144.

The area 50 feet south and 220 feet west of the church was Campo Santo, the first cemetery to be established by the Spanish in Los Angeles. It is currently a parking lot, and all the bodies originally interred there are believed to have been removed. The cemetery expanded beyond the property south of the church, reaching Eternity Street (now Broadway). The remains of the Native Americans who had converted to Catholicism, along with those of the original Spanish and Mexican settlers, were buried here.

An area bounded by Sunset Boulevard, Macy, Los Angeles, Alameda, Arcadia, and Spring streets, the present site of the plaza dates from approximately 1815. It has undergone many changes over time, but the current design was inspired by the original one. The plaza is State Registered Landmark No. 156.

City agencies are prohibited from instituting land-use controls over state and federal properties. Consequently, many buildings of significance here, which are well worth a look, are recognized (but not regulated) by a secondary list maintained by the Cultural Heritage Commission. They include the Pico House (1869, Ezra F. Kysor), the fire house (1884), and the city's oldest extant residence, the Ávila Adobe (1818). Olvera Street, which dates from the establishment of the second plaza, is lined with nineteenth-century buildings. The street was remodeled in 1929 to give the appearance of a quaint Mexican market. Oddly enough, an earlier attempt to establish the plaza as a farmer's market was defeated by Southern California historian Charles Lummis as inappropriate!

The story of the settlement—the birthplace of the city—is a rich one, and while attempts have been made to protect this area of primary historical significance, the results have been mixed, and many of the buildings remain empty. But the future is bright once again: the adjacent Union Station has recently become a subway station. This intensified use of the area may lead to new occupation of the historic plaza buildings.

LA IGLESIA DE NUESTRA SEÑORA
LA REINA DE LOS ANGELES DE
PORNCIÚNCULA

While the area is now part museum, part tourist trap, and a National Register Historic District, there are plans to mark the location of the original plaza, and to restore the hotel, theater, Masonic Temple, firehouse, and Garnier Building to something resembling their original uses. *Nos. 64, 3, 26, declared 4/1/70, 8/6/62, and 3/20/64, respectively*

ELYSIAN PARK

RIVER STATION AREA / SOUTHERN PACIFIC RAILROAD

19TH C.

Between North Broadway on the west, North Spring Street on the east, northward to the Los Angeles River and the southeast corner of Elysian Park, and south to the Capital Milling Company Building.
Elysian Park.
No. 82, declared 6/16/71

The first written description of the Los Angeles basin as "a very spacious valley, well grown with cottonwood and sycamores, among which [runs] a beautiful river" was authored by Father Juan Crespí in 1769, from the vantage point used to photograph the River Station Area. Today, the area is noted for its significance to early transportation, and for its views of the downtown beyond.

This vast area still retains many vestiges of nineteenth-century railroading, including freight yards, warehouses, tracks, switch houses, docks, and cobblestone paving, much of which may be seen in its original setting. When viewed from Elysian Park, with the skyline in the background, the area is a reminder of the significance of the developmental role played by the railroads here, beginning with the completion of the first transcontinental railroad connection in 1876.

MIRACLE MILE

ROCHA RESIDENCE

1828

Gilmore Adobe
Gilmore Lane, off Third Street near Fairfax
Miracle Mile

At the north end of Gilmore Lane, behind a wall, stands an adobe structure that was one of the early buildings of the Rancho La Brea. The ranch, part of the original Los Angeles Pueblo lands, was granted to Portuguese émigré Antonio José Rocha, who built this structure. His son, José Jorge Rocha, later sold the land; subdivision followed, and this parcel came to be purchased by Arthur Gilmore. The discovery of oil in the area made Gilmore a rich man, and his son, Earl, who was born and died in this house, restored it with exceptional care. Today, it serves as corporate offices for the Farmer's Market. Trespassing is prohibited, but a glance through the fence reveals early California as many have dreamed it might have been. *No. 543-A, declared 3/6/91*

MISSION HILLS

MISSION SAN FERNANDO REY DE ESPAÑA

1797

(RECONSTRUCTED 1974)

15151 San Fernando Mission Boulevard
Mission Hills

The seventeenth mission to be constructed, San Fernando was founded by Padre Fermín Francisco de Lausén and named for King Ferdinand of Spain. It was built on ranch property owned by Don Francisco Reyes, then mayor of the Pueblo of Los Angeles. The site was chosen for its agricultural potential and for its congenial Native American inhabitants, who were converted to Catholicism by the padres, and who also provided labor for the construction of the mission buildings. Mission locations were

MISSION SAN FERNANDO

chosen in order to be spaced one day's travel apart, thus providing safe havens at the end of a day's travel along the California coast. A large complex, built over time and often rebuilt following earthquakes and occasional disuse (after secularization), the compound now has the feel of a museum and admission is charged. Nonetheless, for a glimpse into early California, few experiences compare with the mission and the convent (the least altered of the mission buildings). *No. 23, declared 8/9/63*

DE CELÍS RESIDENCE

1834

Pico Adobe
10940 Sepulveda Boulevard
Mission Hills

It is thought that this residence originated as an outbuilding of the Mission San Fernando, and that it was built by Native Americans who labored for the missionaries. First occupied by Spaniard Eulogio de Celís, who returned to Europe in 1853, it was later restored and enlarged (the second floor is not

DE CELÍS RESIDENCE

ROCHA RESIDENCE

original) for Romulo Pico, whose uncle was Governor Pío Pico. His father, General Andrés Pico, utilized the old mission building, which had been abandoned following secularization, as his country home during this period. This, the oldest adobe in the San Fernando Valley, was rescued again from ruin and disrepair in 1929 by Mark Harrington, who was then curator of the Southwest Museum. The building is now owned by the city and houses the San Fernando Valley Historical Society. It is State Registered Landmark No. 362. It is open to the public, though at this writing it is closed for earthquake repairs. *No. 7, declared 9/21/62*

NORTH HOLLYWOOD

FELIZ RESIDENCE

1845

(RECONSTRUCTED)

Campo de Cahuenga (ca. 1939)
3919 Lankershim Boulevard
North Hollywood

As California historic sites go, this one is especially significant: On January 13, 1847, on the veranda of an adobe home owned by Don Tomas Feliz, Mexican General Andrés

Pico surrendered to Lt. Col. John C. ("the Pathfinder") Frémont, thus effectively ceding Mexican control of California. The event is usually referred to as the Cahuenga Capitulation. The formal acquisition of California was later confirmed by the Treaty of Guadelupe Hidalgo. The home eventually disintegrated and was removed by 1900. To mark the site in a manner befitting its historical significance, the Recreation and Park Board commissioned this building, with a front elevation that is a replica of the original adobe house that served as the setting for this auspicious event. Reconstructions such as this are of questionable value in present-day preservation theory, but the efforts here did produce a beautiful compound. This is State Registered Landmark No. 151. *No. 29 declared 11/13/64*

TIMMS LANDING

PACIFIC PALISADES

FOUNDER'S OAK

(DESTROYED 1975)

*Haverford Avenue between Sunset Boulevard
and Antioch Street
Pacific Palisades*

In 1822, a group of men and women met under the oaks in Temescal Canyon to select individual lots from the tract they had jointly purchased. Among these oaks was one they named Founder's Oak to commemorate their gathering. From this modest beginning, Pacific Palisades was founded. Over the years, the original Founder's Oak became infested with termites and had to be destroyed, but other trees in the vicinity still provide a feeling of the presettlement days in the canyon. *No. 38, declared 3/25/66*

SAN PEDRO

TIMMS LANDING

CA. 1837

(DEMOLISHED)

Timms Way at Sampson Street
San Pedro

Named for Captain Augustus W. Timms, who controlled the harbor here and on Santa Catalina Island (which he called Timms Harbor), this area in San Pedro was also known as Timms Point. An engraving from the important Title Guaranty Collection illustrates a simple vernacular structure from the days when Timms Point was the port for the Pueblo of Los Angeles and the surrounding ranches. Cowhides for export were loaded onto ships at this landing, which was also the final destination for stage coaches carrying departing seagoing passengers. No structures remain from the original cluster of buildings, and the first wharf (resembling those found on Nantucket) has vanished. But a plaque locates the center of shipping in the mid-1880s Los Angeles Harbor and confirms that you are in the right place. It was this port that Richard Dana described so vividly in *Two Years Before the Mast. No. 171, declared 2/16/77*

PART II / 1851-1888

During the years 1851 to 1888, Los Angeles matured from village to town. Following the end of the Mexican-American War, the United States Land Commission recognized Los Angeles's title to about 28 miles of land based on the Spanish law that had governed pueblos. Meanwhile, the nature of the economy changed dramatically: the great boom generated by the discovery of gold collapsed, the vast ranchos began to be split up, and the agricultural era of Southern California began. Railroads reached Los Angeles in 1876, ending its relative isolation, and after a rail connection to the East through El Paso was opened up, people poured into the area, causing real- estate development that established much of the present pattern of cities within what is now Los Angeles.

The last of the true Spanish Colonial buildings were built, along with a few Gothic Revival churches, but Los Angeles was soon under the spell of various Victorian-era styles, including the Italianate, Stick, Queen Anne, and Colonial Revival. In the 1870s, architecture of the mid-Victorian era dominated the nation. It was soon to decline, although it hung on in California into the 1890s. Some indigenous California vernacular buildings were built as well, including the Queen Anne variants produced by the Newsom brothers. According to historian W. W. Robinson, as early as 1869 the demolition of existing adobes near the plaza to prepare a site for the Pico House Hotel caused "much local comment on the passing of old landmarks; Pico House became the social and cultural center of Los Angeles," and as Los Angeles expanded in all directions, the pueblo "grew increasingly shabby and isolated."

ST. PETER'S EPISCOPAL CHURCH

ROCHA RESIDENCE

BALDWIN HILLS

ROCHA RESIDENCE

1865

(RECONSTRUCTED 1979)

La Casa de Rocha
2400 Shenandoah Street
Baldwin Hills

This residence was built by Antonio José
Rocha II on a portion of the Rancho Rincón
de los Bueyes ("the corner of the oxen").
Rocha senior was said to have been the first
foreigner to settle in the area following the
establishment of the pueblo, having landed
in Monterey from Portugal in 1815. He was
given a 100-acre parcel of this ranch from
Francisco Higuera, and it was here that this
home was built.

Described as a big, square, one-and-one-
half-story house with a shed-roofed porch on
all four sides and a "gringo" stairway, the
walls were constructed of adobe bricks 23

inches thick. The upper level is constructed
of redwood siding, and the roof is shingled.
The house has been lovingly reconstructed,
and evidence of the original adobe bricks
may be observed on the west elevation.
No. 13, declared 1/28/63

BOYLE HEIGHTS

RESIDENCE

CA. 1870s

(DEMOLISHED 1973)

1620 Pleasant Avenue
Boyle Heights

In the Italianate style, this building became
a silent witness to the cultural erosion of
Pleasant Avenue. Following repeated acts of
vandalism and a fruitless effort by a private
party to relocate it to another site, the richly
detaiied building was demolished. *No. 97,*
declared 2/23/72

CHINESE SHRINE

1877

Evergreen Cemetery
204 North Evergreen Avenue
Boyle Heights

Among the more evocative of Los Angeles' Historic-Cultural Monuments, this small Chinese shrine at the far eastern end of Evergreen Cemetery is well worth a visit. It consists of twin ceremonial ovens and a central altar section; Chinese characters decorate the ovens, but the date of construction is in Arabic numerals. By Chinese tradition, the ovens were used to burn personal effects to transfer them to the "other side." All Chinese bodies were removed from Evergreen and returned to China in 1927, but the shrine remained. Viewed by the cemetery owners as expansion space for additional grave sites, the shrine was recently purchased from Evergreen by the Chinese Historical Society, which plans restorative and protective work at the site. With the destruction of old Chinatown in the 1930s, this remains the oldest reference to the early Chinese presence in Los Angeles. *No. 486, declared 8/20/90*

RESIDENCE

1885

3110 North Broadway
Boyle Heights

This modest residence has all the refinements normally found on middle-brow Queen Anne style residential buildings. Still in good condition, it symbolizes many thousands of similar buildings that have been demolished. *No. 157, declared 7/7/76*

BUNKER HILL

DORN RESIDENCE

1887

(DEMOLISHED 1979)

The Rochester (later West Temple Apartments)
Original Address: 1012 West Temple Street
Bunker Hill

Named for his hometown of Rochester, New York, this rare Second Empire structure was built by Rufus Herrick Dorn. In 1897 it was purchased by the wealthy Van Nuys family, who converted it into fifteen apartment units in 1919. Falling into disrepair through the years, it was another of the Bunker Hill residences to be displaced by the Community Redevelopment Agency (CRA). After a temporary move to Alameda and San Jose streets, it was demolished. *No. 11, declared 1/4/63*

CANOGA PARK

WORKMAN RESIDENCE

1869–72

Shadow Ranch Recreation Center
22633 Vanowen Street
Canoga Park

Australian immigrant Albert Workman is credited with importing the first eucalyptus trees to Southern California. He planted them on his ranch, a small portion of the giant 60,000-acre Los Angeles Farm and Milling Company, which was devoted to raising wheat. It was controlled by the wealthy investors Lankershim and Van Nuys, both names that are well known in the history of the region.

Workman built this adobe and redwood home and lived here for many years. Having passed through other hands over time, by 1932 the house was in serious need of restoration. This project was undertaken by Colin Clements, who named it "Shadow Ranch" to call attention to the beautiful shadowing cast by the towering eucalyptus on the site. Now owned by the city, it is open to the public. *No. 9, declared 11/2/62*

CHINESE SHRINE

CHATSWORTH

STAGE COACH TRAIL

1860s

Approximately 50 acres lying immediately south of Chatsworth Park, north of Oakwood Cemetery, bound on the west by the Los Angeles City and County lines and on the east by the western terminus of Devonshire Street
Chatsworth

Stage coaches actually passed this way during a significant phase in the development of the San Fernando Valley, when the trail linked Los Angeles, Encino, Simi Valley, and Ventura. Today, it resembles nothing so much as a set from a 1940s B-movie western. *No. 92, declared 1/5/72*

PALMER RESIDENCE

1880s

(RECONSTRUCTED 1913)

Chatsworth Park South
Devonshire Street west of Topanga Canyon Boulevard
Chatsworth

A little ranch cottage typical of those built by the homesteaders of the San Fernando Valley with their own hands, the home of Minnie

CHATSWORTH FIRST METHODIST
CHURCH

Hill Palmer is operated today as a museum, staffed with volunteers in period costume. *No. 133, declared 11/20/74*

OLIVE TREES

CA. 1900

Lassen Street between Topanga Canyon Boulevard and Farralone Avenue
Chatsworth

Imported from the eastern Mediterranean region, olive trees were brought to California by Franciscan missionaries. These seventy-six mature trees, with their distinctive gray-green coloration, approximate the age of the town of Chatsworth itself, having been planted in the latter part of the nineteenth century. *No. 49, declared 5/10/67*

CHATSWORTH FIRST METHODIST CHURCH

1903

(RELOCATED 1965)

Chatsworth Community Church
22601 Lassen Street
Chatsworth

This building was relocated from its original site to the cemetery of the second oldest town in the San Fernando Valley. Not only is it the oldest public building remaining in the community but it is also one of only a handful of Gothic Revival churches left in Southern California. The building was erected with volunteer labor from the community. The congregation dates from 1880, when the region's first settlers, under the direction of valley pioneer Ann Johnson, met outdoors. *No. 14, declared 2/15/63*

ROSEDALE CEMETERY

COUNTRY CLUB PARK

ROSEDALE CEMETERY

1884

1831 West Washington Boulevard
Country Club Park

Home of the oldest crematorium in Los Angeles, Rosedale is known for its unusual concentration of pioneer-family grave sites and also for its outstanding examples of Victorian-era funerary architecture. The mature landscaping, including a curving double row of palm trees, evokes the mood of infinity and serenity found in few cemeteries. Reading the markers is like reading a page of California history.

Pictured is the Shatto family monument. A prominent family with a street named for them in Los Angeles, they were also the owners, for a time, of Santa Catalina Island. Still photography is actively discouraged at Rosedale, although the grounds were overrun by a motion-picture caravan and film crew when this photograph was taken. *No. 330, declared 12/7/89*

SANCTA VIBIANA CATHEDRAL

DOWNTOWN

ALBION STREET COTTAGES AND MILAGRO MARKET

1870s

1801-1813 Albion Street
Downtown

A remarkably intact enclave of nineteenth-century working-class cottages, coupled with a neighborhood grocery, this extant row illustrates simply and beautifully how previous generations lived. *No. 442, declared 6/20/89*

SANCTA VIBIANA CATHEDRAL

KYSOR AND MATHEWS 1871-75

St. Vibiana Roman Catholic Cathedral
114 East Second Street
Downtown

This remarkable building, which seats three thousand, is among the largest early churches in the city; it replaced the Plaza Church as the city's Catholic cathedral. The design of Sancta Vibiana, in the academically correct Spanish Colonial style, is said to derive from the Puerto de San Miguel in Barcelona, although the original does not have a belfry. Inside, preserved in a marble sarcophagus, are relics of the early Christian martyr St. Vibiana. Harris Newmark's memoirs describe a feature of the original masonry edifice as a front railing of artificial stone created by Busbard and Hamilton, who founded Los Angeles's first stone factory.

Extensive renovations to the church were completed in 1922 under the direction of veteran church architect John C. Austin. The west front appears much as it did in early lithographs, although it has been moved forward and limestone has been substituted for brick. Today, this entrance is closed and has been appropriated by homeless men, who, incidentally, do not welcome photographers. Parishioners now enter the church through a parking lot on the north side of the block. *No. 17, declared 5/10/63*

FOY RESIDENCE

1873

(RELOCATED TWICE)

633 South Witmer Street
Downtown

Samuel Calvert Foy migrated to Los Angeles in 1854 after a couple of relatively fruitless years in the gold mines of Northern California. He established a harness trade and soon expanded into the livestock business. He married the daughter of Obed Macy (another famous early Los Angeles name), with whom he fathered six children.

His home was built on the corner of Seventh and Pearl (now Figueroa); later it was moved to Wilshire Boulevard and finally to its current address. This sturdy Italianate residence seems once again bound for a new address if the intensity of adjacent development is an indicator. In 1859, Foy joined with other public-spirited businessmen to form the Los Angeles Library Association. Though this first attempt at establishing a library failed, a later proposal succeeded and Foy's daughter Mary became the city librarian. She was the first woman to hold this office. *No. 8, declared 9/21/62*

FORTHMANN RESIDENCE

CA. 1887

629 West Eighteenth Street
Downtown

The case file summary describes this large two-story residence as one of the most elegantly detailed Victorian-era residences remaining in the city. *No. 103, declared 10/4/72*

ECHO PARK / ANGELINO HEIGHTS

The Angelino Heights Historic Preservation Overlay Zone is part of this Echo Park neighborhood, which looks out over the Los Angeles basin. It features a high concentration of Victorian-era residential structures in an area bounded by Bellevue Avenue on the south and enclosed by Kensington Road. In recent years, two homes built during the same period that were slated for demolition have been relocated here. *LA Weekly* says that "Angelino Heights is this city's most significant historic district and Carroll Avenue—with its immaculately restored and stately homes—one of its most famous streets. But Los Angeles is a city that pulps its past without apology, and even though the street has protected status, plans to build a twenty-eight-unit condominium complex on East Edgeware Road have gained approval from the city's Planning Department."

RUSSELL RESIDENCE

CA. 1879

1316 Carroll Avenue
Echo Park

This house was built prior to 1880. The brackets-and-shell motif below the windows and over the porch are noteworthy. *No. 76, declared 2/3/71*

RESIDENCE

CA. 1887

(RELOCATED)

1321 Carroll Avenue
Echo Park

This is a modest cottage that was relocated from 1145 Court Street as an alternative to demolition. *No. 176, declared 7/13/77*

EASTLAKE INN

1887

1442 Kellam Avenue
Echo Park

The surviving twin of mirror-image, side-by-side duplexes, this early residence, with its composition shingle roof, survives as a bed and breakfast inn. The building is named for British designer Sir Charles Eastlake, who strongly disapproved of the "Eastlake" style work that was being built in California. *No. 321, declared 5/20/87*

RESIDENCE

1887

724 East Edgeware Road
Echo Park

This handsome country residence is a rather elaborate Victorian-era expression, particularly notable for its intricate tower, ornamental ironwork, and fish-scale shingles. *No. 206, declared 1/3/79*

RESIDENCE

CA. 1887

1239 Boston Street
Echo Park

This is one of several modest Queen Anne residences with characteristic spool work and decorative shingles. *No. 219, declared 6/6/79*

ALBION STREET COTTAGES

INNES RESIDENCE

CA. 1887

1329 Carroll Avenue

Echo Park

This home was built for the area's council-man, shoe-store magnate Daniel Innes. He and his family occupied the structure for some thirty years. As the Innes's business prospered, the family became one of the first *Blue Book* families of Los Angeles. *No. 73, declared 2/3/71*

SANDERS RESIDENCE

1887

1345 Carroll Avenue

Echo Park

This home was built for Michael Sanders, the operator of a storage warehouse in Los Angeles. His middle-class home sported a characteristic red-brick foundation, Chinese style latticework on the porch, and French style wrought-iron roof crowns, most of which are still in place in this otherwise badly deteriorated residence. *No. 74, declared 2/3/71*

LUCKENBACH RESIDENCE

1887

1441-1443 ½ Carroll Avenue
Echo Park

Little is known about James Luckenbach, who built this Queen Anne style house. The significance of the residence derives from its 1902 acquisition by European immigrant Kaspare Cohn. After establishing his fortune, Cohn founded both the Union Bank and the Kaspare Cohn Hospital, which was a forerunner of the Cedars of Lebanon Hospital. Before these hospitals could be built, however, the house was used for a time as a sanatorium for tuberculosis patients who migrated here from New York City sweatshops. *No. 191, declared 5/3/78*

RESIDENCE

CA. 1887

917 Douglas Street
Echo Park

This is one of the more distinguished buildings of Angelino Heights. Its simple, low retaining wall and entrance steps, flanked by a nearly symmetric pair of mature palms, are quintessential California Victoriana. *No. 216, declared 6/6/79*

RESIDENCE

CA. 1887

1343 Kellam Avenue
Echo Park

This Queen Anne style residence features beautiful detail work, with shingles in diamond and circular patterns, garland trim, and attractive wood turnings on the porch. *No. 220, declared 6/6/79*

RESIDENCE AND CARRIAGE HOUSE

CA. 1887

1347 Kellam Avenue
Echo Park

This residence is almost identical to HCM 220, and it has a matching carriage house. *No. 221, declared 6/6/79*

SANDERS RESIDENCE

PINNEY RESIDENCE

CARRIAGE HOUSE

CA. 1887

1417 Kellam Avenue
Echo Park

Undeniably charming, this structure is one of the best remaining examples of a Victorian era carriage house in Los Angeles. It exhibits wood shingles of various styles, diagonal braces, vertical and horizontal siding, and a cupola surmounted by a weather vane. Viewing requires trespassing onto private property, which is not encouraged. *No. 166, declared 11/3/76*

RESIDENCE AND CARRIAGE HOUSE

CA. 1880s

1411 Carroll Avenue
Echo Park

Both buildings are in the Queen Anne style. The residence is said to have retained fine interior plaster and woodwork. Its carriage house is also in excellent condition, but the front sidewalk, with rose trees, is its most irresistible feature. *No. 190, declared 5/3/78*

SCHEERER RESIDENCE

1887-88

1324 Carroll Avenue
Echo Park

This diminutive cottage derives from a nineteenth-century "plan book" and exhibits the high level of craftsmanship available in that era. *No. 78, declared 2/3/71*

PHILLIPS RESIDENCE

1887

1300 Carroll Avenue
Echo Park

This especially ornate and well-maintained Queen Anne home, built for Aaron P. Phillips, is notable for the spindle work and turned posts at the entry, the stained-glass windows, the textures obtained by the use of shingles, and the shadow play provided by ornamental millwork. *No. 51, declared 5/10/67*

PINNEY RESIDENCE

1887

1355 Carroll Avenue
Echo Park

This relatively unornamented house, with a picturesque witch's hat cupola generally seen on Queen Anne structures, was built for early capitalist Harry L. Pinney. At the time of its designation, the house was still occupied by Pinney's son, Charles, who was mentioned as an eligible bachelor in the 1894 *Blue Book*. *No. 75, declared 2/3/71*

RESIDENCE

CA. 1887

(RELOCATED 1978)

1325 Carroll Avenue
Echo Park

This Stick style residence was originally located at 1123 Court Street and features an unusual arrangement of windows. Little else is known about its history, but in time it should fit comfortably into its new setting. *No. 109, declared 1/3/73*

HEIM RESIDENCE

CA. 1888

1320 Carroll Avenue
Echo Park

This relatively unassuming Queen Anne style house was built with a multitude of architectural elements, including turrets and verandas. The generous proportions of the architectural style were considered charming and unpretentious in their day. *No. 77, declared 2/3/71*

HASKIN RESIDENCE

1888

1344 Carroll Avenue
Echo Park

This remarkably intact and well-maintained home features noteworthy ornamental spindles and scrolls. *No. 79, declared 2/3/71*

COLLINS RESIDENCE

1888

(RELOCATED)

892 Kensington Road
Echo Park

Michael Collins, the first owner of this handsome Stick style residence, owned a livery and stagecoach business. Collins served on the Los Angeles City Council briefly (1887–88) and had a role in bringing the Santa Fe Railroad to Los Angeles. Originally located at 2930 Whittier Boulevard, the building was recently moved and restored, but it now sits somewhat uncomfortably in a new landscape. *No. 266, declared 6/10/83*

COLLINS RESIDENCE

SESSIONS RESIDENCE

SESSIONS RESIDENCE

JOSEPH CATHER NEWSOM 1888

1330 Carroll Avenue

Echo Park

This twelve-room house was built for dairy-man Charles Sessions by Joseph Cather Newsom, one of the enterprising San Francisco architects drawn to Los Angeles by the boom of the 1880s. In 1889, Newsom included a photograph, floor plan, and a description of the interior of this house in his "Picturesque and Artistic Homes and Buildings of California" and featured a sketch of the front elevation in an advertisement for his architectural services. Comparing Newsom's original promotional pamphlet with the present structure reveals that the upstairs porch has been enclosed and an exterior stairway added. Few other design changes have been made.

Newsom thought of this as a "Californian" house, and he chose, as appropriate for the climate, a lacy spindle and lattice ornament in the Moorish Revival manner. Notable are the elaborate shingle patterns, stained glass, and wood carving. Features of this house were elaborated by Newsom in later houses that he designed on Bunker Hill. *No. 52, declared 5/24/67*

RESIDENCE

CA. 1890

1334 Kellam Avenue
Echo Park

This modest residence is another example of the stylistic mishmash that so infuriated Beaux Arts designers. It has been described as being excellent Queen Anne architecture with Colonial Revival touches. *No. 207, declared 1/17/79*

BATES RESIDENCE

1893

(RELOCATED)

1415 Carroll Avenue
Echo Park

This much-moved workingman's Queen Anne style residence is now resting on its third site. Its sunburst gable carvings were ordered out of catalogues and, while not rare, are attractive. *No. 399, declared 11/29/88*

WELLER RESIDENCE

1894

(RELOCATED)

824 East Kensington Road
Echo Park

This Queen Anne residence, with Moorish traces, was relocated from Angelina and Boyleston streets by owner-contractor Z. H.

Weller as oil derricks began to appear in the neighborhood. This was a large, difficult structure to relocate. Only someone who owned an oil field could have considered such a move practical. *No. 223, declared 6/20/79*

WICKS RESIDENCE

1896

1101 Douglas Street
Echo Park

This house was built for Moses Langley Wicks, a Missourian who worked in insurance. Its architecture is described as Queen Anne with Colonial Revival touches. *No. 217, declared 6/6/79*

RESIDENCE

JOSEPH CATHER NEWSOM

CA. 1888-89

1407 Carroll Avenue
Echo Park

This is one of the buildings designed in Newsom's "El Capitan" style, which was largely an outgrowth of his attempts to establish a coherent regional style. It is deceptively simple: close study reveals subtle complexities in the floor plan necessary in order to generate such unusual exterior shapes. *No. 189, declared 5/3/78*

RESIDENCE

CA. 1905

1405 Kellam Avenue
Echo Park

This building was constructed later than much of the neighborhood, reflecting the change in architectural fashion. Unlike its Victorian-era neighbors, this home is in the Mission Revival style. *No. 222, declared 6/6/79*

RESIDENCE

CA. 1908

945 East Edgeware Road
Echo Park

This building, with its dark shingles, rests on a site so overgrown that it is difficult to verify that a Craftsman residence recalling the work of Greene and Greene is located here. *No. 218, declared 6/6/79*

BOB'S MARKET

1910

1234 Bellevue Avenue
Echo Park

This is a rare surviving example of an early vernacular neighborhood grocery, although some see vaguely Oriental details in the building. It is unique primarily because it has survived. *No. 215, declared 6/6/79*

ENCINO

OAK TREE

CA. 1851

Louise Avenue (210 feet south of Ventura Boulevard)

Don Gaspar de Portola and Father Juan Crespí were among the first explorers to glimpse the San Fernando Valley in 1769. Crespí noted in his diary that they had named the area "El Valle Santa Catalina de Bolonia de los Encinos" (the Valley of St. Catherine of Bologna of the Oaks) for the many oaks found in the region. Legend has it that this *Quercus agrifolia* is over a thousand years old. Although probably younger than estimated, the tree is still spectacular. The trunk has a circumference of 24 feet and its branches spread 150 feet. Protected for many years by Michael Lang, who lived nearby, the tree is now revered by the community and attracts visitors from all over the region. *No. 24, declared 9/6/63*

EXPOSITION PARK / WEST ADAMS

WIDNEY HALL

KYSOR AND MORGAN 1880

(RELOCATED THREE TIMES)

650 Childs Way
Exposition Park

The oldest university building in Southern California, Widney Hall has been in continuous use for educational purposes for over a hundred years. Named in 1955 for pioneer educator and the founder of the University of Southern California, Robert Maclay Widney, the building began life as a modest Italianate structure, set amidst mustard fields and approached by horse and carriage. Over time, the building has taken on a faux Colonial Revival expression with green shutters and a widow's walk. It is State Registered Landmark No. 536. *No. 70, declared 12/16/70*

DURFEE RESIDENCE

CA. 1885

(RELOCATED 1899)

1007 West Twenty-fourth Street
Exposition Park

This is a remarkably picturesque and relatively intact two-story country home built for the Richmond Durfee family on a rural site in Florence, California. Durfee had come to California from Illinois, where he had been a dry-goods dealer. Following the death of her parents, their daughter had the house moved to its current location, where she then took up residency. The rural-to-urban movement has rarely been expressed in such literal terms. *No. 273, declared 1/4/84*

ALEXANDER RESIDENCE

1888

2119 Estrella Avenue
Exposition Park

This is a well-maintained Stick/Eastlake style home, built on land surveyed by

early real-estate developer Theodore Weisendanger, as part of the Park Villa Tract. It was built for the family of Richard H. Alexander, a lieutenant colonel in the United States Army who had lived in Arizona before relocating to Los Angeles. *No. 489, declared 5/21/90*

SHORT RESIDENCE

1888

2110 Estrella Avenue
Exposition Park

Like much of the surrounding development in this Park Villa Tract, this two-and-one-half-story pattern-book Queen Anne was built by developer Theodore Weisendanger and contractor Henry Martz. The first owner was Hiram V. Short, a farmer who was moving "uptown." *No. 507, declared 11/2/90*

SEAMAN RESIDENCE

1888

2341 Scarff Street
Exposition Park

This National Register property is another middle-class Queen Anne style residence. It was built for educator William Seaman and his family. In 1896, he moved to Sacramento to become deputy superintendent of public instruction. *No. 408, declared 1/20/89*

ARNOLD RESIDENCE

1888

1978 Estrella Avenue
Exposition Park

Another tract house of the period, this Queen Anne residence was built by contractor Henry Martz and sold to Lois Ellen Arnold. *No. 498, declared 6/12/90*

WRIGHT RESIDENCE

ATTRIB. CARROLL H. BROWN 1888

2121 Bonsallo Street
Exposition Park

Another of the tract homes typical of the proposed St. James Place National Register District, this one was built for the Arthur

Wright family, who lived here for many years. Like its neighbors, it is a modest two-story home in the Queen Anne/Colonial Revival style. It has some unusual detailing and appears to be well cared for. *No. 560, declared 5/26/92*

ALLEN RESIDENCE

ATTRIB. CARROLL H. BROWN 1888

2125 Bonsallo Street
Exposition Park

Following the Wrights' temporary relocation to San Bernardino, their home was rented to the William Allens. While tenants at 2121 Bonsallo, they purchased the home next door, at 2125 Bonsallo. Some time later, members of the Allen family occupied 2125. Similar in quality and detail to its neighbor, today it, too, exhibits a high degree of care. *No. 561, declared 5/26/92*

HIGHLAND PARK HERITAGE SQUARE MUSEUM

3800 Homer Street
Highland Park

Heritage Square was conceived in 1965 as an alternative to demolition for important examples of California Victorian-era architecture. None of these buildings would be here today were it not for this extraordinary project. In fact, two designated buildings that had been relocated here were subsequently torched by vandals.

Originally, Heritage Square was to accommodate about a dozen structures of various architectural styles. Currently, however, the site contains only seven declared monuments and one undesignated building. The complex is operated by the nonprofit Cultural Heritage Foundation of Southern California, whose mission is to restore and interpret these buildings, and the Victorian life-style, for the public.

The problems inherent with collecting and relocating buildings of different architectural styles and functions generate controversy in preservation circles. Site integrity continues to be an important component of historic preservation, but all too often a developer will use the precedent of Heritage Square to justify the removal of a historic structure that stands in the way of his project.

Stylistic juxtaposition also presents some interesting problems at Heritage Square. Choosing to group buildings with such a diversity of style, scale, and function will, most likely, never produce a cohesive feeling in the new environment. Although they were built within a twenty-three-year span (1876–99), the Heritage Square buildings come from several differing contexts (large and small, residential and nonresidential). It is this odd fit, and the lack of an appropriate new context expressed through streetscape and landscape, that sometimes generate criticism of the project. To be understood and appreciated, it must be viewed as an architectural museum. Heritage Square is not really meant to be an example of an appropriate or viable restoration and preservation solution. In recent years, the historic Angelino Heights area has also received some relocated homes, but these buildings

DURFEE RESIDENCE

were set on available sites using an existing street grid, and they seem to achieve a better "fit." Heritage Square is open to the public, and admission is charged. For information call (818) 449-0193.

The buildings of Heritage Square include:

RESIDENCE

1887

(DESTROYED BY FIRE AFTER RELOCATION)

The Salt Box
Original Address: 339 South Bunker Hill Avenue
Bunker Hill

This structure was one of the best-preserved houses on Bunker Hill. It was well designed and well proportioned, a classic example of a turn-of-the-century residence and an elegant reminder of old Bunker Hill. *No. 5, declared 8/6/62*

PALMS DEPOT

1887

Original address not listed
Palms

A nonresidential structure with Dutch Revival gables, this charming depot was built along the Southern Pacific Railroad at a site known as the "grasshopper stop" in what would become the town of Palms, halfway between Los Angeles and Santa Monica. In 1976 the building was moved to Heritage Square, where it now serves as the Museum Visitor's Center. *No. 22, declared 8/9/63*

MORGAN RESIDENCE

SHAW RESIDENCE

RESIDENCE

1882

(DESTROYED BY FIRE AFTER RELOCATION)

The Castle
Original Address: 325 South Bunker Hill Avenue
Bunker Hill

Bunker Hill was a residential suburban development containing many fine examples of late nineteenth-century craftsmanship. In 1969, "the Castle," as it was then known, was moved to Heritage Square. While awaiting restoration, it was burned to the ground by vandals. *No. 27, declared 5/8/64*

MORGAN RESIDENCE

ATTRIB. JOSEPH CATHER NEWSOM 1888

(RELOCATED TWICE)

Hale House
Original Address: 4501 North Pasadena Avenue
Mt. Washington

This house is believed to have been built for G. W. Morgan, about whom little is known. After changing hands a few times, it was purchased in 1906 by James G. Hale. The home is an outstanding example of late Queen Anne style architecture. The building has been restored to its original condition. As it stands today, the home is an architectural symbol of social transition; it represents the passing of a nineteenth-century rural society that gave way to the industrialized urban America of the twentieth century. *No. 40, declared 6/15/66*

SHAW RESIDENCE

1883-84

(RELOCATED TWICE)

Valley Knudsen Garden Residence
Original Address: Mozart Street near Broadway
Lincoln Heights

Renamed for Valley Knudsen, founder of the Los Angeles Beautiful organization, this tiny but elaborate Mansard-roofed jewel box was built by cabinetmaker Richard E. Shaw. Partly in anticipation of criticism about removing buildings from their landscape, the coral tree adjacent to the house was relocated at the same time as the house, through the efforts of the Bel Air Garden Club. *No. 65, declared 4/15/70*

PERRY RESIDENCE

FORD RESIDENCE

CA. 1885

Original Address: Beaudry Avenue near Third Street
Bunker Hill

The elaborate wooden decoration on this modest Italianate residence derives from its original owner, John J. Ford, who was a gifted woodworker. The building was moved from its original site on Beaudry Avenue to make way for an office building. Beaudry Avenue was named for Prudent Beaudry, who was a Quebec native and a pioneer businessman in Los Angeles. He developed "the hills" as the Bunker Hill area was then known. *No. 108, declared 1/3/73*

LINCOLN AVENUE METHODIST CHURCH

GEORGE KRAMER 1897

Original Address: Lincoln Avenue at
Orange Grove Boulevard
Pasadena

This building is noted for its Colonial Revival style, as well as for its nonaxial plan, which was a Methodist tradition. During his career, architect Kramer designed more than two thousand Methodist churches worldwide. *No. 245, declared 6/4/81*

PERRY RESIDENCE

EZRA F. KYSOR 1876

Original Address: 1315 Mount Pleasant Avenue
Highland Park

An ongoing restoration project of the Colonial Dames (and their Los Angeles headquarters), this grand Italianate mansion was built for prominent pioneer Angeleno William Hayes Perry, a carpenter turned furniture maker, who founded Los Angeles's first lumberyard in 1861. He later helped organize the Los Angeles Gas Company and was president of the Los Angeles Water Company for twenty-five years. *No. 98, declared 3/15/72*

LONGFELLOW RESIDENCE

1893

(RELOCATED TWICE)

Original Address: San Pasqual Street
Pasadena

The octagon as an architectural form has a long and noble history. In America, it was first seen as a wing or a projection in Adams style houses of the late eighteenth century. Thomas Jefferson was fascinated with the form and designed his summer home in that shape in 1819. Following the 1849 publication of Orson Fowler's book *The Octagon House, A Home for All*, which extolled the octagon's virtues, several thousand were constructed. This one, built for Gilbert Longfellow, was originally located in

Pasadena. It has been moved twice, and it currently awaits restoration on its current site. *No. 413, declared 1/20/89*

The only structure in Heritage Square not listed with the Los Angeles Cultural Heritage Commission is a carriage barn that was built in 1899 on the grounds of what is now the Huntington Memorial Hospital in Pasadena. It is used here as a utility building. Ironically, a major expansion of this small domestic structure is now planned because Heritage Square's needs have outgrown the existing structure.

OTHER HIGHLAND PARK MONUMENTS

GRIFFITH RESIDENCE AND RETAINING WALL

1880s

141 South Avenue 57
Highland Park

The earliest records available indicate that this structure was originally owned by Charles Griffith on what was then Garvanza Avenue. The first occupant is listed in the 1900 City Directory as John Latter, Sr. The building is positioned at a slight angle from the street, indicating that its construction preceded that of the roadway alignment. It resembles the large vernacular farmhouses of the Midwest. *No. 366, declared 6/21/88*

RESIDENCE

CA. 1885

6028 Hayes Avenue
Highland Park

This rare, undecorated, vernacular residence recalls its predevelopment setting by the orientation of its inviting porch, which wraps the house to the southeast. Far too simple and honest to be classified as a veranda, this shaded outdoor "room" offered views of the river and a cool breeze, before the surround-

ing trees and additional neighboring development converted the property from its country setting to a more urban conformity. Today, surrounded by these other structures, the building still offers a glimpse into the past as the residents gather each evening to porch-sit and gossip. *No. 143, declared 4/16/75*

PETERS RESIDENCE

1887-90

5905 El Mio Drive
Highland Park

This is an imposing, beautifully restored, two-story Queen Anne residence, which is magnificently sited to catch, and reflect, the setting sun. *No. 142, declared 4/16/75*

FORD RESIDENCE

LOS FELIZ

FELIZ RESIDENCE

JOSÉ PACO FELIZ 1853

Feliz Adobe / Park Ranger's Headquarters

4730 Crystal Springs Drive

Los Feliz / Griffith Park

The only remaining adobe structure on the original Rancho Los Feliz, and one of the few remaining in Los Angeles, this simple mud structure is among the oldest in the city. Extensively remodeled in the 1920s, it now serves as a park facility. The area was named for Feliz, one of the soldiers who accompanied the first settlers of the pueblo. *No. 401, declared 11/30/88*

AVOCADO TREES

4400 block Avocado Street

Los Feliz

Of the original twenty-five avocado trees believed to have been planted here over one hundred years ago by Franciscan missionaries, only six remain. A new construction project on the block would have resulted in the loss of two single-family residences and two of these trees. The project was redesigned to allow the historic trees (but not the homes) to remain. Subsequently, however, two of the trees died. *No. 343, declared 1/22/88*

MULLER RESIDENCE

MONTECITO HEIGHTS

BOWMAN RESIDENCE

1885

2425 Griffin Avenue

Montecito Heights

Another early downtown developer, William A. Bowman, commissioned this unusual one-and-one-half-story residence. Although its roof appears to have received at least one too many dormers, the rounded entrance porch recalls a time before air conditioning and television when Californians sought the cool comfort of the outdoors watching the neighbors from this shady and secluded vantage point. *No. 443, declared 6/20/89*

RESIDENCE

ATTRIB. JOSEPH CATHER NEWSOM

CA. 1886

3537 Griffin Avenue

Montecito Heights

Uncharacteristically simple for a Newsom design, this restrained Italianate house seems to have lost its front lawn, but it has retained its unusual double-peaked dormer. *No. 145, declared 5/21/75*

RESIDENCE

CA. 1887

2054 Griffin Avenue

Montecito Heights

It is unusual for Queen Anne decorations to be found on a masonry house in California, but in this case they appear original. The speculation is that the home was built by, and for, a masonry contractor. *No. 144, declared 5/1/75*

SAN PEDRO

ST. PETER'S EPISCOPAL CHURCH

1884

(RELOCATED 1956)

Twenty-fourth Street at Grand Avenue

San Pedro

This small church celebrated its opening on Easter Sunday 1884, when the building was located on Beacon between 2nd and 3rd streets. It is San Pedro's oldest extant church. As an alternative to demolition, the structure was relocated to its present site on the fenced grounds of Harbor View Memorial Park (cemetery). It is available for public use. *No. 53, declared 12/6/67*

DODSON RESIDENCE

CA. 1887

(RELOCATED)

859 West Thirteenth Street

San Pedro

This residence, built for merchant and postmaster James W. Dodson, is one of San Pedro's best examples of late Victorian-era architecture, even though much of its original ornamentation has been removed. *No. 147, declared 9/17/76*

MULLER RESIDENCE

CA. 1899

(RELOCATED 1982)

575 Nineteenth Street
San Pedro

This Colonial Revival structure features exquisite leaded glass, carving, and wood paneling. It was purchased by shipbuilder William Muller, who plied his trade for the Banning transportation interests. A victim of street realignment, it was moved from its original site in 1912.

Recently, it was again relocated to save it from demolition. But in this rare instance, the building's appearance has actually been enhanced by the move. Today, on its spectacular site, the home appears to have been built as an oceanfront cottage. Enhanced by the surrounding light and space, it now serves as a community center. *No. 253, declared 8/25/82*

SAWTELLE

MORETON BAY FIG TREE

1873

11000 National Boulevard at Military Avenue
Sawtelle

This native Australian tree (*Ficus macrophylla*) was reportedly planted by the Smith family, whose cottage it shaded on a portion of what was then La Ballona Ranch. Today it has a span of 120 feet and is the focal point of a modern church complex. In Australia Moreton Bays are considered street trees, which may grow in height from 50 to 100 feet. To this day, the tree on National Boulevard continues to produce generous crops of small purple figs. *No. 19, declared 5/10/63*

MORETON BAY FIG TREE

SOUTH CENTRAL

TROST RESIDENCE

1885

917 East Forty-ninth Place
South Central

The earliest recorded owner of this Queen
Anne style residence was Sophie Trost, who
together with her carpenter husband, Frank,
called this place home for some nineteen
years between 1902 and 1921. *No. 517,*
declared 12/17/90

WESTLAKE

WESTLAKE PARK

1886

General Douglas MacArthur Park
2230 West Sixth Street
Westlake

In 1865, the city began disposing of some of
its public lands at auction, in 35-acre lots.
Included was the area where the park lies,
which consisted of marshy hills, considered
undesirable and which received no bids.
After the surrounding lands became a fashionable residential area (many early structures nearby have become Los Angeles
Historic-Cultural Monuments), a group of
property owners convinced the city to
develop the land as a park by offering to
share the cost of improving the desolate site.
A neglected pond at the site was enlarged
into a lake in 1896, and a bandstand was
erected, providing a focus for the park.
Wilshire Boulevard was rerouted through the
park in 1934, providing an opportunity for
major new development nearby.

WESTLAKE (MACARTHUR) PARK

The park was renamed in 1942 to honor General Douglas MacArthur, then at the height of his wartime popularity. By this time, Wilshire Boulevard was lined with expensive shops (except where it bisected the park) and was considered California's counterpart to New York's Fifth Avenue. Later, as the city continued to expand westward, the MacArthur Park area suffered a much-discussed decline. With its mature landscape, it became a beautiful, if melancholy place, immortalized by the hit song "MacArthur Park."

Many efforts at reversing the decline of the park have been attempted, including the installation of significant public art in the 1980s. The lake was temporarily drained to allow construction of a subway station beneath it, as the Wilshire corridor now prepares for a future that will be less dependent on the automobile. General MacArthur said, "Old soldiers never die, they just fade away"—and one hopes this will not be the destiny of this important historic resource. *No. 100, declared 5/1/72*

RESIDENCE

CA. 1880s

(RELOCATED)

836 South Coronado Street
Westlake

Moved from its original location at 633 West 15th Street, this is a unique example of a Caribbean-influenced Queen Anne style building. Currently undergoing restoration, it has been "shoehorned" onto a lot too small to contain its visual excesses. *No. 167, declared 11/17/76*

CAMP DRUM BARRACKS AND OFFICERS' QUARTERS

WILMINGTON

CAMP DRUM BARRACKS AND OFFICERS' QUARTERS

1859

1053-1055 Cary Avenue (enter from parking lot on Banning)
Wilmington

This is one of two surviving structures of Camp Drum, which was the federal government's western regional headquarters during the Civil War. Originally a large complex of exceedingly plain vernacular buildings costing over one million (pre-Civil War) dollars, it was named for Adjutant General Richard Coulter Drum. Today, the surviving frame building has been modified in the Colonial Revival style. It is said that it was constructed of materials shipped around Cape Horn from the East; milled lumber was not yet available in California.

Famous names in California and United States history are associated with the story of Camp Drum. The land originally belonged to Juan José Domingues through a Spanish land grant. His descendants sold it to Phineas Banning, the founder of the town of Wilmington, who in turn deeded it to the federal government so that an army post might be built to protect the Union. The first telegraph in this part of the country was located here, establishing an important link with other federal fortifications in the Southwest. Camp Drum was closed in 1866 and offered as surplus property by the government in 1873, when it was sold at auction for less than $10,000. It is State Registered Landmark No. 169. *No. 21, declared 6/7/63*

CAMP DRUM POWDER MAGAZINE

1862

1001 Eubank Avenue / 351 Opp Street
Wilmington

Few would recognize this partially demolished structure as anything of value. But, fortunately, someone did. This 20-foot-by-20-foot brick and stone structure is the remnant of a gunpowder magazine that served Camp Drum during the Civil War. Attached to a wooden residential building that was built later, it was rediscovered during demolition of the later building in 1982. Today, it stands, a little forlorn behind its cyclone fence, awaiting a restoration that cannot bring back its context but may allow visitors an insight into the Civil War years in California. *No. 249, declared 8/10/81*

BANNING RESIDENCE

1864

401 East "M" Street
Wilmington

The town of Wilmington, near the southern edge of Rancho San Pedro, was named for the Delaware hometown of Phineas Banning. It was here that Banning, who is considered the father of Los Angeles transportation, built what historian Harold Kirker considers to be "the best extant example of Greek Revival domestic architecture in the state."

Among other early transportation feats, Banning sponsored the construction of the Los Angeles–San Pedro Railroad, which was the city's first rail connection to the harbor. Known for his many contributions to early regional transportation (stagecoach and shipping), Banning became a wealthy man who built this home at the center of what was then a much larger estate. This thirty-room residence, now the focal point of Banning Park, was acquired as a result of a 1927 bond issue voted by the people of Wilmington. It is State Registered Landmark No. 147. *No. 25, declared 10/11/63*

WILMINGTON CEMETERY
CIVIL WAR ERA

605 East "O" Street
Wilmington

A visit to the site of this historic cemetery can be disappointing, for its appearance is that of a new cemetery. Unlike its counterparts closer to the heart of the city, this memorial park has little in the way of monumental funerary statuary or mature landscaping. What it does have are the final resting places of seven Civil War soldiers; the first child born in San Pedro; and many members of the Banning family, who donated the land for the cemetery. *No. 414, declared 1/20/89*

PROTESTANT CHAPEL
1870

(RELOCATED TWICE)

Memory Chapel, Calvary Presbyterian Church
1160 North Marine Avenue
Wilmington

It is surprising how easily and often these little white chapels can be moved. This one, the oldest Protestant church in the harbor area, has served different denominations at different sites for nearly 120 years. Not in regular use for church services, currently it is part of Calvary Presbyterian Church. *No. 155, declared 5/5/76*

MASONIC TEMPLE
1882

(RELOCATED 1912)

227 North Avalon Boulevard
Wilmington

Believed to be the second oldest nonresidential structure in Wilmington, the temple reflects Renaissance Revival detailing. More difficult to move than the frame chapel above, its one-foot-thick walls have allowed this unreinforced masonry structure to withstand two earthquakes with little damage. Phineas Banning helped finance the construction of the building. *No. 342, declared 1/22/88*

ST. JOHN'S EPISCOPAL CHURCH
1883

(RELOCATED 1943)

1536 Neptune Avenue
Wilmington

This simple frame structure is typical of many built around the country during this period; as fewer remain, their significance grows. This one is considered to be the oldest ecclesiastical building in the harbor area that is still used for regular services. *No. 47, declared 3/15/67*

ST. JOHN'S EPISCOPAL CHURCH

BANNING RESIDENCE

PART III / 1889-1908

The discovery of oil in 1892 brought new wealth to Los Angeles, which absorbed Wilmington and San Pedro in order to provide ocean access for the oil shipments.

Los Angeles was still a medium-size, rough-edged town, trying to project a cosmopolitan image. As in the more sophisticated San Francisco, there emerged in the mid-nineties the brash and energetic Beaux Arts style along with the City Beautiful Movement. The Ecole des Beaux Arts in Paris later became the model for the American architectural schools, but during this period America's most important architects were still educated in France. After 1890, another building boom began, and soon office buildings, government buildings, and hotels began to appear in the Beaux Arts style, while varieties of residential structures continued.

The period opened with the Queen Anne/Colonial Revival emerging as a hybrid style in its own right; architects working in both of these styles were still concerned more with the look of a building than its function. In the years after 1900, these frontal assaults on the visitor were beginning to seem a little ostentatious. A few examples of the Shingle style began to appear, and California's first exploration of her Spanish, Portuguese, and Mexican roots reached maturity with the appropriately short-lived Mission Revival style. Both Craftsman and Prairie School architecture made their appearance in Los Angeles during this period.

POWERS RESIDENCE

ALVARADO TERRACE

The following six houses and their park, laid out on a portion of the original Los Angeles Country Club grounds, were built on what became a stylish, curving suburban residential street southwest of downtown. They were developed serially, and some were said to have been lived in by the developer, Pomeroy Powers (who was also City Council president at that time) before being sold to their eventual owners. The buildings represent a variety of architectural styles and are so respectful of one another in scale and refinement that only one really stands out. Oddly enough, it was the last residence built and the one that Powers kept as his own.

KINNEY RESIDENCE

HUNT AND EAGER 1902

1401 Alvarado Terrace

This Colonial Revival residence was designed by architect Sumner Hunt for prominent businessman Arthur W. Kinney, who owned an iron works and was a director of the Oceanic Oil Company. *No. 88, declared 7/7/71*

COHN RESIDENCE

HUDSON AND MUNSELL 1902

1325 Alvarado Terrace

Another Colonial Revival residence, this one was built for Morris Cohn, a clothier who developed the Cole of California line. See also HCM 119, the Cohn-Goldwater Building. *No. 84, declared 7/7/71*

GILBERT RESIDENCE

1903

1333 Alvarado Terrace

This home, built for William F. Gilbert, with its unusual combination of sandstone and shingles and excellent carvings throughout, reflects a correct Shingle style sensibility. *No. 85, declared 7/7/71*

GILBERT RESIDENCE

RAPHAEL RESIDENCE

HUNT AND EAGER 1903

1353 Alvarado Terrace

R. H. Raphael, prominent in the glass business in the early 1900s, asked his architects to incorporate some very elaborate beveled glass into the entrance of this remarkable half-timbered Tudor Revival style home. *No. 87, declared 7/7/71*

BARMORE RESIDENCE

CHARLES E. SHATTUCK 1905

1317 Alvarado Terrace

Constructed for Edmund H. Barmore, president of the Los Angeles Transfer Company, the Medieval Germanic Revival house is cloaked in shrubbery and palm trees. *No. 83, declared 7/7/71*

POWERS RESIDENCE

A. L. HALEY 1905

1345 Alvarado Terrace

This large and exuberant Mission Revival style home was built for Pomeroy Powers, who was president of the Los Angeles City Council from 1900 to 1904 and the developer of the Alvarado Terrace houses. *No. 86, declared 7/7/71*

TERRACE PARK

1904

Powers Place, Fourteenth Street and Alvarado Terrace

Terrace Park resulted from the last subdivision of this area, which was then considered comparable to the exclusive Chester Place. Pomeroy Powers was honored by the city in the naming of Powers Place, the shortest street in Los Angeles, which divides the adjacent Terrace Park. *No. 210, declared 2/21/79*

BOYLE HEIGHTS

RESIDENCE

CA. 1890

1030 Macy Street
Boyle Heights

Unfortunately one of the least documented buildings in Los Angeles, this structure recalls the home of Andrew Boyle (for whom Los Angeles pioneer William Workman named this area), who built his brick house here in 1853. That building was still in place when Harris Newmark completed his memoirs in 1916.

Masonry buildings are a rarity in earthquake-prone Los Angeles. The first kiln for firing brick was built nearby, presumably for Boyle's home. An early accounting indicates that in one year (1859), only thirty-one brick structures were built in the entire city.

It is likely that this structure is older than previously thought, and it is one of about three extant brick domestic structures from the Victorian era in the city. Its appearance and scale suggest that it may be the remaining ground floor of what was probably a two- or three-story home. *No. 102, declared 10/4/72*

RESIDENCE

1890

2700 Eagle Street
Boyle Heights

This two-story Queen Anne style structure features a typical corner tower with an unusual onion-shaped dome. *No. 262, declared 6/3/83*

SIXTH STREET BRIDGE

1898

(DEMOLISHED)

Hollenbeck Park Lake
Boyle Heights

This picturesque wooden bridge was once a decorative and functional feature of a fine residential area. Originally built for both pedestrian and horse-and-carriage traffic and successfully altered for automobiles, it was later declared unsafe, and in 1968, the same year it was designated, it was demolished. *No. 54, declared 5/22/68*

CYPRESS PARK

HURON SUBSTATION

EDWARD S. COBB 1906

2640 North Huron Street
Cypress Park

Never has a city expressed conflict about mass transportation more than Los Angeles. It is currently constructing its third-generation transit system while remnants of its earlier systems remain. Part of the Los Angeles Railway system, the Huron substation was active until 1956, when the last of the conversions from streetcar to bus took place. The simple two-story masonry structure was then sold as surplus for $7,500. Today, the structure appears older than it really is and evokes the small-town nature of its original function. *No. 404, declared 12/20/88*

LEWIS RESIDENCE

DOWNTOWN

LEWIS RESIDENCE

JOSEPH CATHER NEWSOM 1889

1425 Miramar Street
Downtown

Built at the end of the 1880s boom and superbly maintained, this "California-style" house expresses the regional philosophy of Joseph Newsom. The resulting arabesque curves, extensive shingling, veranda, and landscaping derive from his early "California consciousness." This residence, built for Samuel Lewis, is a Queen Anne structure that blends many styles, resulting in a light and comfortable design suitable for California's climate. It is among the best of the extant Newsom structures. *No. 39, declared 6/15/66*

LESLIE RESIDENCE

CA. 1900

767 Garland Avenue

Downtown

A hearty survivor in a neighborhood where few vintage residences remain, this two-story Queen Anne was originally built for an oil executive, Charles C. L. Leslie, about whom little is known. *No. 129, declared 6/19/74*

BRADBURY BUILDING

GEORGE HERBERT WYMAN 1893

304 South Broadway

Downtown

This is considered by many to be the most significant piece of architecture in Los Angeles, and much has been written about the interior of this unique five-story office building with its open corridors, ornamental railings, stairs, and open-cage elevators. Designed and built for mining magnate and architecture aficionado Louis Bradbury, the building features a skylighted interior that, although common in Europe, was rare in the United States and nonexistent in Los Angeles.

The Bradbury Building has been featured in many films. It makes its most memorable impression in the futurist *Blade Runner*, set in 2093, when the Bradbury's light-filled interior has become obsolete in a city whose sky is dark and filled with toxic rain. George Wyman credited his inspiration for the building to Edward Bellamy's socialist/utopian tract *Looking Backward*, which described an office building of the future as being a vast hall filled with golden light.

Like many before him, Wyman came to California for his health and found the light and climate inspirational. He appreticed in the office of Eisen and Hunt, arguably Los Angeles's most important architectural firm of the period. Hunt originally received the commission for the project, and it is unclear how Wyman ended up with it; the Bradbury is the only truly significant building of his career, although two Wyman residences have been declared by the Cultural Heritage Commission.

Usually considered unremarkable when compared with its interior space, the handsome Romanesque Revival exterior of this one-hundred-year-old building has also been restored (along with the interior), and it makes a significant contribution to the Broadway streetscape. *No. 6, declared 9/21/62*

IRVINE / BYRNE BUILDING

EISEN AND HUNT 1894

301 West Third Street

Downtown

Perhaps Hunt's revenge on Wyman, this building is considered to be the first of Los Angeles's Beaux Arts buildings. A masonry structure that has all the distinguishing hallmarks of a style that would become an American commercial standard, it is a tripartite vertical block with distinct top, middle, and base sections. Much of the original storefront material at the base has disappeared, but the restrained cornice at the top section remains intact. This is one of the very few nineteenth-century buildings remaining in the downtown that may still be viewed in a setting resembling its original context. Sadly, the entrance has been converted to a retail shop, rendering the upper levels inaccessible; they are currently vacant and abandoned. *No. 544, declared 7/2/91*

SPANISH-AMERICAN WAR MONUMENT

VAN NUYS HOTEL

MORGAN AND WALLS 1896

Barclay Hotel

103 West Fourth Street

Downtown

Allegedly Los Angeles's oldest continuously operating hotel, the Van Nuys was the city's first hotel constructed in the Beaux Arts style. It boasted exceptional conveniences, including a telephone in each room, electric lights, hot and cold running water, steam heat, and specially designed mattresses. It was developed by Isaac Newton Van Nuys, who was a leading businessman and the founder of the town bearing his name. *No. 288, declared 2/1/85*

SPANISH-AMERICAN WAR MONUMENT

S. M. GODDARD 1900

Pershing Square
Downtown

This uncommon granite statue, in the representational style popular at the turn of the century, is the oldest example of public art in Los Angeles. It commemorates, oddly enough, not those who died in battle but the twenty-one members of the Seventh Regiment who died from diseases caused by unhealthy living conditions while awaiting the call to arms in San Francisco. The soldier's posture is meant to convey a sense of remembrance, and possibly melancholy, but it is difficult not to smile at the Pershing Square pigeons who alight on the soldier's cap and shoulders, and nestle in his arms. *No. 480, declared 2/6/90*

ANGEL'S FLIGHT

COL. J. W. EDDY 1901

(DEMOLISHED 1969)

Third and Hill Street
Downtown

Angel's Flight—315 feet in length and often called "the world's shortest railway"—was a two-car funicular that served as transportation up the 33 percent grade from the Hill Street arch to the Olive Street station house atop Bunker Hill. A shorter counterpart to San Francisco's cable cars, Angel's Flight served an area comprised of Victorian-era residences and businesses. It may be seen adding local color to the neighborhood in films that routinely used this area for exterior shooting. *The Turning Point*, a 1952 William Holden mystery set in Los Angeles, is such a film, with great footage of Holden witnessing a shooting while riding Angel's Flight.

The funicular was disassembled as part of the clearance of Bunker Hill by the Community Redevelopment Agency (CRA). The two cars, named the Olivet and the Sinai, are in storage. For a while, even after all the Bunker Hill buildings were cleared, tourists still queued up at the orange cast-iron portals to buy a ticket for what had, by then, become a ride to nowhere. Similar funiculars existed not only locally (HCM 269 was also a funicular station) but worldwide at the turn of the century. In Pittsburgh, Pennsylvania two similar funiculars are still operating: the Monongahela and Duquesne inclines. The CRA indicates that it will soon complete the restoration of this charming and unique means of transportation. In the interim, the Orient Express at Magic Mountain offers a similar ride. *No. 4, declared 8/6/62*

ANGEL'S FLIGHT

ST. JOSEPH'S CHURCH

BROTHERS ADRIAN AND LEONARD 1901

(DEMOLISHED)

218 East Twelfth Street
Downtown

St. Joseph's was built for a parish established in 1888. It was a simple building with very plain interiors that later received elaborate stenciling.

The design of the building was a collaboration between Franciscan Brothers Adrian and Leonard in Gothic Revival style, featuring three naves, seven altars, thirty-five stained-glass windows, and two towers. *No. 16, declared 5/10/63*

FARMERS AND MERCHANTS NATIONAL BANK BUILDING

MORGAN AND WALLS 1904

401 South Main Street
Downtown

Built by founder Isaias Hellman, this was an early and important institution in the development of Los Angeles. It is the last surviving example of the downtown Beaux Arts banking temples that spoke with architectural eloquence about the solidity of the institutions they housed. *No. 271, declared 8/9/83*

PALM COURT OF THE ALEXANDRIA HOTEL

JOHN PARKINSON 1905

210 West Fifth Street
Downtown

Recognized for its interior decor, the Palm Court originally symbolized the best of early Southern California commercial hospitality.

The Alexandria Hotel was the center of social life in Los Angeles during the 1920s, and the Palm Court, with its stained-glass ceiling panels extending across a 196-foot dining room, was the center of the social activity. The property was owned and developed by Harry Alexander, for whom it was named. Famous guests included Presidents Theodore Roosevelt and William Howard Taft; Edward, Prince of Wales; and film icons Douglas Fairbanks, Mary Pickford, and Charlie Chaplin. Today, the elaborate French interior has been replaced with a pseudo-Victorian decor, which adds a sad and somewhat sour note to what is now a dilapidated residential hotel. *No. 80, declared 3/3/71*

TEMPLE BAPTIST CHURCH AND OFFICE BUILDING

CHARLES WHITTLESEY 1906

(ALTERED 1938, CLAUDE BEELMAN)

(DEMOLISHED 1985)

Philharmonic Auditorium and Office Building,
427 West Fifth Street
Downtown

The Temple Baptist Church was once one of the most beautiful buildings in Los Angeles, and not coincidentally, it contained the first large meeting hall to have a balcony without visible support. Its grand opening took place on November 8, 1907. Originally a Moorish Revival design, it was altered in 1938 to a relatively successful Moderne design in the American Perpendicular style, though a rich roofscape and much beautiful Sullivanesque detail was stripped away. The auditorium was home to the Los Angeles Philharmonic from 1920 to 1964, when it relocated to the Music Center. The site is now a parking lot. *No. 61, declared 7/2/69*

FARMERS AND MERCHANTS BANK

BRADBURY BUILDING

PACIFIC MUTUAL BUILDING

HAMBURGER'S DEPARTMENT STORE

ALFRED F. ROSENHEIM 1907

801-829 South Broadway
Downtown

Once the largest department store in the west, this innovative terra-cotta-covered steel-frame building is seen as a precursor of later downtown stores, including Robinson's and the Broadway. Not only was it pioneering in its scale and concept as a department store—with its stripped-down and relatively undecorated style and large amounts of glass—it was also a precursor to the structural expressionism that would not come into favor for another twenty years. The fledgling Los Angeles Public Library was located here for a time. Architect Rosenheim is credited with some of the city's best buildings, including the Second Church of Christ, Scientist (HCM 57) on West Adams. *No. 459, declared 10/17/89*

PACIFIC MUTUAL BUILDING

JOHN PARKINSON AND EDWIN BERGSTROM 1908
(ALTERED 1929, PARKINSON AND PARKINSON AND DODD AND RICHARDS; GARAGE ALTERED 1936, SHULTZ AND WEAVER)

523 West Sixth Street
Downtown

Pacific Mutual was established in 1868 in Sacramento as the second chartered bank in California. It moved to San Francisco in 1881, merging in 1905 with Conservative Life Insurance of Los Angeles to become the Pacific Mutual Life Insurance Company. After the destruction of the headquarters building in the 1906 San Francisco earthquake and fire, construction began on this building, which housed the company until 1972.

PART III / 1889 1908
66

Unfortunately, the original and incredibly elaborate 1908 white terra-cotta building has been totally lost through subsequent renovations. However, this refined and beautifully restored structure is not without its own importance. *No. 398, declared 11/23/88*

COLE'S PACIFIC ELECTRIC BUFFET

THORNTON FITZHUGH 1908

East Sixth Street
Downtown

This is a rare designation that protects a business use (and an interior) rather than a building. Cole's is the oldest continuously operating restaurant and saloon in Los Angeles. It continues to serve "French dip" sandwiches, which are said to have been invented on the premises by the proprietor, Harry Cole. Cole's interior features a massive mahogany bar, Tiffany light shades, and tables made from wood that was recycled from the sides of the Pacific Electric's "Old Red" cars.

The restaurant is a ground-floor tenant in the Pacific Electric Building (also known as the Huntington Building), built in 1902 by "big four" magnate Henry Huntington. The building is a State of California Point of Historic Interest, which acknowledges that at one time it was the tallest building west of the Mississippi and served as the terminus for the Pacific Electric Railway—the largest interurban railway in the world, serving Los Angeles, Riverside, and San Bernardino counties. *No. 104, declared 10/18/72*

FIRST AFRICAN METHODIST EPISCOPAL CHURCH BUILDING

1902
(DESTROYED BY FIRE 1972)

801 South Towne Avenue
Downtown

Once serving a congregation that was founded in 1872, this was the first African-American church of any denomination in Los Angeles. Inspired by the Gothic architecture he saw in England in 1901 the presiding pastor, Rev. Jarrett E. Edwards, commissioned the new structure in this style. Noted for its pioneering use as both a religious and social structure, First A.M.E. was a significant force in the desegregation movement, beginning in the 1890s. Martin Luther King, Jr. often preached here. *No. 71, declared 1/17/71*

EAGLE ROCK

MEYER RESIDENCE

1890s
(DESTROYED BY FIRE 1992)

4340 Eagle Rock Boulevard
Eagle Rock

Named for original owner/contractor Fred Meyer, this house was originally located on Pasadena Avenue in Highland Park. It was moved in the 1920s to make way for a service station. When designated, the building once again appeared to be standing in the way of progress; it was boarded up and appeared ready to be moved again, or demolished. Instead, it was burned to the ground the night the verdict was announced in the Rodney King beating trial. *No. 461, declared 11/3/89*

OWEN RESIDENCE

EISEN AND HUNT 1897
(DEMOLISHED)

616 North Avenue 66
Eagle Rock

Destroyed by fire within a year of its designation, this unassuming, late nineteenth-century country-style home was designed by prominent architects of the period for Cecilia Owen. Two years later it was purchased by George M. Wilson who, over time, commissioned minor changes by architects Train and Williams. This collaboration resulted in the addition of a fine, curving, Neoclassical porch, which radically altered the style of this house. *No. 418, declared 2/17/89*

GREENSHAW RESIDENCE

JOSEPH CATHER NEWSOM 1906

1102 Lantana Drive
Eagle Rock

This commission was pretty far afield for Newsom, most of whose works were nearer downtown. This one, built for Charles Greenshaw, is uncharacteristically in the Mission Revival style and features elaborate *espadañas. No. 565, declared 8/25/92*

EL SERENO

RESIDENCE

1904
(ALTERED 1929, J. A. WILSON)

Villa Rafael
2123 Parkside Avenue
El Sereno

This appears to be a sentimental designation for a building that possesses little of architectural or historical significance. A stand of mature palm trees testifies to how long this site has been inhabited. *No. 263, declared 6/3/83*

ELYSIAN PARK

CHAVEZ RAVINE ARBORETUM

1892

Grace E. Simons Lodge, entrance off Stadium Way
Elysian Park

Elysian Park was originally called East Los Angeles Park. It was acquired from Julian Chavez, a native-born Angeleno, who owned the property, including the ravine that bears his name. The arboretum was Southern California's first botanical garden and was founded by the Los Angeles Horticultural Society, which originated the planting of rare trees in the upper part of the ravine as early as 1892; by 1895 the double row of date palms (*Phoenix canariensis*) was planted on the west side of Stadium Way between Scott Avenue and Academy Road. A grouping of mature rubber trees further defines one of the most unusual picnic grounds in Southern California. *No. 48, declared 4/26/67*

BARLOW SANITORIUM

1903

2000 Stadium Way
Elysian Park

This compound of Craftsman buildings became the first sanitorium in Southern California to combine a residential atmos-

BARLOW SANITORIUM

phere with health-care facilities. It became a temporary home for indigent consumptives who came to Los Angeles to renew their health in the dry, fresh air. Through the fund-raising efforts of founder Dr. Walter Jarvis Barlow, considerable philanthropic support allowed the sanitorium to grow into a major medical institution, the last of its kind in Southern California. The Mediterranean Revival Administration Building (pictured) differs stylistically from the rest of the complex and was funded and equipped by Mrs. Barlow. *No. 504, declared 10/2/90*

EXPOSITION PARK/ WEST ADAMS

FOSTER RESIDENCE

1889

1030 West Twenty-third Street
Exposition Park

Among the more esoteric occupations of the period was that of windmill manufacturer Henry W. Foster, who built this Queen Anne home, which was one of the original structures in this developing subdivision. *No. 466, declared 10/17/89*

MILLER AND HERRIOT TRACT
RESIDENCE

MILLER AND HERRIOT TRACT RESIDENCE

1890

1163 West Twenty-seventh Street
Exposition Park

Considered the earliest surviving example of tract housing (built by developers) in Los Angeles, the building is noted for its outstanding exterior and its interiors with original fireplaces and staircases. Even today, new home buyers would admire many of the features of this venerable residence. Newer versions of similar homes are still being created in Chatsworth subdivisions. *No. 242, declared 4/9/81*

KELLY RESIDENCE

ATTRIB. BRADBEER AND FERRIS

CA. 1890s

1140 West Adams Boulevard
Exposition Park

A particularly flamboyant Queen Anne variant, the A. E. Kelly residence features the remains of a most unusual red sandstone chimney that encases an arched window. Restoration work, which was underway at the time of the designation in 1985, seems to have stalled. Although the house is in need of repairs, its history is much more "readable" than that of many buildings that have been fully restored. *No. 295, declared 7/12/85*

RESIDENCE

BRADBEER AND FERRIS 1891

2701 South Hoover Street
Exposition Park

This Queen Anne residence is considered to be typical of the large homes constructed for an emerging middle class. *No. 240, declared 4/9/81*

STIMSON RESIDENCE

CARROLL H. BROWN 1891

2421 South Figueroa Street
Exposition Park

Built for an early lumber tycoon, Chicagoan Thomas Douglas Stimson, this mansion is considered to be the best of the few Romanesque Revival buildings in Los Angeles. A four-story, crenelated, octagonal tower; robust red sandstone; and mature semitropical landscaping combine to create a dazzling high-style home. Ironically, this residential display of entrepreneurial excess is now a convent, owned by the nuns of Mount St. Mary's College. *No. 212, declared 5/16/79*

HARRISON RESIDENCE

CA. 1891

1160 West Twenty-seventh Street
Exposition Park

This is an immense, single-towered Queen Anne residence—the largest in the Miller and Herriot Tract development. It was built for John Cleves Short Harrison, a retired Indiana businessman. *No. 296, declared 7/12/85*

FROEBEL INSTITUTE, CASA DE ROSAS

EISEN AND HUNT 1892

Sunshine Mission
2660 Hoover Street
Exposition Park

This building is currently undergoing renovation, and it is difficult to determine if anything remains of Sumner Hunt's original Mission Revival design. Originally a progressive kindergarten, the complex became a collegiate boarding school in 1915, and a haven for destitute women in 1942. *No. 241, declared 4/9/81*

GIBBONS RESIDENCE

1892

2124 Bonsallo Avenue
Exposition Park

This Queen Anne residence was built for Charles Gibbons, who held a secretarial position with a dry-goods company. The property was originally part of the Park Villa Tract. *No. 497, declared 6/12/90*

TEED RESIDENCE

1893

2365 Scarff Street
Exposition Park

This two-and-one-half-story Colonial Revival residence was built for former Los Angeles City Councilman Freeman G. Teed. *No. 457, declared 10/24/89*

KANE RESIDENCE

1893

2133 Bonsallo Avenue
Exposition Park

Another Park Villa lot saw the construction of this Queen Anne style cottage for John Kane, who only occupied the house for a few years. In 1897 it was sold to Alice Patterson. *No. 500, declared 6/12/90*

SHANNON RESIDENCE

1893

1970 Bonsallo Avenue
Exposition Park

A modest two-story residence in the Queen Anne style, this house was built for Irish peace officer Michael Shannon and his wife, Nellie. *No. 501, declared 4/30/90*

HEIMGARTNER RESIDENCE

1894

1982 Bonsallo Avenue
Exposition Park

This one-and-one-half-story Queen Anne cottage was originally inhabited by Agnes B. Heimgartner. It is somewhat obscured from view by a number of very mature yucca trees. *No. 499, declared 6/12/90*

SEYLER RESIDENCE

1894

2305 Scarff Street
Exposition Park

Originally a Southern Pacific agent, Charles Seyler later became cashier at the Farmers and Merchants National Bank. His two-story restrained Queen Anne home was considered a fairly typical white-collar residence when built. *No. 407, declared 1/20/89*

STEVENSON RESIDENCE

1895

Adlai E. Stevenson Student House
of the University of Southern California
2639 Monmouth Avenue
Exposition Park

Adlai E. Stevenson, the internationally known statesman, was born in this subdued Queen Anne style residence in 1900. Unsuccessfully opposing Dwight Eisenhower in the presidential elections of 1952 and 1956, Stevenson subsequently became the acknowledged "conscience" of the liberal wing of the Democratic Party. He was named ambassador to the United Nations by President John F. Kennedy. *No. 35, declared 8/20/65*

BURKHALTER RESIDENCE

1895

2309-2311 Scarff Street
Exposition Park

Most likely built from pattern books imported from the East Coast, this middle-class Queen Anne style home was built for Southern Pacific employee Dennis Burkhalter and his family. *No. 409, declared 1/20/89*

REUMAN RESIDENCE

1896

925 West Twenty-third Street
Exposition Park

Built for a dental-supply company employee, Henry J. Reuman, this is a carefully maintained Colonial Revival residence. *No. 335, declared 12/18/87*

CREIGHTON RESIDENCE

1896

2342 Scarff Street
Exposition Park

A rare Classical Revival structure, now sadly dilapidated, this home was originally occupied by a widow, Jane Creighton, and her daughters, Margaret and Bettie. The building is typical of the fine homes built adjacent to the Chester Place/St. James Park subdivision and is included in the St. James National Register District. *No. 455, declared 10/24/89*

POSEY RESIDENCE

EISEN AND HUNT 1899

Doheny Mansion
8 Chester Place
Exposition Park

One of the few Los Angeles homes in the Spanish Gothic Revival style, this was the "master house" in an exclusive fenced residential park known as Chester Place. It was originally built for the Oliver Poseys, about whom little is known. The entire 20-acre park was purchased shortly after it was built by the newly wealthy oil magnate Edward Doheny (later of the Teapot Dome scandal) who occupied this, the largest house. He commissioned many substantial alterations over the years, including a new dining room which could seat more than one hundred people, and a conservatory to house his enormous collection of rare palm trees and other exotic plant life. Doheny's young second wife, Estelle, a former telephone operator, collected and grew orchids here, amassing the first such collection in Southern California; it numbered over ten thousand plants.

Following the 1958 death of the widowed Estelle (whom Pope Pius XII had elevated to the rank of papal countess), the building was bequeathed to the Catholic Sisters of St. Joseph of Candolet, who call the building Doheny Hall. It is now part of the Doheny Campus of Mount St. Mary's College. Photography is discouraged. *No. 30, declared 1/8/65*

IBBETSON RESIDENCE AND TREE

ROBERT IBBETSON 1899

1190 West Adams Boulevard
Exposition Park

Designed and built by and for Robert Ibbetson, this unconventional residence exhibits an unusual combination of details including its masonry wall, large dormer with double windows, and a rear porte cochere. It is especially scenic with its mature Moreton Bay fig tree. The especially rich interiors have been used for movie locations. *No. 350, declared 3/29/88*

STIMSON RESIDENCE

FREDERICK ROEHRIG 1901

839 West Adams Boulevard
Exposition Park

This residence was built for Ezra T. Stimson, who was treasurer of the family lumber company. He was listed in the 1917 edition of *Condon's Blue Book of Wealth* as one of Los Angeles's wealthiest businessmen. Stimson commissioned Frederick Roehrig to design this large Stick variant home with references to Newport "cottages." *No. 456, declared 10/24/89*

WELLS RESIDENCE

1901

(REMODELED 1909, ELIZA WRIGHT HALLIDAY)

Halliday Residence
2146 West Adams Boulevard
Exposition Park

Although this is one of the approximately two dozen original and extant West Adams mansions, it bears little resemblance to its original design. As built by George Wells, it was in the style of Victorian-era country houses. Sold in 1904 to heiress Eliza Wright, it was enlarged considerably to her own designs. The building, again recently altered, has been described as being in the Dutch Colonial Revival style, with a Craftsman wing. A large Postmodern style health-care institution has been built behind the home.

After Eliza Wright's marriage to W. P. Halliday, she continued to invest in real estate and designed residential structures. She was one of the major shareholders in the Janss Investment Corporation, which developed Westwood. *No. 458, declared 11/3/89*

STEARNS RESIDENCE

JOHN PARKINSON 1902

27 St. James Park
Exposition Park

A remarkable Neoclassical Revival residence, this stately home was commissioned by a descendant of the pioneering family credited with owning the first carriage in Los Angeles. Built by Colonel John E. Stearns, the building is part of the original Chester Place residential park development created by Judge Charles S. Silent in 1895. It was one of the most luxurious residential developments in Los Angeles and saw the construction of thirteen large homes built in a variety of fashionable styles. Today, it is owned by Mount St. Mary's College. *No. 434, declared 5/16/89*

GRANDVIEW PRESBYTERIAN COMMUNITY CENTER AND CATHEDRAL

H. M. PATTERSON 1904-30

First African Methodist Episcopal Zion
Community Center and Cathedral
1449 West Adams Boulevard
Exposition Park

These two buildings evolved for twenty-four years under the direction of the same architect. The original design of the community center was in the Mission Revival style; it was altered later into this Gothic Revival variation. The cathedral retains its original Mediterranean Revival character and the complex is significant for its continued use over the years. Its membership reflects the changing racial makeup of the neighborhood. First A.M.E. is among the earliest African-American congregations in Los Angeles. *No. 341, declared 1/22/88*

POSEY RESIDENCE

LINDSEY RESIDENCE

LINDSEY RESIDENCE AND CARRIAGE HOUSE

IRVING GILL AND CHARLES WHITTLESEY 1905

Our Lady of the Bright Mount Polish Parish Church
3424 West Adams Boulevard
Exposition Park

This elaborate Craftsman complex was built for early Los Angeles businessman Lycurgus Lindsey. The socially prominent, Missouri-born Lindsey became a director of the Los Angeles Trust Company and had numerous other business interests. In 1944, the property was purchased by the Catholic Arch-diocese of Los Angeles, which built the colorful auditorium structure (excluded from the designation) in front of the existing residence. The design is an overwrought confection exhibiting little to none of the style that made architect Gill famous, although the unusual terra-cotta "stone" is of interest.

It is no small irony that Gill's most signifi-cant work, the Dodge residence, has been demolished, while this unusual, but hardly trend-setting building survives. *No. 496, declared 3/30/90*

SECOND CHURCH OF CHRIST, SCIENTIST

ALFRED ROSENHEIM 1905-10

948 West Adams
Exposition Park

This white terra-cotta Classical Revival structure, with its monumental colonnade and pediment, and its broad copper dome, is said to be modeled after the Mother Church in Boston. It is a formidable presence in its West Adams neighborhood; its scale alone insures prominence as a visual landmark. *No. 57, declared 7/27/68*

RESIDENCE

FRANK M. TYLER 1908

2532 Fifth Avenue
Exposition Park

The first owner of this excellent Craftsman residence is not known. It was owned and occupied between 1938 and 1951 by Congressman Gordon Leo McDonough and his family. *No. 417, declared 2/21/89*

WALKER RESIDENCE

CHARLES WHITTLESEY 1908

Olympic Korean Seventh-Day Adventist Church
3300 West Adams Boulevard
Exposition Park

This large (12,000 sq. ft.) half-timbered Craftsman building was one of a row of large homes built along West Adams between 1890 and 1930; only a few of them are extant. It was built for Lucy Walker, but a later owner, William Barker of the Barker Brothers furniture stores, was better known. He purchased it in 1920 and died here two years later. Since the 1940s the building has been in institutional use. *No. 419, declared 3/3/89*

HANCOCK PARK

HIGGINS RESIDENCE

JOHN C. AUSTIN 1902
(RELOCATED 1920s)

Verbeck Residence
637 South Lucerne Boulevard
Hancock Park

Originally located at 2619 Wilshire Boulevard, this exuberant Colonial Revival home was built for Hiram Higgins, a retired Illinois grain dealer who moved to Los Angeles in 1900. Purchased in 1919 by interior designer Howard Verbeck, it became his home and his design showcase. By 1923, Wilshire Boulevard was being redeveloped along the lines it resembles today, and many of the mansions that lined it were being demolished. Verbeck opted to sell his land, but relocate the house to its current address. Today, having settled into its mature landscape, it speaks eloquently for those who view relocation as a viable preservation alternative. Homes such as this will never be built again. *No. 403, declared 12/14/88*

GORDON RESIDENCE

HIGHLAND PARK

GARVANZA PUMPING STATION AND HIGHLAND RESERVOIR

RALPH ROGERS 1889

DEPARTMENT OF WATER AND POWER 1902

420 North Avenue 62

Highland Park

This is the oldest pumping station and reservoir currently serving Los Angeles. A multi-gabled roof structure, which gives the appearance of a buckled hardwood floor, covers some four acres to control evaporation. *No. 412, declared 1/28/89*

RESIDENCE

1890

432 North Avenue 66

Highland Park

This large and distinctive Queen Anne structure seems to have lost its front yard, but is still nicely baffled from the street by good, mature plantings. *No. 107, declared 11/15/72*

WHALEY RESIDENCE

CA. 1890

6434 Crescent Street

Highland Park

This two-story Italianate house, built for Dr. Franklin S. Whaley, may be considered a textbook example of its style. The building received a small addition on the west side in 1907. *No. 528, declared 3/1/91*

GORDON RESIDENCE AND RETAINING WALL

1892

4939 Sycamore Terrace

Highland Park

Early records on this arroyo stone residence are sketchy. It appears that the land was once owned by the prosperous Bent family, but the first sale of the building (1921) was from Elizabeth Young Gordon to the R. K. Voorhies family, who were to occupy the home for sixty years. The patio and garden were decorated with factory-reject tiles from the nearby Batchelder tile factory. *No. 373, declared 1/18/88*

WILLIAMS RESIDENCE
1892

212-214 North Avenue 57
Highland Park

The Charles Williamses were listed as the owners of these buildings beginning in 1896; the original owners are not known. These two structures are among the earliest buildings in the area of Highland Park and represent a vernacular style that has mostly vanished. Some speculate that the rear structure, designed by Henry W. Covas, was an out-building that was converted later to residential use. *No. 556, declared 4/28/92*

LUMMIS RESIDENCE
CHARLES F. LUMMIS 1894

El Alisal / The Sycamore
200 East Avenue 43
Highland Park

Charles F. Lummis, author, historian, librarian for the City of Los Angeles (1905–1910), archeologist, and founder of the Southwest Museum (1907), designed his unusual stone house in the Mission Revival style; it was built largely with his own hands over a fifteen-year period. It is named for a large sycamore tree in the garden (now gone), and is said to have been visited by more famous people than any home in Southern California. Since 1965 it has been the home of the Historical Society of Southern California. El Alisal is State Registered Landmark No. 531 and is open to the public. *No. 68, declared 9/2/70*

DRAKE RESIDENCE

DRAKE RESIDENCE

1894

220 South Avenue 60
Highland Park

This truly modest, if well-preserved, vernacular farmhouse is as evocative of a vanished life-style as any in Los Angeles. Its relative lack of change over time may be attributed to its continuous sixty-year-plus habitation by the Drake family. *No. 338, declared 1/26/88*

RAILROAD BRIDGE

1895

Above the Pasadena Freeway near
162 South Avenue 61
Highland Park

The railroad came to Los Angeles only in 1876, so this early structure is both the oldest and the highest such bridge in the county. Built of steel and supported on concrete footings, the bridge is over 700 feet long and operates as a single-track railroad

RAILROAD BRIDGE

line. It is actually at its most interesting when viewed from its base, near the residential backyards and parkland surrounding the concrete footings. The supporting structures resemble creatures from a George Lucas film. This venerable structure is being studied for an adaptive reuse as a carrier of light rail vehicles (LRVs) as part of Los Angeles's expanding mass transit system. *No. 339, declared 1/22/88*

WHEELER / SMITH RESIDENCE

1897

5684 Ash Street
Highland Park

Former City Engineer Edgar Wheeler commissioned this one-story Victorian-era structure but sold it to the Charles C. Smith family in 1900. A subdivision of the original 5-acre site led to the construction in 1934 of four eclectic Mediterranean Revival style residences that now obscure the view of this historic residence. *No. 378, declared 7/15/88*

COLLEGE OF FINE ARTS AND ARCHITECTURE

TRAIN AND WILLIAMS 1901

Judson Studios
200 South Avenue 66
Highland Park

Beginning as a three-story Islamic Revival style building, the current two-story height reflects a post-fire remodel. This charming and unusual structure was built by William Lees Judson, who founded the school, which later became the School of Architecture of the University of Southern California. The school was relocated to its current central campus in 1920. The building was then occupied by the next Judson generation, this time as the Judson Stained Glass Studios, one of the oldest family-owned businesses in continuing operation in Los Angeles. The studio originally produced opalescent art glass and later nineteenth-century English style art glass. *No. 62, declared 8/13/69*

PUTMAN RESIDENCE

GRIFFITH RESIDENCE

1903

(RELOCATED 1914)

5915 Echo Street

Highland Park

G. W. E. Griffith was a banker who became one of the most prominent and beloved citizens of his neighborhood, earning him the sobriquet of "Mr. Highland Park." Following the construction of a movie theater adjacent to his home, Griffith's building was moved from 110 South Avenue 58 to its current location. It is a two-story Colonial Revival structure featuring both Moorish and Tuscan influences. *No. 374, declared 7/15/88*

PUTMAN RESIDENCE

GEORGE WYMAN CA. 1903

5944 Hayes Avenue

Highland Park

This odd Craftsman home has been described as one of a kind in both design and character. Little is known about its origins, but its three-story pyramidal tower gives it an odd, church-like appearance. *No. 375, declared 7/15/88*

FIELD RESIDENCE AND RETAINING WALL

ATTRIB. PHILIP W. HOLLER 1904

4967 Sycamore Terrace

Highland Park

A well-to-do widow, Mary P. Field, commissioned this one-and-one-half-story Craftsman bungalow as her residence. The building is considered unusual for its barnlike detail. *No. 372, declared 1/15/88*

SPENCER RESIDENTIAL COMPOUND

ALL BY CHARLES C. DODGE, EXCEPT GARAGE

BY FREDERICK ASHLEY 1898

5660 Ash Street

Highland Park

An early vernacular complex in a once-rural setting, the house, carriage house, water tower, and garage have been described as being in the "American Foursquare" style. *No. 564, declared 8/25/92*

REEVES RESIDENCE

1905

219 North Avenue 53

Highland Park

This remarkably intact, modest Colonial Revival residence was built for Mary Reeves, a teacher, and her mother. In a once-popular architectural style and small scale that is increasingly rare, this house is recognized for the degree to which it remains in original condition. *No. 380, declared 7/15/88*

WILLIAMS RESIDENCE

TRAIN AND WILLIAMS 1905

Hathaway House

840 North Avenue 66

Highland Park

Designed as the personal residence of architect Robert E. Williams, this comfortable two-story house, with its many Craftsman features, was converted in 1919 to the Hathaway Home for Children, a service facility for emotionally disturbed or learning-disabled children. The building features stained glass from the Judson Studios, whose building was designed by Williams and his partner. *No. 411, declared 1/18/89*

PIPER RESIDENCE

WILLIAM NEELY 1905

326 North Avenue 53
Highland Park

Significant largely for the degree to which the building remains intact, this Craftsman home was continuously owned by one family from 1905 until the early 1960s. *No. 540, declared 7/19/91*

OLLIE TRACT RESIDENCE

JOHN SCOTT 1907

199 South Avenue 57
Highland Park

The Ollie Tract is made up of six residential lots upon which two houses have been constructed, but only one of them is cited in this declaration. This simple Craftsman home is considered the best surviving example of the work of designer/contractor John Scott, who was known for the construction of many of the homes in Highland Park. This one, with its parklike setting, gives it the feel of a fairy-tale cottage. *No. 377, declared 7/15/88*

MAXWELL RESIDENCE

ARTHUR B. BENTON 1907

211 South Avenue 52
Highland Park

This rather large two-story, shingle-over-clapboard residence displays various Craftsman style details but appears to be more idiosyncratic in its origins. It boasts an odd triple-arched entrance porch and a nearly symmetric front elevation. *No. 539, declared 7/19/91*

SMITH RESIDENCE AND RETAINING WALL

WILLIAM U. SMITH 1908

140 South Avenue 57
Highland Park

Owner-designed and built to resemble a home remembered from his Pennsylvania youth, this vaguely Greek Revival bungalow stands as one man's response to the American dream of do-it-yourself home construction. The house remained in the Smith family for nearly seventy years with virtually no changes. *No. 376, declared 7/15/88*

FARGO RESIDENCE

HARRY GREY 1908

206 Thorne Street
Highland Park

Although this stucco building has often been attributed to Greene and Greene, it was actually designed by one of the many architects influenced by them. It was built for stagecoach line and bank co-founder Dwight Fargo. Esther McCoy, in her ground-breaking *Five California Architects*, calls Greene and Greene pioneers and major contributors to the development of a rich and indigenous American architecture. She also points out that many contemporary copies of their work appeared on the cityscape. While she does not discuss the Fargo residence itself, its date would make it concurrent with the Greenes' most famous work, the Gamble residence, in Pasadena. *No. 464, declared 11/3/89*

FARGO RESIDENCE

JANES RESIDENCE

MERRILL RESIDENCE

CHARLES SHATTUCK 1906

Morrell Residence
215 North Avenue 53
Highland Park

Built for banker and professional organist John B. Merrill, this modest Craftsman bungalow was designed to provide performance space for Merrill, which it evidently did quite handsomely in the cathedral-ceilinged living room. It was sold shortly after completion to Rivers Morrell but continued to be used by Merrill for concerts. *No. 379, declared 7/15/88*

HOLLYWOOD

TAFT RESIDENCE

CA. 1900

(DESTROYED BY FIRE 1982)

7777 Sunset Boulevard
Hollywood

A turn-of-the-century vernacular farmhouse built for Z. A. Taft, who was a prominent figure in the Hollywood community, this structure was moved from its original site on Hollywood Boulevard in 1919. It was destroyed by fire in June 1982. *No. 234, declared 11/3/80*

JANES RESIDENCE

OLIVER DENNIS AND LYMAN FARWELL 1903

6451 Hollywood Boulevard
Hollywood

One of the last remnants of Hollywood Boulevard mansions, this house was purchased by the Janes family from the original developer before Hollywood became home to the film industry. Later, it was operated by the Janes daughters, Carrie, Mable, and Grace, as the Misses Janes' Kindergarten, even while it served as their home. The school was attended by children of the film community, including Agnes de Mille and Geraldine Chaplin. Today, it serves as the centerpiece of an insensitive strip shopping center serving the thousands of tourists who visit the area. Architect Farwell had apprenticed in the office of McKim, Mead and White. *No. 227, declared 4/3/80*

WHITLEY RESIDENCE

OLIVER DENNIS AND LYMAN FARWELL 1903 AND LATER

Whitley Court Apartments
1720-1728 Whitley Avenue
Hollywood

This complex began as a two-story Colonial Revival residence built for the Whitley family. Later, two-story bungalow duplexes were constructed on the front lawn. It is known to have been inhabited by workers in the film industry; actress Theda Bara was rumored to have lived here in the twenties, and Silvia Sydney in the thirties. This property has been found eligible for listing on the National Register. *No. 448, declared 12/13/89*

WHITLEY RESIDENCE

PART III / 1889-1908

SACRED HEART ROMAN
CATHOLIC CHURCH

KOREATOWN

PEET RESIDENCE

1889

1139 South Harvard Boulevard
Koreatown

This is a well-preserved example of a modest
residence built from the plan books of the
Victorian era. It is not known who the original owners were, but it has been in the D. A.
Peet family since 1893. *No. 272, declared
9/1/83*

LINCOLN HEIGHTS

SACRED HEART ROMAN
CATHOLIC CHURCH

1893

2210 Sichel Street
Lincoln Heights

A rarity in Los Angeles, this nineteenth-
century brick Gothic Revival church features
important early stained-glass windows and
an elaborate altar. Though the original
steeple has been removed, the square corner
tower remains. *No. 468, declared 12/5/89*

RESIDENCE

1893

2660 Sichel Street
Lincoln Heights

Little is known about this Victorian-era residence. The immediate area was developed in
the 1880s by John Downey. Originally built
as a single-family residence, the home has
been converted into three rental units. *No.
533, declared 6/11/91*

HOVEY RESIDENCE

1905

Dunning Residence
5552 Carlton Way
Hollywood

Built for Augustus H. Hovey in the style of a
traditional American farmhouse, this
recently restored two-story vernacular structure features clapboard siding, gabled roof,
and a simple rectangular floor plan. Once
surrounded by orange groves, the development tract was named for N. A. Dunning, one
of the original developers of this area before
it became known as Hollywood. *No. 441,
declared 5/31/89*

HYDE PARK

HYDE PARK
CONGREGATIONAL
CHURCH

1901

(DEMOLISHED 1964)

6501 Crenshaw Boulevard
Hyde Park

This site was purchased and the church built
with funds donated by congregation members
Capt. and Mrs. Fred B. Clark. Other
members of the congregation provided the
art-glass windows. The diminutive structure,
built as a Congregational Church, was the
last remaining landmark of the community of
Hyde Park, which is now a neighborhood
rather than a town. *No. 18, declared 5/10/63*

EDISON ELECTRIC COMPANY

JOHN PARKINSON 1904

650 South Avenue 21
Lincoln Heights

Although produced by a firm well known for
its elegant design sensibility, this is a very
utilitarian structure with a monochromatic
brick façade. No longer a power plant, the
building is used today as a warehouse and
for automobile storage. *No. 388, declared
10/21/88*

MID CITY

RINDGE RESIDENCE

FREDERICK L. ROEHRIG 1900

2263 South Harvard Boulevard
Mid City

This is perhaps the best example of a
Châteauesque style residence in Los
Angeles; it was built for noted financier and
real-estate mogul Frederick L. Rindge and
his wife, Mae. Rindge died within a few
years of its completion. Mae, however, continued to live here until her death in 1941.
She was one of Los Angeles's legendary
hostesses.

The residence is located on a cul-de-sac
with a grouping of other fine homes. The
cluster has remained remarkably intact, even
as the neighborhood around it has deteriorated. Other homes on South Harvard are Los
Angeles monuments, but none compare to
the Rindge house. Its perfect symmetry is
reflected not only in the round towers with
conical roofs but also in the dormers, chim-
neys, and lighting standards. After a period
of time as a convent and maternity home, the
building is once again in private hands and
is impeccably maintained. *No. 95, declared
2/23/72*

RINDGE RESIDENCE

BECKETT RESIDENCE

1905

2218 South Harvard Boulevard
Mid City

This residence is a Classical Revival design
built for the educator for whom Beckett Hall
at the University of Southern California is
named. Part of an enclave protected mostly
by restrictive site planning, this cul-de-sac
mansion housed in recent years the Veteran's
Light House and Cultural Center. The building fell into disrepair after a roof fire in 1981
and is now in poor condition. *No. 117,*
declared 4/4/73

PHILLIPS RESIDENCE

HUNT AND EAGER 1905

2215 South Harvard Boulevard
Mid City

Another of the large residential structures
built on this quiet cul-de-sac, this was the
home of early bond investor Thomas W.
Phillips. The half-timbered Craftsman home
has eight bedrooms. Phillips was an early
business associate of Frederick Rindge,
whose home was built nearby. Presumably,
this influenced Phillips's decision to acquire
this prestigious building site. *No. 551,*
declared 3/18/92

FITZGERALD RESIDENCE

JOSEPH CATHER NEWSOM 1903

3115 West Adams Boulevard
Mid City

Although little is known of J. T. Fitzgerald, who commissioned this home, its architect is quite well known. While it has been said that Newsom's work did not adhere to any particular style, it is consistent with other buildings of the period in which he worked. This house is a significant departure from his usual style. Newsom's product was most often built of wood, as opposed to the masonry found here (his work also generally fit into the Queen Anne mold), yet this oddly idiosyncratic home has vaguely Gothic details. It remains an unusual and interesting home, in remarkable condition except for some insensitive window alterations. *No. 258, declared 11/5/82*

DURFEE RESIDENCE

FREDERICK L. ROEHRIG CA. 1908

Villa Maria
2425 South Western Avenue
Mid City

Built for an early Los Angeles family, this distinguished example of a large Tudor Revival residence, which contained nine bedrooms, is now the centerpiece of a large seniors housing complex. The other Durfee residence is HCM 273. *No. 230, declared 6/12/80*

MERRILL RESIDENCE

FIRE STATION NO. 18

JOHN PARKINSON 1904

2616 South Hobart Boulevard
Mid City

A survivor from the horse-drawn fire engine days, this delicious twin-towered Mission Revival style building has been refurbished and converted to an art center. *No. 349, declared 3/29/88*

MT. WASHINGTON

MERRILL RESIDENCE

H. M. PATTERSON 1908

815 Elyria Drive
Mt. Washington

The second Craftsman residence built for John Merrill to be named an HCM, this home was among the first to be built in the Mt. Washington neighborhood. As with his other residence, this house was also built to accommodate Merrill's organ concerts in the large living room. *No. 483, declared 2/26/90*

JUDSON RESIDENCE

GEORGE HERBERT WYMAN 1895

(DEMOLISHED 1993)

4911 Sycamore Terrace (formerly Pasadena Street)
Mt. Washington

In one of Los Angeles architecture's more compelling mysteries, George Wyman, who was the architect for the Bradbury Building, produced no other visionary architecture during the remainder of his career. He did design this unusual Colonial Revival home for real-estate pioneer Albert Judson. Judson was known for his part in creating the title insurance business; he founded the Title Insurance and Trust Company, the first of many title companies in Los Angeles. *No. 437, declared 5/19/89*

HORNBECK RESIDENCE

THOMSON RESIDENCE

1902

215 South Avenue 52
Mt. Washington

This unusual building, with its long, covered porch and simple, rustic detailing, reflects its Queen Anne affinity in its two semi-conical roof elements. It was built for the Reverend Williel Thomson, who was a founder and the first president of Sierra Madre College. *No. 541, declared 7/19/91*

HORNBECK RESIDENCE

1904

Zeigler Residence
4601 North Figueroa Street
Mt. Washington

The original owner, real-estate broker Charles Hornbeck, had this elaborate and idiosyncratic Craftsman home built for his family. But he soon sold it to businessman Louis B. Zeigler, who owned it until 1959. In 1960, the home was acquired by Carl Dentzel for the nearby Southwest Museum. *No. 416, declared 2/21/89*

BENT RESIDENCE

HUNT AND EAGER 1904

161-169 South Avenue 49
Mt. Washington

Another example of Sumner Hunt's residential architecture, this secluded, half-timbered, Tudor Revival structure was built on a hilltop for noted historian and second-generation Angeleno, Arthur Bent, whose family was quite prominent at the turn of the century. This is one of four homes built for the extended family in the Mt. Washington neighborhood. Bent was a trustee and founder of Pomona College. The building is now part of a school complex and is very difficult to locate; it can be glimpsed briefly from the Pasadena Freeway. *No. 482, declared 5/1/87*

RESIDENTIAL COMPLEX

CHARLES E. BENT 1906

Treehaven
4211 Glenalbyn Drive
Mt. Washington

In keeping with the Craftsman philosophy, Treehaven was constructed by owner/builder Charles Bent, who was also a successful insurance broker active in the Rotary Club and the Chamber of Commerce. Together with his half-brothers, Stanley and Ernest, they built this family compound. A guest house was the first to be completed. Charles and his family lived here until the main residence was completed. A pavilion was also constructed for Mrs. Bent for use as an art studio. The entire complex, including walkways, a gazebo, and other hand-wrought features, displays the rustic appeal of the Craftsman style. *No. 392, declared 11/4/88*

PHILLIPS RESIDENCES

IVAR PHILLIPS 1907

4200 and 4204 North Figueroa Street
Mt. Washington

Near-twin Craftsman style homes, designed and built by Ivar Phillips, an architect, contractor, and developer, both were rental properties; Phillips maintained his own residence nearby. It is theorized that these buildings were built as models for a subdivision that he built later in another part of the city. *Nos. 469, 470, declared 12/20/89*

BURNS RESIDENCE

ATTRIB. EDWARD SYMONDS 1907

369 North Avenue 53
Mt. Washington

Beautifully sited on a steep slope of Mt. Washington, this Tudor Revival residence was designed for original owner/builder James Burns by his brother-in-law Edward Symonds, a talented architect whose promising career was cut short by his untimely death at twenty-seven. *No. 554, declared 3/18/92*

BURNS RESIDENCE

FIRE STATION NO. 18

BENT-HALSTEAD RESIDENCE

ERNEST BENT 1908

4200 Glenalbyn Drive

Mt. Washington

Construction of this element of the Mt. Washington Bent family began in 1908. The main house bears strong resemblance to its neighbors, with its low-pitched r oof, wide eaves, and shingle walls. It also features a fence with distinctive Craftsman style heart-shaped cutouts. *No. 394, declared 11/4/88*

WACHTEL RESIDENCE

1906

315 West Avenue 43

Mt. Washington

Elmer and Marian Kavanaugh Wachtel were both proficient Southern California landscape painters who worked in the Craftsman style. They commissioned this classic bungalow with its unusual studio space, nestled into a eucalyptus grove, as an extension of their involvement in the American Arts and Crafts movement. Elmer developed his understanding of the movement through his work in sculpture, metalwork, and furniture carving. Well-known within the movement in Southern California, their work happily remained idiosyncratic and free from influence by their colleagues. They lived and worked in the area until 1921. *No. 503, declared 10/9/90*

PALMS

IVY SUBSTATION

1907

9015 Venice Boulevard

Palms

This superb Mission Revival building, until recently just a shell, provided power for the ever-expanding Los Angeles Pacific Railway.

Originally these substations were set in beautifully landscaped grounds. Empty for more than ten years, the building has been recently converted to Park and Recreation Department use and has been beautifully restored and landscaped. It is listed on the National Register. *No. 182, declared 2/1/78*

SAN PEDRO

GREY / COLEMAN RESIDENCE

1906

383 West Tenth Street
San Pedro

A charming row house from another era, this Colonial Revival home is larger than it appears because of its fully developed attic. Dormers and an arched, recessed balcony at this upper level add considerable appeal to this deservedly well-maintained residence. It is named for its original owners, John Grey and E. Coleman. *No. 514, declared 12/7/90*

SILVER LAKE

SILVER LAKE AND IVANHOE RESERVOIRS

WILLIAM MULHOLLAND 1906

Between West Silver Lake Drive and
Silver Lake Boulevard
Silver Lake

The largest of these reservoirs—and ultimately the whole district—was named for Herman Silver, first president of the city Water Commission. When built, these reservoirs were capable of supplying Los Angeles's water needs for twenty days. Originally covered to delay evaporation, Ivanhoe's roof was removed during earthquake-proofing in the 1970s. *No. 422, declared 3/31/89*

SOUTH CENTRAL

PAUL HAUPT BUILDING

CA. 1889

"Cast Iron Building"
740-748 South San Pedro Street
South Central

Not one of the famous cast-iron buildings of the East Coast, which feature slim structural members and lots of glass, this period commercial block derives its name from the one remaining cast-iron column cover extant on the front façade. A more distinctive feature of this simple Queen Anne commercial structure is its corner bay surmounted by a sheet-metal witch's cap, which has a sensational view of downtown high rises. *No. 140, declared 3/19/75*

VENICE

VENICE CANAL SYSTEM

MARSH AND RUSSELL 1905

(PARTIALLY DEMOLISHED)

Public right-of-way in an area bounded by
Venice Boulevard, Washington Street, Ocean Avenue,
and Strongs Drive

VENICE ARCADES (DETAIL)

VENICE ARCADES, COLUMNS, AND CAPITALS

MARSH AND GRAHAM 1905

(PARTIALLY DEMOLISHED)

67-71 Windward Avenue

Influenced by tobacco magnate Abbot Kinney's vision to create an American Venice, the development company of Strong and Dickerson commissioned Norman J. Marsh to plan the conversion of 160 acres of marshy flatland into a residential subdivision with canals and waterways. An intricate system of roadways and bridges, as well as imported gondolas (and, reportedly, an imported gondolier), were meant to approximate a Venetian atmosphere.

The development, however, was not a success, and in the 1930s many of the canals were filled in. On a foggy evening, even if you squint, you will find it next to impossible to conjure up memories of the real Grand Canal or any of its tributaries. But historic photographs show a richly detailed architecture. Remnants of the romantic image that was promoted here still have exceptional appeal for some.

As of this writing, the canals are undergoing a multimillion-dollar restoration to provide a flushing system to eliminate the polluted waters. New sidewalks, banks, and a boat ramp complete the repairs, which will see the waters restocked with fish and ducks. The Venice Canal System has been listed on the National Register. *No. 270, declared 7/15/83*

Marsh was also commissioned to design an Italianate town center on Windward Avenue, which became Venice's widest street. Conceived and built in only one year as a prestigious locale, Venice boasted expensive hotels and a Chatauqua hall. But the concept proved to be too intellectual for Angelenos, who preferred the beach and sunshine to the various cultural amenities of the town.

In a surprising show of flexibility, the format was changed, and Venice was developed instead as a prototypical adult amusement park. Vestiges of the grander days remain in a few of the arcaded walkways, columns, and particularly the Ionic capitals, the faces of which were modeled after a beauty queen and local businessman. *No. 532, declared 4/8/91*

VENICE CANAL SYSTEM

SILVER LAKE AND IVANHOE
RESERVOIRS

FORGET RESIDENCE

WESTLAKE

GREEN RESIDENCE

ROBERT BROWN YOUNG CA. 1890

(RELOCATED 1909)

1851 West Eleventh Street
Westlake

An integral part of the South Bonnie Brae Street National Register Historic District, this beautifully restored Queen Anne home was built for Richard Green. Displaced by downtown business expansion, it was moved to its current location from its original site on South Olive Street. Young was known for his designs for early downtown hotels. *No. 431, declared 5/5/89*

FORGET RESIDENCE

ROBERT BROWN YOUNG 1890

(RELOCATED 1909)

1047 South Bonnie Brae Street
Westlake

The similarity between this home, built for Alphonse J. Forget, and the Green Residence, located around the corner on West Eleventh Street, is not coincidental: both were built at roughly the same time and by the same prominent builder/designer Robert Brown Young. This one, too, has been relocated from its original location on South Olive Street. *No. 433, declared 5/5/89*

BOOTHE RESIDENCE AND CARRIAGE HOUSE

1893

824-826 South Bonnie Brae Street
Westlake

This early and extremely unusual Victorian-era residence features an oddly Islamic style domed roof over a cylindrically shaped room on the second floor. It was built for pioneer businessman Charles Boothe who, like so many others, came to California seeking sunshine and restored health. Boothe was instrumental in assisting with the passage of the National Irrigation Act in Congress, which made possible the reclamation of arid Western lands. *No. 491, declared 7/13/90*

MOOERS RESIDENCE

1894

818 South Bonnie Brae Street
Westlake

Built for Frederick Mitchell Mooers, who made his fortune with the discovery of the famous Yellow Aster gold mine of Randsburg (Kern County), this remarkably well-preserved residence may be considered a prototype of the buildings constructed during the real-estate boom of the 1880s. Represented here are the various styles of eclectic architecture that were popular during this period. Proponents of the Beaux Arts style, which would soon emerge, saw buildings like this as the embodiment of the lack of discipline in American architecture. The building's architect is unknown, but the high quality and quantity of woodcarving on this Mannerist expression are reminiscent of the works of Joseph Cather Newsom. Mooers's home is listed on the National Register. *No. 45, declared 2/8/67*

COCKINS RESIDENCE

BRADBEER AND FERRIS 1894

2652 South Hoover Street
Westlake

This large and graceful two-and-one-half-story residence was built for William Cockins. It features most of the signature Queen Anne details, including an asymmetric front elevation dominated by a round tower. At this writing, the building is boarded up and appears to be awaiting either demolition or relocation. *No. 519, declared 12/7/90*

RESIDENCE

1896

1036-1038 South Bonnie Brae Street
Westlake

The exterior of this unusual home, with its wooden "château" detailing, clearly registers its history and its "mileage." This is not a new home, and it has seen a lot of living. Nonetheless, its current owners have lovingly repaired and painted the structure to enhance its weathered countenance. Nearly a hundred years old, it remains remarkably photogenic. *No. 99, declared 4/5/72*

HILL RESIDENCE

1898

Grier-Musser Residence
403 South Bonnie Brae Street
Westlake

This simplified Queen Anne/Colonial Revival style residence was built by Jonathan A. Hill. Having undergone many conversions to various uses over time, including a maternity hospital and a boarding house, the recently restored building now serves as a house museum, featuring an installation that suggests how the current owner's grandmother, Anna Grier-Musser, might have lived. Admission is charged. *No. 333, declared 12/18/87*

DORIA APARTMENTS

AUGUST HANSON 1902

1600 West Pico Boulevard
Westlake

Named for Mrs. John (Doria Deighton) Jones, this Mission Revival apartment building survives with much of the original exterior intact, although the street-level storefronts have been altered over the years. The Joneses were prominent wholesale merchants, developers, and philanthropists. *No. 432, declared 5/5/89*

BERNARD RESIDENCE

JOHN B. PARKINSON 1902

845 South Lake Street
Westlake

An opulent turn-of-the-century Château-esque home and carriage house, with both Gothic and Art Nouveau touches, it was constructed for Swiss émigré Jean Bernard's widow (née Susana Machado) and their seven children. Mrs. Bernard was early Los Angeles landed gentry (Rancho Ballona), and she built here to raise her large family by herself after her husband's untimely death. Her grandfather, José Manuel Machado, was one of the founding settlers of the Pueblo of Los Angeles in 1781, under Governor Felipe de Neve.

After the Bernard family moved, the building served as a rest home for nearly thirty years. Today, it is once again a private residence. The mature landscaping makes it difficult to see this very early work by architect Parkinson. *No. 208, declared 1/17/79*

BEYRLE RESIDENCE

1906

1866 West Fourteenth Street
Westlake

Noted for the fine Craftsman detail of its interior, this dark-shingled building, on a heavily wooded site, was built for lumberman Andrew Beyrle. *No. 244, declared 4/30/81*

POTTER RESIDENCE

HUDSON AND MUNSELL 1906

1135 South Alvarado Street
Westlake

This ten-room Tudor Revival style residence was built for entrepreneur Thomas Potter. Both this building and its neighbor at 1147 are now in institutional use. *No. 327, declared 9/22/87*

WINSTEL RESIDENCE

JOHN PAUL KREMPEL 1907

1147 South Alvarado Street
Westlake

In what may be one of the more bizarre Los Angeles examples of imitation being the sincerest form of flattery, August Winstel commissioned and built this Tudor Revival style residence the year after his neighbor (see Potter Residence above) finished his. *No. 328, declared 9/22/87*

RESIDENCE

1908

(DEMOLISHED FOLLOWING A FIRE IN 1978)

919 West Twentieth Street
Westlake

This building, with its finely crafted interior, was moved to this site in 1918. Following a major fire less than a year after its designation (which was opposed by the owners), it was subsequently demolished. Unhappily, this is not a particularly rare occurrence in Los Angeles preservation annals. *No. 179, declared 8/17/77*

PART IV / 1909-1928

During this period the foundations of the modern City of Los Angeles were laid: the harbor area, Hollywood, and the San Fernando Valley were annexed; the movie industry moved to California—and the era of the talkies began; and, most significantly, the Owens Valley Aqueduct was completed, thus providing the water necessary to sustain both the growing urban population and the still highly profitable agricultural business. By 1922, Wilshire Boulevard had become a major six-lane thoroughfare, signaling how much the city had grown and presaging the great network of roadways that would characterize Los Angeles in the years to come.

Los Angeles saw many architectural styles during this period. The first service station was opened (1912). Significant architectural influences emerged from San Diego's 1915 Panama-California Exposition, which popularized Spanish Colonial Revival buildings. Although architects were still designing in the Craftsman style, glimmerings of the modern movement were seen with the construction of the Barnsdall Residence (1919). The Hollywood Bowl was built on the site of an early Native American camp (1920s). Olvera Street was saved (1928).

FINE ARTS BUILDING (DETAIL)

ATWATER VILLAGE

FLETCHER DRIVE BRIDGE

MERRILL BUTLER 1928

Between Larga Avenue and Crystal Street
Atwater Village

One of three bridges funded by a 1925 bond issue and designed by a bridge engineer in the civil service, this low-lying, reinforced concrete structure, in the Neoclassical style, has a particularly romantic feel when its street lamps are burning. *No. 322, declared 7/21/87*

BEVERLY HILLS / BEL AIR ESTATES

LLOYD RESIDENCE

WEBBER, STAUNTON AND SPALDING 1928

Greenacres
1040 Angelo Drive
Beverly Hills / Bel Air Estates

Lying exactly on the border of the communities of Beverly Hills and Bel Air Estates, and reputed to be one of the finest residential and garden complexes in the region, Greenacres was developed by silent-screen comedian Harold Lloyd. Its landscaping and siting make it impossible to view from a public right-of-way. Much of the original acreage has been subdivided and sold off, but the home has been elaborately restored. Currently owned by Marshall Field's heir and film producer Ted Field (*The Hand that Rocks the Cradle*), at this writing the property is on the market for a reported $45 million.

Greenacres is listed on the National Register and is also State Registered Landmark No. 961. It is not open to the public, and uninvited visitors are quickly turned away. *No. 279, declared 7/24/84*

BOYLE HEIGHTS

LINCOLN PARK CAROUSEL

BUILDING DESIGNED BY THE LOS ANGELES BUREAU OF ARCHITECTURE 1914

(DEMOLISHED 1976)

Mission Road and Valley Boulevard
Boyle Heights

There seems to be a problem keeping a carousel in this location. The original one was moved to San Francisco's Golden Gate Park in 1930, where it remains in operation to this day. It was replaced by another carousel (built in 1924), with hand-carved horses, goats, and a giraffe, but this one was burned by vandals four months after its designation. *No. 153, declared 4/21/76*

CONGREGATION TALMUD TORAH

A. M. EDELMAN AND LEO W. BARNETT 1923

247 North Breed Street
Boyle Heights

Dating from a congregation formed in 1904, this Renaissance Revival masonry shul became the spiritual center for a large Jewish population living in the then-fashionable Boyle Heights district. The structure's exterior has a distinct East Coast architectural quality and patina that belies its more recent vintage. Its interior was conceived and executed in the folk art tradition of Eastern European synagogues. Currently empty and deteriorating, this handsome building is in need of restoration. *No. 359, declared 6/7/88*

CANOGA PARK

CANOGA RAILROAD STATION

1912

21355 Sherman Way
Canoga Park

This simple vernacular building recalls a lost era of the west Valley. This was the first railroad station built there and, as a transfer point, it was extremely significant to pioneer inhabitants of the region. The building is currently boarded up and derelict after interim use as a hardware store, but it is said that much of the original interior remains. A sign nearby offers only "Land for Sale," which does not bode well for the historic structure it supports. *No. 488, declared 5/21/90*

CASTELLAMARE

SYCAMORE TREES

1926

Bienvenada Avenue
(south from Sunset Boulevard
to the cul-de-sac) Castellamare

These street trees were planted as part of the original subdivision when this land was converted to residential use. The trees are now mature and contribute greatly to the feeling of the area. Further subdivision, proposed in 1989, would have replaced one of the trees with a gate house for new development. This planned removal, coupled with the potential pollution damage to the trees resulting from increased traffic to the new subdivision, resulted in the designation. *No. 465, declared 10/27/89*

MILBANK RESIDENCE

COUNTRY CLUB PARK

MILBANK AND McFIE RESIDENCES AND GROUNDS

G. LAWRENCE STIMSON 1913

ONE Institute of Homophile Studies
3340 Country Club Drive and
1130 Arlington Avenue
Country Club Park

This three-and-one-half-acre site was part of a large development on lands once occupied by the Los Angeles Country Club. The property was acquired by business executive Isaac Milbank as a location for his own Beaux Arts style residence, which is a near twin to the William Wrigley home in Pasadena. Later he had a Colonial Revival style home built on the grounds for his daughter, Phila Milbank McFie. The beautifully landscaped grounds allow only glimpses of the homes from the public right-of-way.

Today, the homes are in institutional use as the campus of the ONE Institute, which offers classes, lectures, and masters and doctoral programs in homophile studies. ONE published the first American periodical for homosexuals, a magazine that ultimately figured in the Supreme Court ruling that such publications are protected under the First Amendment.

The impressive main house is used for receptions and fundraisers, and it also houses one of the world's largest libraries of publications relating to homosexuality. The house has occasionally been used for movies, including *Protocol* with Goldie Hawn and *Farewell, My Lovely* with Robert Mitchum. It is privately owned and maintained. For information call (213) 735-5252. *No. 420, declared 12/13/89*

DONOVAN RESIDENCE

I. EISNER 1913

"Sunshine Hall"
419 South Lorraine Boulevard
Country Club Park

Built for New Yorker Jeanette Donovan, this building is a rare example of the Neoclassical Revival residence that was popular on the East Coast at the turn of the century. Donovan was a friend of the developer, a man named Rowan, who named the street for his daughter and who called the district "Windsor Square." The exterior is dominated by a Roman temple portico with Ionic columns. *No. 115, declared 3/21/73*

MORENO RESIDENCE

CA. 1918

(DEMOLISHED 1986)

The Masquer's Club
1765 North Sycamore Avenue
Country Club Park

This Tudor Revival residence was built for silent-screen star Antonio Moreno. With its landscaped gardens, it reflected the era when Hollywood was becoming the film capital of the world. Moreno's career peaked in the twenties, when he played opposite such leading ladies as Greta Garbo and Gloria Swanson. But with the advent of talkies, his thick Spanish accent relegated him to supporting roles. Alas, his best-known film is probably *Creature from the Black Lagoon*.

In 1923, at the height of his career, Moreno married oil heiress Daisy Canfield and moved from this residence to the Silver Lake estate she had built for them (Canfield-Moreno Residence, HCM 391). Subsequently, Moreno's house became the headquarters of the Masquer's Club, which was one of Hollywood's earliest (founded in 1925) and most respected theatrical organizations. A home for priceless movie memorabilia, the club occupied the Moreno home for more than sixty years until the building was razed. *No. 226, declared 8/29/79*

STILL RESIDENCE

CA. 1920S

1262 Victoria Avenue
Country Club Park

William Grant Still was born in Woodville, Mississippi in 1895. In 1936, Still became the first African American to conduct a major symphony orchestra. He is credited with at least 150 compositions, including operas, symphonies, ballets, chamber works, and arrangements for traditional black spirituals. His work continues to be performed by top-ranking conductors and musical organizations throughout the world. According to Leopold Stokowski, "Still is one of America's greatest composers. He has made a real contribution to music." Still lived in this modest stucco residence in his later years. *No. 169, declared 12/1/67*

WILSHIRE CONGREGATIONAL CHURCH

ALLISON AND ALLISON 1924

Wilshire Methodist Church
4350 Wilshire Boulevard
Country Club Park

While this building's interior reflects distinct Gothic motifs, its exterior is pure Romanesque Revival, with a tower that recalls Seville's cathedral, La Giralda, or perhaps San Francisco's Ferry Building. The structure is beautifully sited at a turn on Wilshire Boulevard. *No. 114, declared 3/7/73*

WILSHIRE BOULEVARD TEMPLE

A. M. EDELMAN, S. TILDEN NORTON, AND DAVID C. ALLISON 1928

3663 Wilshire Boulevard
Country Club Park

Built for a congregation dating from 1862, this imposing Byzantine Revival temple was dedicated in 1929 and is one of the largest and most influential Reform synagogues in the country. Among the notable artistic features of the edifice are the symbolic murals by Hugo Ballin, which depict episodes in the biblical and post-biblical history of the Jewish people. The temple is listed on the National Register. *No. 116, declared 3/21/73*

CROWN HILL

WITMER RESIDENTIAL COMPOUND

DAVID J. WITMER

CA. 1920s

208-210½ Witmer Street
1422 West Second Street
Crown Hill

Built on property owned by the Witmer family since the 1880s, these interesting residences, constructed of reinforced concrete with an exposed aggregate finish and tile roofs, are reminiscent of Italian/Mediterranean architecture, although they hint at modern origins. Part of the original design concept for these structures included a high wall and dense landscaping, which conceal the buildings from view. *No. 538, declared 7/2/91*

CULVER CITY

FURTHMAN RESIDENCE

CA. 1915

(RELOCATED 1990)

3771 Lenawee Avenue
Culver City

Built for well-known screen writer (*To Have and Have Not*) Jules Furthman (who wrote under the less Germanic pseudonym Stephen Fox for many years), this large Neoclassical country home has been recently restored and relocated to a different portion of the site to provide additional development space on the grounds. *No. 502, declared 6/20/90*

DOWNTOWN

COHN-GOLDWATER BUILDING

1909

525 East Twelfth Street
Downtown, south

Unusually bare for a period when factories and loft buildings were often enhanced with decoration, this is the first modern, Class A reinforced concrete factory building in Los Angeles. It was built by Morris ("Cole of California") Cohn and Lemuel Goldwater, who were pioneers in the Los Angeles garment trade. The building is virtually a concrete cage, infilled originally with factory-sash windows that have been replaced with green fiberglass. The building, first used for clothing manufacture, is now a storage facility. *No. 119, declared 5/16/73*

SINAI TEMPLE

S. TILDEN NORTON 1909

Welsh Presbyterian Church
1153 South Valencia Street
Downtown

This rare Greek Revival temple with interiors of exceptional merit was sold to a Presbyterian congregation in 1926. *No. 173, declared 4/20/77*

SINAI TEMPLE

COHN-GOLDWATER BUILDING

CLUNE'S BROADWAY THEATER BUILDING

A. F. ROSENHEIM 1910

Cameo Theater
526 South Broadway
Downtown

This small free-standing theater was among the first to be built solely for motion-picture exhibition. It was the longest continuously operating movie theater in the state until recently, when the building was converted to retail use. This modest cast-iron structure was commissioned by the pioneer motion-picture producer/exhibitor and real-estate developer William H. Clune, who owned Raleigh Studios and was a financial backer of the film *The Birth of a Nation*. The large billboard above the building dates from a later period. *No. 524, declared 2/25/91*

PANTAGES THEATER BUILDING

MORGAN AND WALLS 1910

Arcade Theater Building
532-536 South Broadway
Downtown

This is one of three theaters built in Los Angeles by renowned vaudeville producer Alexander Pantages. "Big-name" acts appeared here, including Sophie Tucker and Stan Laurel. The existence of the auditorium in this building is concealed behind its well-ordered, seven-story, tripartite, Renaissance Revival façade. The current marquee is not original, and the signage of the current retail tenants does little to showcase the value of this very handsome structure, on which the Pantages name may still be read. *No. 525, declared 2/25/91*

CLUNE'S BROADWAY THEATER,
ROXIE THEATER,
AND PANTAGES THEATER BUILDING

FIRE STATION NO. 28

FIRE STATION NO.23

HUDSON AND MUNSELL 1910

255 East Fifth Street
Downtown

This modest Renaissance Revival building
was retired from active service in 1960 when
it became the training headquarters for the
fire department. Its combination of living and
working spaces was considered an advanced
design at the time. *No. 37, declared 2/18/66*

ORPHEUM THEATER

G. ALBERT LANSBURGH WITH R. B. YOUNG 1911

Palace Theater
630 South Broadway
Downtown

This Renaissance Revival vaudeville theater
and office building is said to have been
modeled after the Casino Municipale de
Venezia. It has a rich surface of terra-cotta
and masonry featuring laughing faces, floral
friezes, swags, and gremlins. It was the third
building in Los Angeles to operate under the
Orpheum name, and the oldest surviving
Orpheum theater in the world. It showcased
the nation's most important stars during the
time when the Orpheum and the nearby
Pantages made Broadway the premier theater
district in Los Angeles. *No. 449, declared*
8/16/89

LOS ANGELES ATHLETIC
CLUB

JOHN PARKINSON AND EDWIN BERGSTROM 1912

431 West Seventh Street
Downtown

The club was founded in 1880 by forty
socially prominent men. When this Beaux
Arts style building was built, it received
worldwide publicity for the placement of a
100-foot-long swimming pool on the sixth
floor, rather than the usual basement location. This design decision may be "read" on
the exterior by observing the blank walls,
which indicate the location of the pool.
No. 69, declared 9/16/70

FIRE STATION NO.28

KREMPLE AND ERKES 1912

644 South Figueroa Street
Downtown

One of the few early fire stations to survive downtown, this charming Renaissance Revival structure has been lovingly refurbished and converted for restaurant and office use. Its front elevation reflects the original street width; neighboring buildings on both sides are set back farther from the current street boundary. *No. 348, declared 3/29/88*

BRUNO STREET PAVING

1913

Between Alameda and North Main streets
Downtown

This short industrial street located between the Civic Center and Chinatown reveals remnants of the last-known surviving hand-hewn granite street pavements in Los Angeles. Sadly, the blocks are mostly covered with asphalt paving, and the surrounding area is so barren that recalling its history is difficult, at best. *No. 211, declared 3/7/79*

CHOCOLATE SHOPPE

1914

Finney's Cafeteria
217 West Sixth Street
Downtown

Located in a simple four-story loft building, the original first-floor tenant was the Chocolate Shoppe, a prototype for a projected chain of soda shops. The shop featured Dutch designs, and each successive shop was to suggest a different European country. Interior decorations by Ernest Batchelder, including his famous custom ceramic tile, proved so costly that plans for additional stores were dropped. Today the shop is operated by Finney's Cafeteria, which is also an old-time Los Angeles business name. The Batchelder tiles remain intact. *No. 137, declared 1/15/75*

EXAMINER BUILDING

JULIA MORGAN 1915

1111 South Broadway
Downtown

Brought into existence by the team that later created San Simeon (William Randolph Hearst and his pioneering woman architect, Julia Morgan), this building (a near-literal copy of A. Page Brown's California Building at the 1893 World's Columbian Exposition in Chicago) has been the subject of considerable public debate regarding its future. The late Mission Revival edifice currently sits empty, and its owners are said to have considered the possibility of replacing it with a parking lot. It is in nearly original condition except for the filling-in of the arched windows on the ground floor, which occurred during the blackout following the Japanese invasion of Pearl Harbor. The building has been empty since the *Los Angeles Herald Examiner* ceased publication in 1989. *No. 178, declared 8/17/77*

EXAMINER BUILDING

BOSTON STORE

1915

(ALTERED 1934, ALLISON AND ALLISON)

Robinson's
600 West Seventh Street
Downtown

Founded in 1883 by Bostonian J. W. Robinson, the Boston Store (now Robinson's) provides a direct link to one of the city's earliest mercantile establishments. It was, originally, a very elegant store, but its prestige was challenged by the opening of Bullock's Wilshire in 1929. The Boston Store was subsequently remodeled in American Art Deco, most likely in an attempt to compete with Bullock's and to lure shoppers back downtown, a struggle that has been won by Robinson's—Bullock's Wilshire is closed. *No. 357, declared 4/26/88*

CHURCH OF THE OPEN DOOR

WALKER AND VAWTER 1915

(DEMOLISHED)

550 South Hope Street
Downtown

Another victim of changing demographics and vanishing urban congregations, this much-loved Renaissance Revival auditorium (4,000 seats), flanked by two thirteen-story dormitories, has been demolished. Of major significance to Christian fundamentalists, the organization was founded by Union Oil magnate Lyman Stewart, who also established the Union Rescue Mission. The build-

ing is best remembered by Angelenos for its large 1935 neon sign, which bore the legend "Jesus Saves." *No. 323, declared 7/28/87*

YOUNG APARTMENTS

ROBERT BROWN YOUNG 1921

1621 South Grand Avenue
Downtown

The Young apartment building was recognized for the elaborate quality of the scrolled brackets supporting its cornice and many other decorative exterior details. A Renaissance Revival design with a rusticated base and a heavily corniced top layer, this once-prestigious building (no longer "young," but still on Grand) has fallen on hard times. Its decline reflects the changes that occurred in the area following the construction of the Santa Monica Freeway. The building is currently empty, graffiti-covered, and secured by chain-link fencing. *No. 317, declared 1/7/87*

LOEW'S STATE THEATER BUILDING

WEEKS AND DAY 1921

701-713 South Broadway
Downtown

Beginning as a vaudeville house, the State introduced, among others, the Gumm Sisters, one of whom was the adolescent Judy Garland. Builder Marcus Loew was one of the founders of MGM Studios. As a movie palace, it was the most successful theater on Broadway for more than fifty years, often premiering MGM films. The theater is but one function housed in the imposing Spanish Renaissance Revival office block, which even today lends a dark presence to the carnival atmosphere of the street. San Francisco architects Charles Weeks and William Day designed the Mark Hopkins Hotel and the San Diego Fox Theater. *No. 522, declared 3/4/91*

ODDFELLOWS TEMPLE

MORGAN, WALLS AND CLEMENTS 1924

Casa Camino Real
1828 South Oak Street
Downtown

The Oddfellows commissioned this combination meeting lodge, dining and dancing hall, and retail space. While much of the interior is considered bland, the two-story-high social hall is quite elaborate. The building is a lesser work by an important architectural firm that drew its inspiration from the 1915 Panama-California Exposition in San Diego. *No. 300, declared 10/29/85*

NISHI-HONGWANJI BUDDHIST TEMPLE

EDGAR CLINE 1924

Japanese-American National Museum
355-369 North Central Avenue
Downtown

Built on a triangular corner site within the Little Tokyo National Register Historic District, this building combines two utilitarian structures, one in the Second Egyptian Revival style (the presence of this style on a Japanese temple is unexplained). An elaborate *karahafu* entrance roof structure on this building is located near a series of columns with lotus capitals. Both buildings are otherwise typical of the surrounding neighborhood, but the contemporary history of these buildings reveals that they are among the earliest religious structures in Los Angeles' Asian community. *No. 313, declared 10/24/86*

THE PANTRY

1924

(RELOCATED)

The Original Pantry
877 South Figueroa Street
Downtown

In an unusual marketing sleight-of-hand, the Original Pantry is *not* located in the Original Pantry building. Beginning in one room with a fifteen-stool lunch counter at 9th Street near Figueroa, the Pantry was relocated here when its previous site was acquired for a freeway ramp. The move is said to have taken place without an interruption in service. "I'll bring your coffee if you will move to the new building."

This quintessential Los Angeles cafe has expanded over the years to become one of Los Angeles's legendary brunch spots. Customers wait in line to sample its old-fashioned food and hearty servings. Their slogan is "Never Closed—Never Without a Customer." *No. 255, declared 10/5/82*

LOS ANGELES MAIN LIBRARY

BERTRAM GOODHUE AND

CARLETON M. WINSLOW 1922-26

630 West Fifth Street
Downtown

This distinctive structure was the last major work of Bertram Goodhue, one of the outstanding American architects of the period. It remains one of the most distinctive visual landmarks in Los Angeles, an internationally recognized example of transitional twentieth-century architecture. Included in the designation were the grounds, which provided one of the few significant open spaces within the downtown area. Following a fire, and a proposed demolition, new construction was allowed on a portion of the open space, in exchange for restoration of the main building. At this writing, the new construction is complete, and the revitalization project seems to be aware and respectful of Goodhue's work, but the lost open space will be missed. *No. 46, declared 3/1/67*

BANK OF ITALY

MORGAN, WALLS AND CLEMENTS 1922

Giannini Place / Bank of America
649 South Olive Street
Downtown

A successful design from the premier corporate architectural firm of the period, this building is conceived as a Neoclassical base supporting an office block. Its most successful feature is a three-story monumental colonnade, which is well integrated into the rusticated base. Remodeled in 1968, the banking hall has been replaced with a women's apparel store, but subtle and sensitive alterations and restrained signage allow the building to retain much of its original appearance. *No. 354, declared 4/16/88*

BILTMORE HOTEL

SCHULTZ AND WEAVER 1922-23

515 South Olive Street

Downtown

Central Park (later Pershing Square) was located on the south edge of the four square leagues comprising the original Pueblo of Los Angeles when, with the shift in population, it became the center of downtown. As the area became important, history repeated itself as significant religious buildings were built here, including a frame Episcopal cathedral. Later the cathedral was demolished to make way for the Biltmore Hotel.

The twenties were a time of explosive growth and development in the area, and with the increase in land values, commercial development edged out all of the ecclesiastical buildings. Of all the new construction during that time, nothing rivaled the scale and opulence of the Biltmore. Named for George Vanderbilt's lavish estate in Asheville, North Carolina, the Biltmore opened to acclaim as the "greatest hotel ever conceived by man," according to one publication of the period.

Designed by the renowned New York architects who created both the Waldorf-Astoria and the Sherry Netherland, the Biltmore featured interiors derived from Italian Renaissance palaces. The largest and fanciest hotel west of Chicago, for many years the Biltmore had no peer. *No. 60, declared 7/2/69*

BILTMORE HOTEL

BROCK JEWELERS

DODD AND RICHARDS 1922

Clifton's Cafeteria
513 West Seventh Street
Downtown

This building dates from the period when this four-story jewelry business was located in the most fashionable commercial sector of the city, the jewelry district. Its Mediterranean Revival "picture frame" architecture and its ornate interiors restated the richness of the objects sold within. When it was threatened with demolition in the early 1970s, the street level was converted into a cafeteria that maintained many of the original interior finishes. A morning at Clifton's may be the Los Angeles equivalent of breakfast at Tiffany's.

The Clifton name is also a long and distinguished one in Los Angeles culinary history. In an earlier incarnation at 618 South Olive, Clifton's façade presented an outrageous tropical garden, replete with faux rock, luxurious planting, and a waterfall! Designed by Welton Becket, and painted by muralist Einar Petersen (see Studio Court, HCM 552), the original Clifton's was the outrageous concept of Clifford E. Clinton. This entrepreneur founded a chain of seven cafeterias that advertised "Dine free unless delighted" and "No guest need go hungry for lack of funds." *No. 358, declared 4/15/88*

CATHEDRAL HIGH SCHOOL

BARKER AND OTT 1923

1253 Stadium Way
Downtown / Chinatown

Although relatively new, Cathedral High is the oldest Catholic high school in the Archdiocese of Los Angeles. Situated on lands that were deeded to the Church by the city for burial grounds in 1844, the cemetery was officially closed in 1910. Re-interment took place in 1925 in New Calvary Cemetery in east Los Angeles. Cathedral High is an outgrowth of the Christian Brothers School of Sacred Heart Parish. *No. 281, declared 8/7/84*

TRINITY AUDITORIUM BUILDING

THORNTON FITZHUGH 1923

Embassy Auditorium and Hotel
851 South Grand Avenue
Downtown

A truly interesting and unusual design, this massive steel and concrete structure reflects a wonderful Beaux Arts sensibility with its four-story-high incised colonnade centered on the front elevation beneath a four-story-high Baroque dome. It was originally built to contain a church, a 1,500-seat meeting hall/auditorium, and a hotel. Unsympathetic, free-standing, green canvas awnings sound the only dissonant note on this terra-cotta wonder. *No. 299, declared 10/4/85*

JAPANESE UNION CHURCH

H. M. PATTERSON 1923

120 North San Pedro
Downtown

This was the first structure designed to house a Protestant congregation of the Japanese-American community in Los Angeles. In the Classical Revival style, with its colonnaded entrance porch, it resembles a banking institution as much as a religious one. The building serves as both a community center and a religious center. *No. 312, declared 10/24/86*

FRIDAY MORNING CLUB

ALLISON AND ALLISON 1924

Variety Arts Center Building
940 South Figueroa Street
Downtown

This stately five-story theater and clubhouse was built for a women's organization established in 1891. Their gatherings began with Friday morning "klatches" and developed, by the time their building was finished, into an important Friday morning lecture series. Recently restored, the well-designed Renaissance Revival building seems to be preparing for a new life. *No. 196, declared 8/9/78*

TRINITY AUDITORIUM BUILDING

ST. PAUL'S EPISCOPAL CATHEDRAL

REGINALD JOHNSON, ROLAND COATE, GORDON
KAUFMANN, AND CARLETON WINSLOW 1924
(DEMOLISHED 1979)

615 South Figueroa Street
Downtown

This is a remarkably restrained design, which was undoubtedly a compromise resulting from all of the design talent involved. Although the exterior of this simple cathedral building derived from Italian Romanesque designs, its major architectural feature was its single, tall, arched entryway with a rose window. The cathedral was the replacement for its predecessor, which was demolished to make way for the construction of the Biltmore Hotel. In recent years, the diocese has witnessed a declining urban churchgoing population; following years of attempts at preservation, this church, too, was demolished. *No. 66, declared 5/6/70*

SUBWAY TERMINAL OFFICE BUILDING

SHULTZ AND WEAVER 1925

417 South Hill Street
Downtown

This ten-story Renaissance Revival office block is an odd remnant of Los Angeles's first subway. The building housed the downtown terminal for the single mile of underground rail lines (from First and Glendale) actually constructed. At its peak use in 1944, the trains of the Pacific Electric Railway carried some 65,000 passengers daily, but not all of them came through this building.

The subway and tunnel have long been abandoned, but the building continues to be an important downtown structure. Its architecture certainly complemented adjacent Philharmonic Hall, which has been demolished, allowing the rear of the building to face nearly onto Pershing Square. The sides have been decorated with trompe l'oeil to compensate for their lack of finish. *No. 177, declared 7/27/77*

STANDARD OIL BUILDING

GEORGE KELHAM 1925

605 West Olympic Boulevard
Downtown

This Renaissance Revival office block was designed by the same hand that produced the similar, but superior Standard Oil corporate headquarters in San Francisco in 1922. Beautifully rendered, with fine materials and exquisite detailing, both buildings evoke a period of quality and pride that remain unequaled. *No. 340, declared 1/26/88*

ROOSEVELT BUILDING

CURLETT AND BEELMAN 1925

727 West Seventh Street
Downtown

Named for Theodore Roosevelt, this is one of the most significant of the older downtown buildings. This block-long Renaissance Revival office and retail block offers some of the best architecture to be found in Los Angeles. It is part of a stately Seventh Street ensemble that includes the Barker Brothers and Fine Arts buildings. The architectural continuity of these important structures virtually defined the City of Los Angeles at the time they were built. *No. 355, declared 4/26/88*

BARKER BROTHERS BUILDING

BARKER BROTHERS BUILDING

CURLETT AND BEELMAN 1925

818 West Seventh Street

Downtown

Displaying great affinity for its neighbor in the next block, this is another of the fine, monumental Renaissance Revival structures that are part of the downtown ensemble. This building was commissioned to house Southern California's largest home-furnishings company. *No. 356, declared 4/26/88*

FINE ARTS BUILDING

WALKER AND EISEN 1925

811 West Seventh Street

Downtown

A more romantic expression than its neighbors, this wonderful building was originally described as "a building for artisans, for the molders of taste, for the craftsmen and middlemen of culture . . . embodying in its exterior and interior ornament the finest work of craftsmen in bronze and iron, in ceramics, in furnishings and in terra-cotta." Recently refurbished, it has been converted to conventional office space, although its stunning and unconventional lobby, complete with Ernest Batchelder tile work, remains. The languorous figures of Sculpture and Architecture, reclining atop the neo-Gothic base, indeed represent an integration of sculpture and architecture rarely found in the design of American buildings. *No. 125, declared 4/17/74*

BELASCO THEATER

MORGAN, WALLS AND CLEMENTS 1926

Metropolitan Community Church
1046-1054 South Hill Street
Downtown

Built by the New York theatrical-production family, this was the second Los Angeles theater building to bear the Belasco name. The façade is an elaborate four-story confection in a Spanish-Moorish Revival style, fabricated in terra-cotta by the Gladding McBean Company. The auditorium is noted for its acoustic qualities; other interior features include a large "green room" and a mezzanine-level gallery/ballroom that can accommodate up to four hundred people. The city and the building itself would benefit from a judicious pruning of the hugely overgrown street trees that currently obscure the view of this handsome and original structure. *No. 476, declared 10/30/89*

MAYAN THEATER

MORGAN, WALLS AND CLEMENTS 1926

1044 South Hill Street
Downtown

Designed in a rare style that utilizes Pre-Columbian inspired motifs, the heavily textured front façade features a cast stone entablature composed of rows of Mayan chieftain heads alternating with slim concrete columns. All of this is topped with an even richer casting in a geometric motif. The Mayan operated for years as a musical-comedy theater, opening with a production of George Gershwin's *Oh, Kay* on August 15, 1927. After a stint as a motion-picture theater, the building became a nightclub. The raw precast concrete work has been colorfully hand-painted, resembling the style originally employed in the Mayan temples of the Yucatán, but it was not part of the original theater architecture. This could be corrected, but the paint would have to be removed by hand to avoid damaging the concrete. The interior was recently featured in the Kevin Costner film *The Bodyguard*. *No. 460, declared 10/17/89*

HARRIS NEWMARK BUILDING

CURLETT AND BEELMAN 1926

127 East Ninth Street
Downtown

Much of the history of Southern California would be lost if it were not for the writings of Harris Newmark, an early merchant-philanthropist whose published memoirs (*Sixty Years in Southern California*) dealt with the years when the region was being developed. It is one of the great autobiographies of the American Jewish experience, and a must-read for those interested in Southern California's past.

Commissioned by Newmark's estate, this twelve-story Renaissance Revival commercial/office building was designed by an important architectural firm that was soon to design some of Los Angeles's most important Art Deco structures. Yet this building, appropriately for its namesake, resembles those designed at the turn of the century. For some, this structure may represent an architectural changing of the guard. *No. 345, declared 2/23/88*

FINE ARTS BUILDING

MAYAN THEATER

PACIFIC NATIONAL BANK

MORGAN, WALLS AND CLEMENTS 1926

Coast Federal Savings Building
314 West Ninth Street
Downtown

A typical Renaissance Revival, three-part, vertical office block with a rusticated base and a cap featuring two-story arched windows, the building also offers a rich palette of interior materials and finishes. Like the previously cited Harris Newmark Building, this was also a design throwback from a firm that was about to emerge as the creator of some of the best Art Deco designs of all time. *No. 346, declared 3/11/88*

MACY STREET VIADUCT

1926

Macy Street spanning the Los Angeles River
Downtown

Both the street and the bridge recall the pioneering family of Nantucket native Obed Macy, who arrived in Los Angeles in 1850. A shallow riverbed was chosen as the most promising site for crossing the ever-changing Los Angeles River, beginning with the Yang-na villagers, who crossed here to reach the San Gabriel Mission. In 1867, a footbridge made the first connection to the lands east of the river, but it succumbed to "turbulent waters" in 1870, and a series of bridges continued to be built at this site until the current one was completed.

Technically speaking, a viaduct is defined as a bridge consisting of short spans, supported on piers or towers. This bridge is anchored by towers on either side of the river, but its distinguishing characteristic is a series of short spans, resting upon the longer span of a graceful concrete arch. The towers represent an odd variation in bridge design: the portals are turned sideways, a visual invitation to step off rather than pass through. *No. 224, declared 8/1/79*

MAYFLOWER HOTEL

CHARLES WHITTLESEY 1927

Checkers Hotel
535 South Grand Avenue
Downtown

This elaborate Moorish-influenced Spanish Colonial Revival hotel was conceived as one of the most elegant buildings in downtown Los Angeles. Its location near the main library enhances its unique qualities. It was originally owned by millionaire importer William Anderson and operated by hotelier Charles DeLong. Recently refurbished by the Philippine-based Ayala family and currently part of the Kempinski chain, it continues to be among the most stylish downtown hotels. *No. 286, declared 10/5/84*

UNITED ARTISTS THEATER BUILDING

WALKER AND EISEN 1927
THEATER: C. HOWARD CRANE

927-939 South Broadway
Downtown

A Spanish Gothic Revival cum American Perpendicular style steel-framed office block, with a reinforced concrete theater set into the base, this was the first theater commissioned by the United Artists Corporation, and the one it used for special screenings and premieres. Its outstanding interior features included a reflective dome covered in leaded crystal and preset controls that automated all lighting in the auditorium. Murals by Anthony Heinsbergen (see the Heinsbergen Studio, HCM 275) depicted leading actors of the day, including United Artists founders Douglas Fairbanks, Mary Pickford, and Charles Chaplin. Today, the theater is used as the "Church of the City," the media home of televangelist Dr. Eugene Scott. *No. 523, declared 12/17/90*

PACIFIC NATIONAL BANK

MACY STREET VIADUCT

TOWER THEATER

S. CHARLES LEE 1927

800 South Broadway
Downtown

Utilizing a prominent corner site and power-ful Baroque architecture, S. Charles Lee designed this late "Movieland Mannerist" homage to architectural history. He utilized windows that evoke the Paris Opera, columns from LeDoux, Moorish details, Spanish arches, and miscellaneous Italian elements—all executed in gleaming terra-cotta—to complete one of the most com-pelling buildings along Broadway. Although empty, this 1,000-seat theater building con-tinues to command respect and maintain a significant place in the downtown cityscape. *No. 450, declared 8/16/89*

RIALTO THEATER BUILDING

WILLIAM LEE WOOLETT 1927 (ALTERED 1930s)

808 South Broadway
Downtown

In the 1930s, Sid Grauman assumed opera-tions of this theater and commissioned a new box office and an elaborate new neon marquee (obliterating the original façade), which remain to this day. The entire interior has been destroyed, but the exterior of the building continues to remind one of the heyday of the Broadway theater district. The Rialto currently reveals a disturbing trend concerning the preservation of downtown theaters: the abandonment of the auditorium and the conversion of the lobby to retail space. This building designation protects only the marquee, box office, and the entrance floor. *No. 472, declared 12/20/89*

TITLE INSURANCE AND TRUST COMPANY BUILDING AND ANNEX

JOHN PARKINSON 1928

Design Center of Los Angeles

433 and 419 South Spring Street

Downtown

Putting to rest one of those urban myths that surface from time to time, the relatively neutral Zigzag Moderne design of these buildings should be attributed to the Parkinson firm and not Walker and Eisen. Taken together, the buildings provide a well-mannered background complement for some of the more spectacular designs of the Spring Street National Register Historic District. 433 Spring is particularly notable for the rich materials utilized in the public areas; even the toilet rooms feature elaborate marbles. Hugo Ballin contributed murals, and the lobby interior was designed by Herman Sachs. The Los Angeles Cultural Heritage Commission is located here. *No. 385, declared 8/5/88*

GARFIELD BUILDING

CLAUDE BEELMAN 1928

403 West Eighth Street

Downtown

Known primarily for its elaborate and opulent Art Deco lobby, the twelve-story terra-cotta-clad office block is significant as an example of the stylistic transition that Los Angeles's downtown underwent during the twenties. *No. 121, declared 8/22/73*

GARFIELD BUILDING

OVIATT BUILDING

WALKER AND EISEN 1928

617 South Olive Street
Downtown

Commissioned by James Oviatt, this building is internationally recognized as a fine example of French-influenced Art Deco architecture and interior design. It is twelve stories in height. The ground floor, with its sensational open-air lobby, originally housed Alexander's, a men's clothing store that utilized considerable amounts of Lalique crystal in its interior. Today this same space is occupied by Rex, Il Restaurante, an elaborate Italian restaurant that has frequently been used in films. When Rex opened, the dining experience was likened to being on an ocean liner from the period. The middle portion of the building is still offices. In the upper portion, behind the clock tower, exists one of the most beautiful Art Deco apartment interiors ever built. Its ten rooms look out onto a roof garden that includes both a swimming pool and tennis courts. *No. 195, declared 7/19/78*

LOS ANGELES CITY HALL

JOHN C. AUSTIN, ALBERT C. MARTIN,
AND JOHN PARKINSON 1928

200 North Spring Street
Downtown

This early tower provides an important visual focus for the center of government in Los Angeles, and in the original *Superman* series it housed the "Daily Planet." Its classical temple base and "skyscraper" tower place it squarely in the transitional architectural tra-

dition embodied in buildings designed by the brilliant Bertram Goodhue, whose work it resembles. Nonetheless, it is a significant building in its own right, with interiors that are Byzantine in mood—a style that seems uncannily appropriate for a big-city bureaucracy. *No. 150, declared 3/24/76*

EAGLE ROCK

EAGLE ROCK WOMEN'S TWENTIETH CENTURY CLUBHOUSE

1914

1841-1855 Colorado Boulevard
Eagle Rock

Although the Craftsman style was more prevalent in residential work, some small institutional buildings were constructed in this style as well. During this pre-feminist period, many women's organizations found comfort in these residentially scaled and detailed structures. Julia Morgan designed many such buildings for women's clubs, but this is not one of hers. The building, which organized a lounge and banquet kitchen into a large meeting hall, also features a massive central fireplace. *No. 537, declared 6/11/91*

SWANSON RESIDENCE

EMIL SWANSON 1921

2373 Addison Way
Eagle Rock

This is the only log-cabin style structure in Los Angeles to receive recognition as a Historic-Cultural Monument, and one of the very few ever built in the city. Emil Swanson, the owner, designer, and builder, was the founder of the Eagle Rock Lumber Company, which offered siding that had the appearance of whole logs yet could be fastened to a structure like conventional siding. Mercifully, this concept did not meet with wide public acceptance. *No. 542, declared 7/2/91*

EAGLE ROCK CITY HALL

1922

2035 Colorado Boulevard
Eagle Rock

This three-level, Spanish Colonial Revival, tile-roofed building was constructed eleven years after Eagle Rock was incorporated as a city. Later Eagle Rock was annexed to the City of Los Angeles, and the building became the first of many city halls in Los Angeles to be acquired through this process. *No. 59, declared 2/26/69*

ARGUS COURT

TAYLOR AND TAYLOR 1923

1769 Colorado Boulevard
Eagle Rock

This courtyard complex consists of sixteen Tudor Revival style bachelor cottages surrounding a common court. Period details include open eaves, exposed rafters, half-timbering, and original plumbing! At this writing, the buildings are boarded up and awaiting demolition. *No. 471, declared 12/20/89*

"STORYBOOK HOUSE"

H. A. EDWARDS 1920s

1203-1207 Kipling Avenue
Eagle Rock

Only the (undeclared) garage of this complex is visible from the street, and it appears to be extremely fragile. It is reported that the other buildings in this Period Revival complex include a cottage, artist's studio, and playhouse. *No. 383, declared 8/5/88*

EAGLE ROCK WOMEN'S CHRISTIAN TEMPERANCE UNION HOME

A. GODFREY BAILEY 1927

2235 Norwalk Avenue
Eagle Rock

It is buildings such as this that serve to remind one of the history of the women's rights movement. This building is emblematic of the struggle not only for female equality but against alcohol.

Unusual, both in plan and expression, the building appears to be a squat hexagonal tower (four stories with a cupola) topped with red tile, to which two residential wings are attached. There is another, lower wing attached to the rear, but it is from a later time and not included in the designation. The building's windows are being replaced, unfortunately with aluminum, but otherwise the Mediterranean Revival style residence hall appears to be in nearly original condition. *No. 562, declared 5/28/92*

EXPOSITION PARK / WEST ADAMS

BRITT RESIDENCE

A. F. ROSENHEIM 1910

Los Angeles Amateur Athletic Foundation
Headquarters
2141 West Adams Boulevard
Exposition Park

Originally attorney Eugene W. Britt's residence, this elaborate building in the Jeffersonian Classical mode has been successfully converted into the headquarters of this nonprofit foundation. *No. 197, declared 8/23/78*

GUASTI RESIDENCE

HUDSON AND MUNSELL 1910

Busby Berkeley Residence
3500 West Adams Boulevard
Exposition Park

The same firm that was responsible for the design of several of the West Adams mansions designed this rare Beaux Arts style home for Secundo Guasti and his family. Guasti was an immigrant viticulturist, who established Rancho Cucamonga Vineyard. In 1937, the home and its furnishings were purchased by legendary film director and choreographer Busby Berkeley, where, it is said, he created an elaborate life-style that mimicked his escapist fantasy films. The building was enlarged with a huge masonry addition on the rear, and it is currently owned by a religious institution that is said to be restoring the building to its original grandeur. One hopes this will include restoration of the front lawn, which is currently a parking lot. *No. 478, declared 1/30/90*

BRITT RESIDENCE

BRIGGS RESIDENCE

HUDSON AND MUNSELL 1912

3734 West Adams Boulevard
Exposition Park

This example of a Craftsman / Tudor style residence was built for an important pioneer family. The neighboring building, at 3726 West Adams, built at the same time, in the same style, by the same architects, offers an illustration of the relative importance of scale. This building, though decorated with many of the same details, is dwarfed by its neighbor in a manner that suggests a remarkable display of independence on the part of these architectural partners. *No. 477, declared 1/30/90*

MACGOWAN RESIDENCE

HUDSON AND MUNSELL 1912

Korean Church
3726 West Adams Boulevard
Exposition Park

The MacGowan Residence may be described as the Briggs Residence on steroids. This is the larger of the two side-by-side residences built for two generations of a pioneering family. The larger home was built for the Grandville MacGowans, next door to that of (Mrs. MacGowan's mother) Mary Hoover Briggs, an early Los Angeles real-estate developer. Dr. MacGowan, who was educated in Europe, had moved to Los Angeles from Iowa. He and his wife were socially prominent Angelenos who hosted many events in their home. *No. 479, declared 1/30/90*

OVIATT BUILDING

LOS ANGELES
CITY HALL

ST. JOHN'S EPISCOPAL CHURCH

F. PIERPONT AND WALTER S. DAVIS WITH
HENRY WITHEY 1921

514 West Adams Boulevard
Exposition Park

This is a sometimes undervalued architectural treasure that suffers by comparison with its neighbors, the Southern California Automobile Association Building, St. Vincent de Paul Church, and the Stimson Residence. Nonetheless, this church, winner of an architectural competition, was modeled after the eleventh-century Tuscan church of San Pietro. Italian sculptor Cartiano Scarpitta is credited with directing the building's sculpture, as he also did on the Stock Exchange Building and City Hall. As is the case with European church buildings, St. John's is perpetually under construction: a

stained-glass window depicting Dr. Martin Luther King, Jr. was installed in 1977 by the Judson Art Glass Studio. Not included in this designation is the existing social hall. *No. 516, declared 1/7/91*

WEST ADAMS GARDENS

1920

1158-1176 West Adams Boulevard
Exposition Park

These six identical two-story, half-timbered, Tudor Revival apartment buildings, arranged around a private street, provide some of the more interesting student housing in the neighborhood of the University of Southern California. *No. 297, declared 8/13/85*

AUTOMOBILE CLUB OF SOUTHERN CALIFORNIA

HUNT AND BURNS 1922

2601 South Figueroa Street
Exposition Park

This Spanish Colonial Revival headquarters complex was built for the Automobile Club, which in the early days lobbied for the construction and maintenance of good roads to accommodate the automobile. Subsequently, Los Angeles has become the most automobile-oriented city in the world, and the automobile club has become a commonplace necessity. The building is particularly notable for its characteristic courtyard and main lobby. *No. 72, declared 2/3/71*

ST. VINCENT DE PAUL CHURCH

ALBERT C. MARTIN 1923

621 West Adams Boulevard
Exposition Park

Albert Martin's career and firm span a remarkable period in Los Angeles's architectural history, reflecting, along the way, significant expertise in the varying styles it attempted. This dazzlingly Churrigueresque

WEST ADAMS GARDENS

church recalls Goodhue's California Building at the 1915 Panama-California Exposition in San Diego, but nonetheless his work stands the test of time. St. Vincent's is as popular and beautiful today as it was when it was built.

The Doheny family, who lived nearby, was deeply committed to charitable and religious enterprises—as personified by the seventeenth-century French priest for whom the church is named. They also gave generously to St. Vincent's Hospital. Doheny was a self-made millionaire, and he and his second wife were considered nouveau riche by Los Angeles society. They sought respectability through their religious and charitable commitments, ultimately garnering the papal titles of Knight and Lady of the Equestrian Order of the Holy Sepulchre in 1925 for their good works. *No. 90, declared 7/21/71*

CHALET APARTMENTS

FRANK M. TYLER 1913

2375 Scarff Street
Exposition Park

Although bungalow cottage clusters enjoyed a brief popularity, there were very few apartment buildings designed in this style. This one resembles a single-family residence but actually contains nineteen units, offering a unique home-style atmosphere to apartment dwellers. *No. 467, declared 10/27/89*

ST. VINCENT DE PAUL CHURCH

CLARK LIBRARY

ROBERT D. FARQUHAR 1926

2520 Cimmaron Street
Exposition Park

A visually seductive building set in superb formal grounds, the Clark Library is one of three buildings that once existed within this walled compound. The library, built to house the personal collections of eccentric millionaire William Andrews Clark, Jr., is extant; Clark's residence has been demolished, and an adjacent garage/servants' quarters building has been relocated elsewhere on the grounds.

Clark, who was the fabulously wealthy heir to a Montana copper fortune—which grew even larger in the stock market—was a bibliophile and a great patron of the arts. His library houses the world's most comprehensive public collection of the printed works and manuscripts of Oscar Wilde; it also features an important collection of the works of John Dryden. An inveterate collector, the twice-widowed Clark spent his later years with a companion, Harrison Post.

The building is French Renaissance Revival, and shares some of the exquisite scale and setting of the legendary jewel, the Château Bagatelle (sans Mansard roof); it too is something small and delightful. Close analysis reveals that the compulsive symmetry of the interior of the reading rooms results

CLARK LIBRARY

in a cramping of the fenestration on the back, which is a surprising gaffe on the part of the elegant Farquhar.

Deceptively simple on the exterior—its masses of undecorated surface reflect some insights into the modern movement—the building's complex and layered interior features designs by noted muralist Allyn Cox. Bequeathed to the University of California at Los Angeles in 1934, with a $1.5 million endowment, as a memorial to Clark's father, former Montana Senator William A. Clark, Sr. (who died in 1925), the library is open to the public and tours may be arranged by appointment. Unfortunately, these tours originate at the side entrance, rather than from the sensational formal front entrance hall, blunting the brilliant experience of Farquhar's axial composition. For an appointment call (213) 731-8529. *No. 28, declared 10/9/64*

DISTRIBUTION STATION NO.31

PACIFIC GAS AND ELECTRIC STAFF ARCHITECTS
1924

1035 West Twenty-fourth Street
Exposition Park

This is an archetypal 1920s industrial building, oddly out of place in the modest neighborhood of frame vernacular homes. To a certain extent its significance derives from its contextual incompatibility. The original masonry parapet has been replaced with pipe-rail. *No. 410, declared 1/20/89*

SECOND BAPTIST CHURCH BUILDING

PAUL R. WILLIAMS 1925

2412 Griffith Avenue
Exposition Park

This church has been one of the hubs of the cultural life of the black community since its founding in 1885. The present building is recognized for its historical associations and is considered an excellent example of the Romanesque Revival style. *No. 200, declared 10/18/78*

CHURCH OF THE ADVENT

WILLIAM E. YOUNG
DATE UNKNOWN
ALTERED 1925, ARTHUR BENTON

4976 West Adams Boulevard
Exposition Park

Former congregation members here include James Roosevelt, Lyle Talbot, Alexander Summerville, and Nat "King" Cole, each of whom sought spiritual comfort in this large, single-story masonry church. Resembling an English parish church, on a Los Angeles scale, this Craftsman building displays Gothic elements. *No. 512, declared 1/16/91*

SHRINE CIVIC AUDITORIUM

JOHN C. AUSTIN, A. M. EDELMAN,
G. ALBERT LANSBURGH 1926

665 West Jefferson Boulevard
Exposition Park

This Moorish Revival structure, with twin cupolas at each end of the front elevation, is among the largest in Los Angeles, seating 6,700. It has been a popular venue for opera, concerts, conventions, and other events that draw large crowds. The cupolas and loggia along the western elevation are suggestive of the Arabian-Egyptian costumes and symbolism affected by the Masonic organization. Adjoining the auditorium is a pavilion ballroom with space for 7,500 dancers or 5,200 diners, with a mezzanine that seats an additional 3,200. *No. 139, declared 3/5/75*

EXPOSITION PARK CLUB HOUSE

CA. 1928

3990 South Menlo Avenue
Exposition Park

This building is part of the complex of recreation buildings that has evolved into Exposition Park, which was originally established in 1872 as a privately owned fairgrounds. A modestly scaled Spanish Colonial Revival building, it continues to serve the community for events sponsored by the Park and Recreation Department. *No. 127, declared 5/1/74*

HANCOCK PARK

CHURCHILL RESIDENCE

F. PIERPONT DAVIS 1909

215 South Wilton Place
Hancock Park

Built for Thomas A. Churchill, Sr., in a classic English Arts and Crafts style, this beautiful home was designed by an important architect of the period. *No. 568, declared 10/27/92*

FIRE STATION NO.29

JAMES J. BACKUS 1913

158 South Western Avenue
Hancock Park

This abandoned, graffiti-covered fire station, in a classically correct Italian Renaissance Revival style, awaits someone with enough vision to discover a use for such a wonderful and unique building. Architect Backus made a specialty of fire stations. *No. 310, declared 10/1/86*

RESIDENCE

1913

1443 North Martel Avenue
Hancock Park

Considered an outstanding example of the California bungalow, inside and out, this structure was completed with especially fine Tiffany fixtures and stained-glass windows. *No. 246, declared 11/25/81*

RESIDENCE

1913

1437 North Martel Avenue
Hancock Park

Little is known about this Craftsman bunga-low, with its redwood exterior, other than that its builder also built 1443 North Martel (HCM 246) in a complementary fashion.
No. 527, declared 3/11/91

EL ROYALE APARTMENTS

WILLIAM DOUGLAS LEE 1920s

450 North Rossmore Avenue
Hancock Park

The apartments in this tall and elegant twelve-story Spanish Renaissance Revival style building overlook the grounds of the Wilshire Country Club. A logical destination for transplanted Easterners, the El Royale's

height makes it a visual beacon in the district and continues to exert its confident presence on the street and neighborhood.
No. 309, declared 9/2/86

MEADE RESIDENCE

LESTER SCHERER 1928

La Casa de las Campañas
350 North June Street
Hancock Park

Now owned by Pepperdine University, this was originally the home of Lucille Meade Lamb. It features a clock tower containing four massive bronze bells, hence the name *La Casa de las Campañas* ("The House of the Bells"). Deceptive in appearance, what looks to be a modestly scaled, if beautifully land-scaped, Spanish Colonial Revival home

MEADE RESIDENCE

actually contains thirty-seven rooms. Architect Scherer had a rather eclectic career; he completed a "New Orleans Mansard style" medical center in Pasadena in 1948. *No. 239, declared 4/9/81*

STUDIO COURT

EINAR C. PETERSEN 1922

Hansel and Gretel Court
4350-4352½ Beverly Boulevard
Hancock Park

This studio court complex, originally designed in the European tradition, as work space for artists, by Danish-born muralist Einar Petersen, is a picturesque, if somewhat kitschy, compound of Period Revival bungalows, which are tenanted today by such businesses and services as chiropractor Dr. (Robert) Goodbar. At the rear is Petersen's residence, an oddly out-of-place two-story, split-level tract house, dating, it appears, from the forties or fifties. The buildings that front on Beverly Boulevard suffered some damage following the April 1992 riots. *No. 552, declared 3/18/92*

EBELL AUDITORIUM

HUNT AND BURNS 1924

4400 Wilshire Boulevard
Hancock Park

The Spanish Colonial Revival club building, with its auditorium and gardens, is the outgrowth of a cultural, educational, and philanthropic women's organization that began in Los Angeles in 1894. Somewhat altered over time, the complex remains an outstanding example of the later work of these important architects. *No. 250, declared 8/25/82*

LOS ALTOS APARTMENTS

E. B. RUST 1925

4121 Wilshire Boulevard
Hancock Park

A huge double-loaded, double-block apartment building in the Spanish Colonial Revival style with Italian-influenced orna-

mentation, the Los Altos was, in its day, a prestigious address. *No. 311, declared 10/17/86*

13TH CHURCH OF CHRIST, SCIENTIST

ALLISON AND ALLISON 1925

1750 North Edgemont Street
Hancock Park

Beaux Arts-trained architect David Allison proved conclusively with this commission that he understood the potential for the various decorative uses of concrete. This handsome and richly colored Renaissance Revival ecclesiastic structure is among his best. Dating from a congregation that began in 1920, this church was conceived as a quality structure, characteristic of Christian Science church architecture. As a matter of principle, this denomination always pays cash for its buildings, and it is respected for the quality of the architects it employs. *No. 559, declared 4/21/92*

HIGHLAND PARK

BROWNE RESIDENCE

CLYDE BROWNE 1909

Oldstone Abbey or San Encino Abbey
6211 Arroyo Glen
Highland Park

Browne, a printer by trade, whose hero was British writer and designer William Morris, constructed his home/studio as a place to live and work in an atmosphere of Medievalism, which he loved. Morris's controversial ideas regarding the work ethic and the value and importance of hand-crafted goods influenced Browne's building. The building was featured prominently in the California Design–1910 Exhibition of the Pasadena Center. Browne continued to work on the building until it was completed in 1925. Like Lummis's El Alisal, it is one of the few buildings that may be seen to bridge the Mission Revival and Spanish Colonial Revival styles. *No. 106, declared 11/15/72*

MT. WASHINGTON CABLE CAR STATION

1909

200 West Avenue 43
Highland Park

Deriving from a long tradition of Mission Revival style railway stations, this building served a funicular that climbed the eastern slope of Mt. Washington until 1919. Today the funicular is gone, but the building serves, in altered form, as a private residence that illustrates the adaptability of the romantic but short-lived style. *No. 269, declared 6/28/83*

KELMAN RESIDENCE AND CARRIAGE BARN

1910

5029 Echo Street
Highland Park

This Craftsman Bungalow style residence was built for Joseph N. Kelman, who owned a manufacturing company. It features a practical, screen-enclosed patio, which detracts somewhat from its appearance. *No. 494, declared 7/2/90*

TUSTIN RESIDENCE AND STONE WALL

MEYER AND HOLLER 1910

4973 Sycamore Terrace
Highland Park

Built for Mary Tustin, a member of a pioneer California family, this house was occupied by her relatives for over thirty years. She was the widow of Columbus Tustin, for whom the town of Tustin was named. Together with the two neighboring structures, the Tustin residence is considered to be among the very best Craftsman homes built in Los Angeles. *No. 371, declared 7/15/88*

13TH CHURCH OF CHRIST,
SCIENTIST

JOHNSON RESIDENCE AND STONE WALL

MEYER AND HOLLER 1911

4985 Sycamore Terrace
Highland Park

This two-story Craftsman home was one of three designed and built on Sycamore Terrace by Meyer and Holler. It was built as a wedding present, given to John Cherry Johnson and his bride by Johnson's parents. *No. 369, declared 7/15/88*

JOHNSON, SR. RESIDENCE AND STONE WALL

MEYER AND HOLLER 1912

4979 Sycamore Terrace
Highland Park

In a remarkable display of family unity, John Johnson built his own house next to the one he commissioned for his son, utilizing the same style, as well as the same architects and contractor. Later, tennis courts were built spanning the rear yards of both homes. *No. 370, declared 7/15/88*

SOUTHWEST MUSEUM AND ENTRANCE PORTAL

HUNT AND BURNS 1912 AND 1920

234 Museum Drive
Highland Park

Founded in 1903 by Los Angeles booster Charles Lummis to preserve Native American artifacts of the Southwest, this was the first museum in Los Angeles. The museum building is in the Mission Revival style. The entrance portal is in a rare and odd Pre-Columbian Revival style. *No. 283, declared 8/29/84*

CHURCH RESIDENCE

H. J. KNAUER 1912

5907 Echo Street
Highland Park

Another of the two-story bungalows constructed of river stone, this one was built for Clyde M. Church, a prominent member of

EBELL CLUB

the community who worked in the Security Pacific Bank in Highland Park. *No. 389, declared 10/4/88*

EBELL CLUB

HUNT AND BURNS 1913

131 South Avenue 57
Highland Park

Another Ebell Club, this time in the rare (for California) Prairie style, the building has hosted symphony concerts, lectures, and other programs of a cultural nature. The club is considered by many to be the premiere cultural center of Highland Park. *No. 284, declared 8/29/84*

ASHLEY RESIDENCE

FREDERIC ASHLEY 1914

740-742 North Avenue 66
Highland Park

Frederic Ashley is best known for his designs (with John Austin) for the Griffith Observatory. For his own home, he chose to work in the Colonial Revival style. This interesting essay in rigorous symmetry has a few oddly jarring notes, like the unique, mismatched windows on the first floor, and a strange third Tuscan column peeking around from the east side—all in all, a fascinating home, currently undergoing restoration. *No. 402, declared 12/9/88*

ARROYO SECO BANK

JOHN AUSTIN AND FREDERIC ASHLEY 1920s

Highland Federal Savings
6301 North Figueroa Street
Highland Park

A simplified Churrigueresque style entrance (by the designers of the Griffith Observatory), set on a diagonal at the corner of the site, defines this unusual early bank. The building has always housed a financial institution, with little discernable change to the exterior, save for some insensitive anodized aluminum trim and remarkably ungainly signage. *No. 492, declared 6/2/90*

ASHLEY RESIDENCE

CASA DE ADOBE

PISGAH HOME

1915

Christ Faith Mission
140 South Avenue 59
Highland Park

Pisgah Grande, a utopian colony with a religious basis, was founded by Finis Yoakum in the mountains north of Chatsworth around 1914, and a small colony of masonry buildings was erected there. About the same time, this large two-story Tudor Revival house was built for Father Yoakum as a halfway house called Pisgah Home. The massive triple-arched masonry entrance porch seems to belong to a previous building, so out of character is it with the delicacy of the half-timbered Tudor detailing of the rest of the building. But with its handsome row of cypress trees lining the drive, the compound continues as a well-maintained visual delight. Today, the home not only provides accommodations for traveling missionaries but it shelters men, women, and adolescents temporarily in need. *No. 287, declared 1/18/85*

DEPARTMENT OF WATER AND POWER

FREDERICK ROEHRIG 1916

Distributing Station 2
225 North Avenue 61
Highland Park

Frederick Roehrig, whose residential work has long been recognized, also designed this nonresidential structure for the City of Los Angeles. Its Beaux Arts design seems an odd choice and rests somewhat uncomfortably in this hilly residential community. *No. 558, declared 4/21/92*

CASA DE ADOBE

THEODORE EISEN 1920

4605 North Figueroa Street
Highland Park

Casa de Adobe was built to replicate a Mexican Colonial home as a project of the Hispanic Society of Southern California. By 1925, it had been deeded to the nearby Southwest Museum, which furnished it with traditional style furnishings and used it for receptions and fiestas. It is now a house museum which exhibits the furnishings and landscaping typically found in an early land-grant home. *No. 493, declared 4/21/92*

MADISON RESIDENCE

ARTHUR G. LINDLEY 1920

148-150 South Avenue 56
Highland Park

Highland Park contains what few examples of Prairie School architecture exist in Los Angeles. This home, built for A. J. Madison, is one of the few in this style that have been declared a Historic-Cultural Monument. It features extensive use of beautiful wood on the interior. After a period of neglect, when the building was converted into four residential units, it was recently restored as a single-family residence. *No. 550, declared 10/2/91*

SUNRISE COURT APARTMENTS

1921

5721-5729 Monte Vista Street
Highland Park

It is interesting to compare a building like this one to something like the Roman Gardens Apartments (HCM 397) or the Andalusian Apartments (HCM 435) to see the differences not only in styles and flourishes but also in the accommodations made available to differing classes. Like many (perhaps thousands) of the garden-court apartment complexes, the Sunrise Court catered to a working-class clientele and offered few luxuries. It survives as a reminder of life in a different time. *No. 400, declared 11/23/88*

HINER HOUSE

1922

4757 North Figueroa Street
Highland Park

The distinctive architecture of this residence has been variously described as California Chalet style with Oriental influences and Stone Tudor. It was built for Edwin M. Hiner, who founded the music school at the University of California at Los Angeles. Stone from the adjacent Arroyo Seco was used in its construction. *No. 105, declared 11/15/72*

MASONIC TEMPLE

JEFFERY SCHAEFFER 1922

104 North Avenue 56
Highland Park

The institutional use of this lodge building was subsidized by commercial use at the street level of the two-story Renaissance Revival structure. A recessed balcony at the second level features a delicately scaled colonnade. *No. 282, declared 8/29/84*

SECURITY TRUST AND SAVINGS BANK

JOHN AND DONALD PARKINSON 1923

5601 North Figueroa Street
Highland Park

This is a competent, but unexciting, two-story Renaissance Revival Branch Bank, designed by a firm that would continue to be among the most prominent in the city for several decades. *No. 575, declared 2/09/93*

HIGHLAND THEATER

L. A. SMITH 1924

5600-5608 North Figueroa Street
Highland Park

Relatively unchanged over time, this Spanish Colonial Revival theater was the centerpiece of a group of six theaters built in this neighborhood when movie-going was at the height of its popularity. The opening of the Highland featured a personal appearance by the actress Norma Shearer. The current marquee is not original. *No. 549, declared 10/2/91*

HINER HOUSE

PISGAH HOME

NORTHEAST POLICE STATION

1926

6045 York Boulevard

Highland Park

Considered the last of the traditional police stations, this institutional Renaissance Revival building is currently undergoing a restoration from which it will emerge as the Los Angeles Police Museum. The building is listed on the National Register. *No. 274, declared 1/4/84*

HOLLYWOOD

HOLLYWOOD(LAND) SIGN

1923

(RECONSTRUCTED, 1978)

2428 Beachwood Drive

Hollywood

There may be no symbol more universally recognized or associated with Los Angeles and the movie business than the Hollywood sign. While some find it tacky, others associate it with the glamour and mystique that the name "Hollywood" implies. The sign was originally constructed as advertising for the 500-acre residential subdivision (Hollywoodland) located at the top of Beachwood Canyon. The first 50-foot-tall letters were made of wood and outlined with light bulbs. A replica may be seen in the recent filmed biography of Charles Chaplin. Today each letter (minus the original "land") has been reconstructed in steel; the total length is 450 feet. Built on public land, the sign is owned and maintained by the Hollywood Chamber of Commerce.

Restricted access, with a $103 fine for violators, has not deterred the many graffiti artists whose work is displayed on the backs of the individual letters. Appreciation of the sign is not dependent upon being up close. It is actually far more interesting when viewed from afar. The landmark's most gifted biographer is artist Ed Ruscha, whose images of the sign are widely known. But starlet Peg Entwistle, who committed suicide from atop the last letter of the original sign, made the landmark infamous.

Restoration work on the sign was funded by the subscription of prominent members of the entertainment community, including rock star Alice Cooper, who reputedly paid for the last "O" in memory of Groucho Marx. *No. 111, declared 2/7/73*

TOBERMAN RESIDENCE

RUSSELL, ALPAUGH AND DAWSON 1924

1847 Camino Palmero
Hollywood

C. E. Toberman was a prominent and theatrically minded real-estate developer who commissioned this nineteen-room gated Mediterranean Revival residential complex with a three-story villa, guest house, pool house, and tennis court. Occasionally used for film locations, the complex is only barely visible behind walled gates guarded by a black Doberman. Called "Mr. Hollywood," Toberman was well known for his involvement as the developer of the Roosevelt Hotel and the Egyptian, Chinese, and El Capitan theaters. His son James was a three-term mayor of Los Angeles. *No. 285, declared 10/3/84*

HOLLYWOOD SIGN

STORER RESIDENCE

FRANK LLOYD WRIGHT 1923

8161 Hollywood Boulevard
Hollywood

This exquisite residential pavilion was built for surgeon John B. Storer, who came to California from Wisconsin to retire. Larger than it appears, this five-bedroom, three-bathroom house extends literally and visually into the terrain with a series of retaining walls that provide changing vistas of the house as one approaches. Unlike some homes that ultimately disappear as the landscape matures, this house seems to improve as it settles into its site. One can detect Lloyd Wright's talented hand here; he not only supervised the construction but was the building's landscape designer. In an odd lapse of confidence during the construction of the house, the senior Wright was said to have agreed with his son that the Storer house "lacked joy." Perhaps true then, or perhaps simply a reflection of the temporary mood of the architect, that situation has clearly changed. Lovingly restored by its sixth owner, motion-picture producer Joel Silver (*Lethal Weapon*, *Die Hard*), the interior features furnishings and accessories from the period. On a summer day, when its decorative fabric canopies are floating in the breeze, the home is a visual feast, a party waiting to happen. *No. 96, declared 2/23/72*

STORER RESIDENCE

LANE RESIDENCE

OLIVER P. DENNIS 1909

Magic Castle
7001 Franklin Avenue
Hollywood

Built as a residence for Rollin B. Lane, this seventeen-room Châteauesque structure is a copy of the Kimberly Residence (of the Kimberly-Clark fortune), now a house museum in Redlands, California. This home was occupied by the Lane family into the 1940s. After a period of decline, it was reopened in 1963 as the Academy of Magical Arts, a private club for magicians and their supporters and admirers. It featured, among other entertainments, "invisible Irma and her magic piano." *No. 406, declared 1/17/89*

LANE RESIDENCE

KOREATOWN

TEMPLE SINAI EAST

S. TILDEN NORTON 1926

Korean Philadelphia Presbyterian Church
407 South New Hampshire
Koreatown

Built for a congregation that dates from
1906, this domed structure seats 1,400
people. Its grand synagogue architecture is
eclectic, including elements of Romanesque,
Moorish, and "California Hollywood."
Though somewhat flamboyant in its style, the
temple is considered the birthplace of
Conservative Judaism in Los Angeles. The
building was used as a set in the second film
version of *The Jazz Singer*. *No. 91, declared*
11/17/71

FIRST BAPTIST CHURCH
OF LOS ANGELES

ALLISON AND ALLISON 1927

760 South Westmorland Avenue
Koreatown

If Baptists had cathedrals, this would be one.
Already called a notable work of eclectic
architecture, it is tempting to add the word
"bombastic" to the building description. It is
one of the least user-friendly designs to come
from the pen of these noted church and
school architects. It is, in a word, unforgettable. *No. 237, declared 4/9/81*

MOVIE STUDIOS

Five motion-picture studios have been declared Monuments. The first is in nearby Silver Lake, but the rest are in Hollywood:

KEYSTONE STUDIOS
1912

1712 Glendale Boulevard
Silver Lake

By 1912, Mack Sennett's insatiable curiosity about film led him, along with two partners, to form his own production company, Keystone. Built as work space for the production of Mack Sennett comedies, these studios were among the first motion-picture studio complexes in Los Angeles. By 1915, the successful Keystone was assimilated into a much larger conglomerate, Triangle Film Corporation, which combined the talents of Sennett, D. W. Griffith, and William Ince.

Buried by the staggering losses generated by Griffith's monumental film *Intolerance*, Triangle closed its doors within three years. Much of the original Keystone complex has been demolished, and the property functions today as a storage facility. *No. 256, declared 11/5/82*

CHAPLIN STUDIOS
1919

A and M Record Studio
1416 North La Brea Avenue
Hollywood

This is one of the first motion-picture studios built in Hollywood. When the "Little Tramp," Charlie Chaplin, built his home on La Brea Avenue, facing Sunset Boulevard, he built this studio behind it. Chaplin's childhood years were spent in poverty in England. With the completion of the studio, the "Little Tramp" now owned his own version of a picturesque English village. This Tudor Revival complex is a reflection of the magic and illusion inherent in "the business." A remarkably detailed re-creation of the studio was built at a rural site for use in the recent film *Chaplin*, showing Hollywood during the early years of filmmaking. *No. 58, declared 2/5/69*

WARNER BROS. STUDIO
1919

5800 Sunset Boulevard
Hollywood

The sound era of motion-picture production dates from 1927, the year of *The Jazz Singer* and the talkie revolution. Although *The Jazz Singer* was basically a silent picture with occasional musical and spoken passages presented on a synchronized phonograph, it was revolutionary for its time. Warner Bros./Vitaphone filmed *The Jazz Singer* on this site, now home of television station KTLA. The extant colonnaded administration building, designed in the manner of southern Greek Revival plantation houses, concealed the stage where the actual filming took place. Ironically, new (sound) stages were soon built, replacing the structure where the first talkie was made. *No. 180, declared 9/21/77*

SITE OF FIRST WALT DISNEY STUDIO
CONSTRUCTION DATE UNKNOWN
(DEMOLISHED)

Griffith Park Shopping Center
2725 Hyperion Avenue
Griffith Park

As tenants in a cluster of small, generic stucco buildings, Walt and Roy Disney created both the character of Mickey Mouse and the award-winning *Snow White and the Seven Dwarfs*, which was the first animated full-length feature film. As the company became successful, the studio outgrew the space, ultimately leading the Disneys to build new studios in Burbank, where they relocated in 1940. The old buildings were

CHAPLIN STUDIOS

LUBIN FILM STUDIOS

demolished to make way for one of Los Angeles' four thousand strip shopping centers, and no evidence of the Disney presence remains today. *No. 163, declared 10/6/76*

LUBIN FILM STUDIOS

1922

KCET Broadcasting Headquarters
4401 Sunset Boulevard
Hollywood

Only a few remnants remain of the old film studio built on this site. Originally Lubin Film, the building was subsequently purchased by Monogram, and then by Allied Artists. The complex has a distinguished lineage in "the business": the Keystone Cops, Charlie Chaplin, and Fatty Arbuckle all made movies here. Since 1971 it has been owned by KCET. While much of the site has been rebuilt, some of the early buildings can still be seen on the north side of the property. *No. 198, declared 9/20/78*

HIGHLAND-CAMROSE VILLAGE

VARIOUS ARCHITECTS 1916-23

2103-2115½ North Highland / 6819 Camrose
Hollywood

One of the most scenic and unusual residential communities in Los Angeles, this is a charming complex of fifteen Craftsman and Dutch Colonial Revival style buildings. There is also a dash of Lloyd Wright and a pinch of San Gimignano, Italy (the 1920 tower), thrown in for good measure (the designation covers only the listed addresses). It is difficult to find and difficult to climb, but the experience is worth the effort, although the elevator is tempting. Traditionally home to people who worked in the film community, this neighborhood was featured in the films *The Long Goodbye* and *Dead Again*. *No. 291, declared 4/23/85*

HIGHLAND-CAMROSE VILLAGE

BARNSDALL RESIDENCE

BARNSDALL ESTATE

Three designations have occurred at
Barnsdall Park; one is for the park itself, the
others are for two Frank Lloyd Wright-
designed buildings:

BARNSDALL RESIDENCE

FRANK LLOYD WRIGHT 1917-20

Hollyhock House
4800 Hollywood Boulevard
Hollywood
No. 12, declared 1/4/63

STUDIO RESIDENCE "A"

FRANK LLOYD WRIGHT 1919

Arts and Crafts Building
No. 33, declared 2/26/65

BARNSDALL PARK

No. 34, declared 2/26/65

Arguably the earliest extant "modern" residence in Los Angeles (Wright's work has
been described by Philip Johnson as "half-
modern"), Hollyhock House was commissioned by oil heiress and "parlor Bolshevik"
Aline Barnsdall. It was the second of several
Wright residences to be built in Southern
California, and the first to be built in Los
Angeles.

Barnsdall was a patroness of avant-garde theater in conservative Chicago, where she first met Wright. She commissioned him to design this elaborate residence as the centerpiece of her 36-acre Olive Hill estate. Barnsdall hoped to develop the property as an artist's colony, which would also include a 1,200-seat theater.

Described as a "brooding" home at the crest of the hill, Hollyhock House was named for Barnsdall's favorite flower, the hollyhock, which Wright abstracted into three-dimensional concrete ornamentation that appears as a leitmotif throughout the house.

Wright designed and built two other buildings on the site, Studio Residences A and B. Wright lived in Studio B (now demolished) when in residence in California, during construction of the main house.

While doing the work for Mrs. Barnsdall, Wright often traveled to Japan to oversee the construction of the Imperial Hotel. As a result, the construction supervision of Studio A was done by Wright's employee, Rudolf M. Schindler (some actually credit Schindler with the design under Wright's supervision, an allegation that loses credibility with repeated viewing). The landscaping was done by Lloyd Wright, Frank's talented eldest son. Together with Richard Neutra, Schindler designed the pergola and wading pool in 1925.

Barnsdall occupied the house for only a short time. Conflicts with Wright soured her on the project, which she ultimately abandoned, leaving the theater unbuilt. She donated her home to the artists of California for use as the California Arts Club, and in 1922 she left the United States for Europe. Studio B served as her home on subsequent visits to Los Angeles, and it was here that she died in 1946. Olive Hill ultimately reverted to city ownership. After Barnsdall's death, the buildings went through several years of neglect before a $500,000 city-funded restoration. Somewhat in keeping with Barnsdall's original vision, the compound now serves as an art colony, with the addition of two buildings designed in a neo-Wrightian style. The first was the Junior Art Center (1967) by Hunter, Benedict, Kahn and Tarrell; the other is the Municipal Art Gallery (1971) by Wehmueller and Stephens.

GARDEN COURT APARTMENTS

FRANK L. MELINE 1919

(DEMOLISHED CA. 1982)

7021 Hollywood Boulevard
Hollywood

To quote from its National Register nomination, "The building was the first of the 'modern' luxury residential hotels in Hollywood, built to accommodate the demands of the burgeoning movie industry." "Modern" in this context meant a Beaux Arts design, which housed, in its early years, a veritable Who's Who of Hollywood movers and shakers, including such luminaries as Louis B. Mayer, Mae Murray, and John Gilbert. Later the building went into decline, and after a few years as the American School of Dance, it was abandoned. Ultimately trashed by squatters, it became known in the neighborhood as "Hotel Hell." *No. 243, declared 4/28/81*

STAIRS AND RETAINING WALLS

Various locations in Hollywoodland Subdivision
Hollywood

STONE ENTRANCE PORTALS

1920s

Beachwood at Belden Drive
Hollywood

These stone portals marked the official entrance to the Hollywoodland subdivision. They were built by immigrant European stonemasons who quarried and dressed the stone on the site, while living in tents located in work camps in the wild terrain of this undeveloped canyon. In addition to the portals, they built many graceful stairways descending the hillsides. They are also credited with the construction of many of the retaining walls in the area, as well as the stone facing of several of the homes. *Nos. 20, 535, declared 5/24/63 and 6/11/91, respectively*

SECURITY TRUST AND SAVINGS BUILDING

SECURITY TRUST AND SAVINGS BUILDING
PARKINSON AND PARKINSON 1920

Security Pacific Bank
6381 Hollywood Boulevard
Hollywood

Hollywood's first high rise, this rather plain and somber Beaux Arts office block sits amid the more energetic action now taking place on the boulevard, as a reminder of how Hollywood has changed in the last seventy-odd years. Architect Charles Moore describes this building as a "reprise of an early Louis Sullivan skyscraper." *No. 334, declared 12/18/87*

FRANKLIN GARDEN APARTMENTS

L. H. BALDWIN 1920
(DEMOLISHED 1978)

6233 Hollywood Boulevard
Hollywood

This well-known neighborhood landmark was considered an outstanding example of Spanish Colonial Revival architecture which also incorporated beautiful landscaping. The owners were unresponsive to efforts aimed at preserving the structures; the permit for demolition was authorized within a month of the designation. *No. 192, declared 6/7/78*

HOLLYWOOD MASONIC TEMPLE

JOHN C. AUSTIN 1921

6840 Hollywood Boulevard
Hollywood

This Neoclassical colonnaded, terra-cotta-fronted structure sits vacant, in rather somber repose, adjacent to the El Capitan theater. It bears witness to the changing rituals of Hollywood Boulevard, which must have seemed unusual even to the ritualistic Masons who first occupied the building. Founded in 1903, the Hollywood chapter had many famous and prestigious members. *No. 277, declared 6/12/84*

BOLLMAN RESIDENCE

LLOYD WRIGHT 1922

1530 North Ogden Drive
Hollywood

One must examine the design drawings to appreciate fully what the architect had in mind here. An elaborate formality with richly detailed fenestration originally gave this relatively chaste, vaguely Mayan pavilion a forcefulness that belied its size. The base was constructed of unfinished, exposed concrete block that has since been whited-out, skewing the original proportions. Still a handsome, early-modern home, which Lloyd Wright considered the first commission of his practice, it was built for Henry Bollman. A simultaneous Lloyd Wright commission for the Otto Bollman Residence is located in the Highland-Camrose Village (HCM 291).
No. 235, declared 11/3/80

WEID CANYON DAM

1924

Mulholland Dam and Lake Hollywood Reservoir
2460 Lake Hollywood Drive
Hollywood

Accessible these days only by foot, the monumental arcaded dam structure in Weid Canyon, with its castings of the California Bear, rises about 70 feet above a dirt bank dam that collects water to a depth of 186 feet. Its base is 160 feet thick, tapering to a 16-foot-wide walkway at the top. It was dedicated to Irish immigrant engineer William Mulholland, who had a forty-three-year career in public works. He is remembered for his long tenure as chief of the Los Angeles Water Department, during which time he was personally credited with the designs of the Elysian, Solano, Silver Lake, and Ivanhoe reservoirs, and the Buena Vista Pumping Station. He was also intimately involved with the creation of the Owens Valley aqueduct, which brought water to Los Angeles from 255 miles away. Tragically, four years after being honored with the dedication of this dam, Mulholland's last dam (San Francisquito Canyon) failed due to poor soil conditions. Mulholland bravely accepted responsibility for the failure, which is considered Los Angeles's most devastating natural disaster. More than 450 people lost their lives when that dam gave way. (See also Mulholland Fountain, HCM 162.) *No. 421, declared 3/31/89*

LAKE HOLLYWOOD

AFTON ARMS APARTMENTS

LELAND BRYANT 1924

6141 Afton Place

Hollywood

This is a picturesque work from the pen of apartment architect Leland Bryant, who was to become famous for his brilliant Art Deco Sunset Towers apartments. This Mission Revival style was attempted much too late for any intellectual credibility. A tall arched entrance, topped by an *espadaña*, leads to a central courtyard that charms but does not convince. *No. 463, declared 11/3/89*

FREEMAN RESIDENCE

FRANK LLOYD WRIGHT 1924

1962 Glencoe Way

Hollywood

Samuel and Harriet Freeman relocated to California from the East in the early 1920s. Wealthy and progressive, they were quite attracted to Wright's reputation when they chose him to design their home on this steep site. Wright enjoyed the challenge presented by the intellectually stimulating clients and the difficult site. He responded with a very

FREEMAN RESIDENCE

vertical, knit-block house that exploited the views from each level as it stepped down the hill.

Harriet Freeman, who seemed to enjoy the role of architectural patroness, was the sister of Leah Lovell, who together with her husband commissioned masterpieces by both Neutra and Schindler. Both of the Freemans lived in their house for more than fifty years. Harriet induced Schindler to design furniture for the home, which evidently caused Wright some consternation (his own furniture designs were notoriously uncomfortable). It has been suggested that Harriet was in love with Schindler, as were many Los Angeles women during the twenties and later. The letters between these architects, their clients, and each other certainly make interesting reading.

As directed by her will, Harriet Freeman's house was donated to the University of Southern California with an endowment for restoration. The University's School of Architecture will use it to house distinguished visitors. *No. 246, declared 11/25/81*

HOLLYWOOD STUDIO CLUB OF THE YWCA

JULIA MORGAN 1926

1215 Lodi Place
Hollywood

High-quality, low-cost housing was offered by the Studio Club for young women who migrated to Los Angeles hoping to participate in the exciting and fast-growing motion-picture industry. Designed by the prominent and successful architect Julia Morgan, who did many projects for the YWCA, this inviting Mediterranean Revival structure was once home to both Marilyn Monroe and Kim Novak. *No. 175, declared 5/4/77*

VILLA CARLOTTA

ARTHUR HARVEY 1926

5959 Franklin Avenue
Hollywood

Eleanor Ince, youthful widow of legendary film producer Thomas Ince (1882-1924), commissioned this elaborate apartment building across the street from her home. Her residential property was soon to become the site for her second project, the Château Elysée Hotel. Thomas Ince, who was one of the most important and influential figures in the history of film, died under mysterious circumstances on William Randolph Hearst's yacht, two years before the construction of the Villa Carlotta. Advanced for its day, Villa Carlotta featured elaborate soundproofing, water filtration, and a ventilation system that generated complete air changes in each apartment every five minutes. The building's star resident was Louella Parsons, who was married in the lobby. *No. 315, declared 10/28/86*

HOLLYWOOD STUDIO CLUB

CHÂTEAU ELYSÉE

ARTHUR HARVEY 1928

5930 Franklin Avenue
Hollywood

Like the neighboring Villa Carlotta, this impressive structure was commissioned by the Ince Development Company, and built as a residential hotel. It was constructed on the site of what had been Eleanor Ince's home during her marriage. The eclectic building reflects a grandiose French Renaissance Revival sensibility, and it is far more elaborate than the Carlotta. Residing here during its years of prominence were Clark Gable and Carole Lombard, Cary Grant, Humphrey Bogart, Elizabeth Taylor, and many, many others from the film colony. During the fifties and sixties the building was renamed Fifield Manor while it served as a retirement home for the elderly. Today, it is the "Celebrity Centre" of the Church of Scientology. *No. 329, declared 9/23/87*

ANDALUSIA APARTMENTS

ARTHUR AND NINA ZWEIBEL 1926

1471-1475 Havenhurst Drive
Hollywood

The Andalusia is among the very best Spanish Colonial Revival courtyard apartment complexes built in Southern California. Los Angeles's balmy climate encouraged the construction of many similar compounds with interior courts, pools, and fountains; but none was as believable or as livable as this. Although the exercise pool at the rear of the site is gone, no changes have taken place in the central courtyard, which is complemented by mature landscaping and has a feeling of quiet and calm. Refreshingly restored, the building was once a favorite of the movie colony, boasting such famous residents as Clara Bow, Jean Hagen, John Payne, Caesar Romero, and Teresa Wright. The Zweibels were known for a number of similar projects. Although unlicensed, Mr. Zweibel designed them for signature by an architect, while Mrs. Zweibel decorated the interiors. During the Depression, they became set designers for the movies, an occupation for which they were obviously highly qualified. *No. 435, declared 5/16/89*

ANDALUSIA APARTMENTS

CHÂTEAU ELYSÉE

ROMAN GARDENS APARTMENTS

ROMAN GARDENS APARTMENTS

WALTER S. AND F. PIERPONT DAVIS 1926

Villa Valentino
2000 North Highland Avenue
Hollywood

A truly eclectic garden-apartment complex, this one exudes a kind of funky charm. Not exactly run-down, but clearly past its prime, it is the sort of place one expects to find a struggling writer or aspiring ingenue. It is heavily shaded and has a rich variety of mature landscaping, yet the gardens feel somehow empty and slightly melancholy. Varying somewhat from the axial orientation of most courtyard complexes, the apartments are arranged around a series of informal courts and terraces. A nonfunctioning tower, of African origin, is but one of the many romantic details that give the Spanish Colonial Revival complex its resonant character. The tower is also the only part of the complex that is visible from the street. It is said that Valentino secretly maintained an apartment here for his amorous adventures. *No. 397, declared 11/23/88*

ROOSEVELT HOTEL

FISHER, LAKE AND TRAVER 1926

7000-7016 Hollywood Boulevard
Hollywood

Named for President Theodore Roosevelt, this lavish twelve-story Spanish Colonial Revival pastiche was the design responsibility of H. B. Traver. A 1940s addition surrounding a swimming pool is uncredited. "Mr. Hollywood," developer C. E. Toberman, put together this project with financing from prominent members of the film community, including Mary Pickford, Douglas Fairbanks, Louis B. Mayer, and Joseph Schenck, among others. Their involvement assured the hotel's success; it was often the site of post-premiere parties, and from 1927 to 1935 it was home to the Academy of Motion Picture Arts and Sciences. The first "Oscar" presentations were held here in 1929. *No. 545, declared 6/17/91*

ROOSEVELT
HOTEL

ARTISAN'S PATIO SHOPS

MORGAN, WALLS AND CLEMENTS 1926

6727-6733 Hollywood Boulevard
Hollywood

It is hard to see what is being singled out for protection here. Ostensibly an open-air patio complex, today it feels more like an alley, pressed into service in a greedy attempt to exploit the pedestrian tourist market. It was allegedly created by an important architectural firm, but little evidence of their presence remains. A tacky fountain complements one mature palm tree. The complex is associated with "noted clown painter" Leon Franks, which says it all. *No. 453, declared 10/17/89*

EL CAPITAN THEATER BUILDING

MORGAN, WALLS AND CLEMENTS 1926
(RESTORED 1991, FIELDS AND DEVEREAUX)

6834 Hollywood Boulevard
Hollywood

Unlike the movie theaters built during this period by C. E. Toberman (Grauman's Chinese and Egyptian), the El Capitan was designed and built for theatrical productions rather than movies. The Period Revival exterior with East Indian detailing enclosed a shallow 1,500-seat auditorium decorated in a South Seas motif by San Francisco architect G. Albert Lansburgh, who designed many Los Angeles theater interiors as well as that of the San Francisco Opera House. A mixed-use building, the giant Barker Brothers Furniture Company, occupied the retail frontage and upper floors.

The theater was recently restored by its current owners, the Walt Disney Company, at a cost of $8.65 million. The elaborate marquee (not original) is an appropriate addition to the building (the inflatable Mickey Mouse in our photograph was a tem-

porary installation for the re-release of *Fantasia*). Another appropriate addition at the "El Cap" is the fanfare that precedes the showing of each film. The furling of seven brightly colored scrims and a sensational sound system make going to the movies a special experience.

In their restoration efforts, the Disney organization and their architects have made a significant contribution to the culture and history of Los Angeles. Recent discussions have taken place regarding a controversial

proposal to install a large mural depicting pop-music icon Michael Jackson on the eastern wall of the building. *No. 495, declared 6/12/90*

GRAUMAN'S CHINESE THEATER

MEYER AND HOLLER 1927

Mann's Chinese Theater
6925 Hollywood Boulevard
Hollywood

This building was showman Sid Grauman's second theater in Hollywood. It opened with Cecil B. DeMille's film *King of Kings*. Its sinocized architecture, with Art Deco touches, features a formal forecourt designed to allow parades of arriving movie stars during premieres. Grauman's sensational publicity stunt, setting in concrete the hand and footprints of Hollywood "royalty," remains a top tourist attraction today.

Early photographs indicate that the building has undergone few exterior alterations over time, but it definitely suffers from wear and neglect. The entire complex is in need of restoration, including the removal of excessive and inappropriate signage. The current owners would do well to follow the lead established by the sensitive restoration of the El Capitan Theater across the street. *No. 55, declared 6/5/68*

STROMBERG CLOCK

1927

6439 Hollywood Boulevard
Hollywood

A neighborhood landmark for many years, the clock was installed as advertising in front of William Stromberg Jewelers, one of the boulevard's early retail stores. Two generations of Strombergs worked here until 1986. Known as "Jewelers to the Stars," the Strombergs numbered among their clients

Bette Davis, Marilyn Monroe, Elizabeth Taylor, and Peter Lorre. Today, the clock is maintained by the Hollywood Chamber of Commerce. *No. 316, declared 1/7/87*

HOLLYWOOD THEATER

G. ALBERT LANSBURGH 1928

6433 Hollywood Boulevard
Hollywood

Another important theater design from the rich imagination of theater designer Lansburgh, this Renaissance Revival theater, office, and retail complex was built for Warner Brothers. *No. 572, declared 2/9/93*

HOLLYWOOD WESTERN BUILDING

S. CHARLES LEE 1928

5510 Hollywood Boulevard
Hollywood

This sadly dilapidated four-story Art Deco structure was commissioned by Louis B. Mayer and was, for a time, one of the most prestigious buildings in Hollywood. Over the years, it was visited by many of the famous names in Hollywood because it housed the Central Casting Corporation and the Motion Picture Producers Association, the latter better known as the "Hayes Office," the official watchdog of on-screen Hollywood morality. *No. 336, declared 1/6/88*

PALM TREES

1928

Highland Avenue between Wilshire Boulevard and Melrose Avenue
Hollywood

The residents of Highland Avenue arranged with the city for the construction of a median strip down the center of Highland Avenue. The plan included the planting of a single row of Queen and Washington Robusta palm trees down the center of the median, at the expense of the residents, as a neighborhood beautification project. Spaced roughly 50

HIGHLAND TOWERS APARTMENTS

feet apart on a 16-foot-wide median strip, these trees are now mature and have become a truly memorable visual landmark, not only for the residents but also for the rush-hour commuters who make Highland a challenging pedestrian experience. *No. 94, declared 1/26/72*

HIGHLAND TOWERS APARTMENTS

SELKIRK AND STANBERG 1927

1920-1928 Highland Avenue
Hollywood

The perfect "background building" in a prominent location, this L-shaped Spanish Colonial Revival apartment tower with its small, shaded north garden is passed by thousands of motorists daily, with little recognition. It is but one of the increasingly rare examples of the many apartment buildings of this style built to house personnel for the growing movie industry. *No. 475, declared 10/16/90*

EL CAPITAN THEATER
BUILDING

JARDINETTE APARTMENTS

SAMUEL / NOVARRO RESIDENCE

LLOYD WRIGHT 1926

5609 Valley Oak Drive
Hollywood

This is the first of two homes designed by Wright for Louis Samuel, who was silent-film star Ramon Novarro's agent. (Samuel's second Wright home was built on Bundy Drive in 1935.) Novarro also commissioned a house from Wright about this time for a site on 22nd Street, but the home was never built. How Novarro came to own this house is not clear, but he asked Wright to make some minor changes almost immediately after he acquired the property, which is why the house is referred to by both names. Evidently Samuel and Novarro never shared the house.

An early work in Wright's independent career, this house is a stunning display of the influence on his work of the 1925 Paris Exposition Internationale des Arts Décoratifs et Industriels Modernes (from which Art Deco derives its name). The design also incorporates his ongoing concerns about relating interior space to the landscape and his preoccupation with integrating more sophisticated structural solutions into his work. His genius for landscape and environment undoubtedly contributed to what may be the most beautifully sited home in Los Angeles.

The house, as remodeled for Novarro, suggests the renegade sensibilities of this "Latin lover," who chose to live in an Art Deco masterpiece in the Hollywood Hills at a time when other stars were choosing the more eclectic aesthetics then popular in Beverly Hills. Novarro's fame and fortune declined. A lifelong bachelor, his name made headlines one last time in 1968, when he was beaten to death by two young men. By this time, the glamorous life he once led in this sybaritic playground was only a distant memory. Recently refurbished, the home is now owned by actress Diane Keaton.
No. 130, declared 7/17/74

JARDINETTE APARTMENTS

RICHARD NEUTRA 1927

5128 Marathon Street
Hollywood

This was the first International Style multi-family residence to be built in the United States. It was also Neutra's first independent commission in this country (though it began as a joint venture with Schindler). Architects from the modern school consider this to be among the seminal pieces of modern American architecture. It is an austere design, made more so by the absence of the original colored banding, which emphasized the horizontality of the building. To this day, it continues to fulfill the European dream of architecture as a machine for housing the masses. Closer study of some of the design elements suggests that Neutra was not yet in complete understanding of the California climate: large balconies, which would have floor-to-ceiling glass today, are accessed only by small windows. *No. 390, declared 10/4/88*

CHÂTEAU MARMONT

ARNOLD WEITZMAN 1928

8221 Sunset Boulevard
Hollywood

An eclectic building with Gothic Revival overtones, long associated with the film industry, the Château Marmont is a brooding symbol of Hollywood's tarnished glitter. The building is alternately described as "genteel-shabby" and "recently restored" (you be the judge), while its gardens offer a surprising oasis on "the Strip." As an urban-design element, it gives visual focus to a curve on Sunset Boulevard, and its interiors reveal their twenties origins. It is perhaps best known today for its association with comedian John Belushi, who died of a drug overdose in 1982 in one of the hotel bungalows. *No. 151, declared 3/14/76*

SAMUEL / NOVARRO
RESIDENCE

DESMOND RESIDENCE

1928

1803-1811 Courtney Avenue
Hollywood

Said to be influenced by the hillside houses of Taxco, Mexico, this cluster of five red tile-roofed homes has a distinctive Mexican/Beverly Hills flavor. With elaborate iron gates and a beautifully landscaped swimming pool, this property was developed by descendants of early Los Angeles émigré and wildly successful hat-merchant-turned-real-estate-developer Daniel Desmond. The street was named for Desmond's eldest son, Courtney. Desmond's daughters were said to have commissioned a project by Frank Lloyd Wright, but it never materialized. *No. 445, declared 6/20/89*

HYDE PARK

PRESIDENT'S RESIDENCE

1912

(DEMOLISHED 1978)

7581 Budlong Avenue
Hyde Park

To delay demolition, this Mission Revival compound on the Los Angeles campus of Pepperdine College became a Historic-Cultural Monument. The building's primary significance was its interior, which featured tile work and hardware of distinguished craftsmanship. In an all-too-common scenario, the structure was demolished shortly after designation. *No. 185, declared 4/19/78*

DESMOND RESIDENCE

McKINLEY RESIDENCE

GRANADA BUILDINGS

LAFAYETTE PARK

MCKINLEY RESIDENCE

HUNT AND BURNS 1917

The Mansion
310 South Lafayette Park Place
Lafayette Park

This generously proportioned Renaissance Revival home is the last remaining single-family residence in what was once a beautiful row of similar estates. Falling victim to changing zoning and land-use patterns—which allow more than one hundred units on this site—the home was proposed for replacement by an apartment building which would have been similar in size and scale to those flanking this stalwart survivor. Currently protected by the mitigation requirements of the California Environmental Quality Act, restoration may follow. For now, cyclone fencing borders the site, the porte cochere has collapsed, and a wall sign bears the plaintive hand-painted words "Save this Landmark." *No. 326, declared 9/9/87*

GRANADA BUILDINGS

FRANKLIN HARPER 1925

672 South Lafayette Park Place
Lafayette Park

Suggested by the massed structures of a historic village near Ronda, Spain, this surprising and unusual complex of buildings is organized along a landscaped interior street with open corridors and bridges. Like a mythical village, perceptions of the complex constantly change: when viewed from the sidewalk, the upper, less-articulated floors totally disappear. This upper level, with its large-scale arches, is visible from Lafayette Park, located across the street. Recently and handsomely restored, this complex is among the best of its type. *No. 238, declared 4/9/81*

LINCOLN HEIGHTS

FEDERAL BANK BUILDING

OTTO NEHER AND C. F. SKILLING 1910

2201 North Broadway
Lincoln Heights

It is unusual to find such a finely detailed banking temple at such a distance from downtown, and yet here it is. Prominently located, this building served as a gateway to what was then one of Los Angeles's first stylish suburban shopping areas. The copper dome and granite base give this terra-cotta-faced, unreinforced-masonry building a presence that belies its location. The building is vacant and appears to be awaiting demolition. *No. 396, declared 11/23/88*

LOS FELIZ

CEDAR TREES

1916

Los Feliz Boulevard between Riverside Drive
and Western Avenue
Los Feliz

An unusual choice for street trees, these cedars (*Cedrus Deodara* and *atlantica*) were planted here as part of a beautification endeavor, a joint venture of the Los Feliz Improvement Association and the Los Feliz Women's Club. *No. 67, declared 5/20/70*

FEDERAL BANK BUILDING

ENNIS RESIDENCE

ENNIS RESIDENCE

FRANK LLOYD WRIGHT 1924

2607 Glendower Avenue
Los Feliz / Griffith Park

The largest of Wright's Los Angeles houses was built for Mr. and Mrs. Charles Ennis, about whom little is known. A wealthy couple who added many rich interior materials to the building (to Wright's consternation), they sold the house after only a few years' occupancy. The design is considered the most monumental of Wright's experiments with concrete-block construction, and the house possesses little sense of a domestic interior. Criticism of Wright regarding the house stemmed from seeming philosophical contradictions: he advocated the integration of architecture with the terrain but then sited this structure atop an outcropping, which required substantial site modifications in the form of retaining walls. Soon these walls began to bulge away from the hillside, presaging structural problems that plague the house to this day.

Used for films like television's *An Inconvenient Woman*, some sixty years after it was completed the home retains a futurist look. It was neglected for years and sometimes stood empty, and indeed, demolition was contemplated until its 1968 purchase and subsequent restoration by August Oliver Brown. Unfortunately, the purity of the building's concrete exterior has been muddied by what appears to be a thick coat of beige paint. *No. 149, declared 3/3/76*

TAGGART RESIDENCE

LLOYD WRIGHT 1922-24

5423 Black Oak Drive
Los Feliz

Built for Martha Taggart, who would later become Wright's mother-in-law, this innovative residence is significant, at least in part, for the ways in which it anticipates the soon to arrive Art Deco style. This unique home has an expressionist aesthetic that seeks the integration of interior with exterior. It also uses interior plantings that reflect Wright's training in landscape architecture. *No. 521, declared 3/15/91*

MONTEREY APARTMENTS
C. K. SMITHLEY 1925

4600 Los Feliz Boulevard
Los Feliz

The second-oldest deluxe court in Los Angeles, this modest courtyard complex recalls the early Monterey style in an urban context. With its mature landscaping and giant street trees, it is a late example of the graciousness offered by this uniquely California building style. *No. 353, declared 5/11/88*

MID CITY

PACIFIC BELL GARAGE
1922

2755 West Washington Boulevard
Mid City

It is unusual to find such a small and handsome utility-type building in a residential neighborhood. The garage is a modest, but nicely detailed Spanish Colonial Revival building featuring an elaborately decorated entryway in the Churrigueresque style. *No. 331, declared 12/8/87*

WESTMINSTER PRESBYTERIAN CHURCH
1926

2230 West Jefferson Boulevard
Mid City

This traditional Renaissance Revival church with its distinctive bell tower is home to the oldest black Presbyterian congregation in Los Angeles. It was founded in 1904 and is the largest in the West. *No. 229, declared 6/11/80*

TAGGART RESIDENCE

MONTECITO HEIGHTS

RESIDENCE

LESTER S. MOORE 1909

Montecito View House
4115 Berenice Place
Montecito Heights

An unusual example of a Craftsman residence perched on a steep hillside, the style seems better suited to flat sites. This particular building was featured in advertising promoting the Montecito Heights real-estate development. Unfortunately, without trespassing it is impossible to see this building or to assess its architectural merit. *No. 529, declared 3/1/91*

MT. WASHINGTON

WILES RESIDENCE

WILLIAM WILSON WILES 1911

4224 Glenalbyn Drive
Mt. Washington

Designed and hand-built by brass-bed manufacturer William Wiles, this two-story Craftsman style "Butterfly Bungalow"—so-named for its symmetrically "winged" roof shape—features many characteristic details of the style including wide eaves, a low-pitched roof, wooden casement windows, and dark-stained wooden shingles and trim. The house has remained virtually unchanged during sixty years of ownership by subsequent generations of the Wiles family. *No. 393, declared 11/4/88*

BENT RESIDENCE AND CARRIAGE HOUSE

ATTRIB. HUNT AND BURNS 1914

4201 Glenalbyn Drive
Mt. Washington

The last of the homes built by the prominent Bent family, this one was for H. Stanley Bent and his wife, Grace Sitherwood. Unlike his brothers' homes, this one is built in the Prairie Style with cream-colored stucco walls and a flat roof with wide overhanging eaves. It is simpler, but similar in style to the Highland Park Ebell Club (HCM 284). *No. 395, declared 11/4/88*

BENT RESIDENCE

NORTH HOLLYWOOD

EL PORTAL THEATER

L. A. SMITH 1926

5265-5271 Lankershim
North Hollywood

An important early shopping center concept, the El Portal includes retail and office space in its Spanish Colonial Revival theater complex. *No. 573, declared 2/9/93*

ST. SAVIOR'S CHAPEL, HARVARD SCHOOL

REGINALD JOHNSON 1914

(RELOCATED 1937)

3700 Coldwater Canyon Avenue
North Hollywood / Studio City

St. Savior's Chapel re-creates (in plan) the chapel at Rugby School in England, with the pews that face a center aisle. The Harvard School campus and St. Savior's Chapel were originally located at Venice and Western streets. In 1937 the chapel was cut into sixteen sections, brought over the hills via Sepulveda Boulevard, and reconstructed on its current site. *No. 32, declared 2/5/65*

ST. SAVIOR'S CHAPEL

LANKERSHIM MONUMENT

LANKERSHIM MONUMENT
CA. 1920

North end of Nichols Canyon Road
North Hollywood / Studio City

The final resting place of Col. J. B. Lankershim of the California militia is marked by a simple stone obelisk, on a small, unkempt sliver of ground, bordered by a riot of bougainvillea at the crest of Mt. Olympus. Lankershim, together with I. N. Van Nuys and a group of investors, purchased the southern half of the Mission San Fernando property, where this parcel is located. This purchase signaled the end of the Mission era and the beginning of modern development.

The monument is marked with bronze plaques that describe the events concerning the "Cahuenga Capitulation" and suggest that Andrés Pico passed this way, en route to meeting Frémont at Campo de Cahuenga (HCM 29) for the signing of the surrender of Mexican forces in Southern California. Lankershim was a key player in the development of the North Hollywood/San Fernando Valley area. From this site, both the Los Angeles basin and the valley can be seen. *No. 181, declared 1/18/78*

NORTHRIDGE

NORWEGIAN LUTHERAN CHURCH
1917

Faith Bible Church
18531 Gresham Street
Northridge

Another Gothic Revival church of the "this is the church, this is the steeple" white clapboard school, it was the first to be built in the community of Zelzah, which later became Northridge. The universality of this architectural style is illustrated by the origins of this one, which is considered Norwegian, by way of the farmers from Norway who settled originally in the Dakotas, and later California. *No. 152, declared 4/7/76*

PACIFIC PALISADES

SANTA MONICA LAND AND WATER COMPANY BUILDING
CLIFTON NOURSE 1924

Pacific Palisades Business Block
15300 Sunset Boulevard
Pacific Palisades

This crisply detailed Spanish Colonial Revival business block is considered to be one of the most architecturally distinguished commercial structures in the western portion of the city. Today, it serves as both anchor for the old, and inspiration for the new development nearby. *No. 276, declared 4/24/84*

PARK LA BREA

HEINSBERGEN STUDIO
CLAUDE BEELMAN 1924

7415 Beverly Boulevard
Park La Brea

This superbly maintained Period Revival structure was the studio of noted muralist and interior designer Anthony B. Heinsbergen who created interiors and murals for more than seven hundred theaters, including the Pantages, Wiltern, Los Angeles, and Million Dollar. Oozing with eclectic charm, it was one of the last theatrical re-creations, for a theatrical client, by an architect who would soon develop a specialty in the American Art Deco. *No. 275, declared 1/4/84*

PARK LA BREA APARTMENTS

The following buildings represent a grouping of Park La Brea apartment buildings built in the 1920s and 1930s. As a grouping, they have come to represent the transition from later Period Revival to some of the post-rationalist styles.

APARTMENTS

1926

450 South Detroit Avenue

Park La Brea

Adding to the "back-lot" quality of these Miracle Mile apartment buildings, this early one is an elaboration called French Château Court apartments. What it may lack in architectural honesty, it more than compensates for in continuity—a good, solid contributor to an archetypal Los Angeles multifamily residential neighborhood. *No. 439, declared 5/19/89*

APARTMENT BUILDING

1931

607 Burnside Avenue

Park La Brea

Like its fraternal twin (HCM 473) at 613 Ridgeley Drive, this is also a turreted, Normandy style apartment complex. This one appears to have undergone some rooftop alterations, but they are well-integrated and sensitively done, resulting in architectural compromise. *No. 423, declared 3/31/89*

RHINOCK-MITCHELL APARTMENTS

1930s

613 Ridgeley Drive

Park La Brea

This, another eclectic, but well-crafted, turreted, Normandy style apartment building, is a twin to 607 Burnside (HCM 423). But unlike its twin, this complex appears to have undergone no exterior alterations. The original owners were Emma Rhinock and Lorna Mitchell. *No. 473, declared 6/7/89*

VILLA CINTRA APARTMENTS

J. A. GUNDFOR 1928

430 Cloverdale Avenue

Park La Brea

Named for a town in northern Portugal, this is a Portuguese Colonial Revival architectural derivation that has been translated into an American expression. It remains true to its stylistic origins in having a symmetric plan that is only two stories in height and centers around an open court. The Villa Cintra is one of six apartment buildings constructed by developer Raul Pereira. *No. 428, declared 4/7/89*

APARTMENT BUILDING

LELAND BRYANT 1928

601 Cloverdale Avenue

Park La Brea

Leland Bryant was a master who had not quite hit his stride with this one. He will always be best known for his lavish High Art Deco Sunset Tower apartment building, which was completed only two years after this modest 28-unit building. Clearly, his intent here was to blend sympathetically into this quietly elegant apartment neighborhood. He accomplishes this goal with relative ease in this low-key Norman expression of an apartment block. *No. 429, declared 4/7/89*

626 BURNSIDE APARTMENT BUILDING

CORNELL APARTMENTS

CORNELL APARTMENTS

MAX MALTMAN 1928

603 Cochran Avenue

Park La Brea

This was the largest of the works designed by Maltman, who subsequently retired these eclectic and picturesque building designs in favor of Art Deco. This large and formal complex with Tudor Revival details recalls a period when perceived propriety was a necessary component for architecture if the building was to attract the upper-middle-class tenants who were just beginning to trade their homes for the relative security of expensive apartment living. *No. 430, declared 4/7/89*

APARTMENT BUILDING

CLARENCE J. SMALE 1930

364 Cloverdale Avenue

Park La Brea

Similar in size and detailing to Max Maltman's apartment blocks, Smale's work as seen here is more refined in its integration of the fire escape but less robust in its use of

Art Deco motifs. Smale was the designer of the exuberant Loyola Theater (HCM 259). *No. 427, declared 4/7/89*

APARTMENT BUILDING

1932

445 South Detroit Avenue

Park La Brea

A rich, picturesque Mediterranean Revival apartment block, which blends quietly into its neighborhood, this eight-unit building was among the last to be constructed in the district. *No. 438, declared 5/19/89*

APARTMENT BUILDING

MILTON J. BLACK 1933

654 Burnside Avenue

Park La Brea

Another picturesque apartment building derived from Spanish Colonial roots, this tile-roofed structure conveys a truly romantic feeling with its unusual massing that develops two-, three-, and four-story elements. *No. 426, declared 3/31/89*

APARTMENT BUILDINGS

MAX MALTMAN 1930

626 Burnside Avenue and 636 Burnside Avenue
Park La Brea

These two structures were built by apartment developer Samuel Pollack and designed by Maltman. The mild Art Deco façades give a subtle elegance to what were otherwise fairly ordinary apartment blocks. Each building contains eight two-bedroom units and twenty-four one-bedroom units. When constructed, each of these buildings cost about $55,000. *No. 424 and 425, declared 3/31/89*

SAN PEDRO

HARBOR YWCA

JULIA MORGAN

CA. 1918

Morgan House
437 West Ninth Street
San Pedro

Now named for its distinguished architect, this inconspicuous Craftsman building, often remodeled, was one of many designed by Morgan for the YWCA. *No. 186, declared 5/3/78*

BATTERY OSGOOD-FARLEY

ARMY CORPS OF ENGINEERS 1919

Fort MacArthur
3601 Gaffey Street
San Pedro

It is interesting to observe that fortifications from one period in time can become playgrounds in another. Owned today by the Department of Recreation and Parks, and listed on the National Register, these obsolete concrete bunkers, with their unusual pre-modern sculptural shapes, are now used in such a way as would have completely dumbfounded brigadier generals Osgood and Farley, for whom they were named. The battery is a significant example of coastal-defense technology in the days prior to the emergence of the airplane as a military weapon. *No. 515, declared 1/7/91*

FIRST BAPTIST CHURCH

NORMAN F. MARSH 1919

555 West Seventh Street
San Pedro

Church and school specialist Norman Marsh, who often worked in a historicist mode (see Venice Arcades, HCM 532), imbedded in the front elevation of this Second Egyptian Revival church a homage to the Temple of Karnak in Egypt. In an unhappy compromise, the church administrators have decided to demolish this building, while saving only the front elevation and the stained-glass windows. The commission participated in this decision by designating only those parts proposed for retention! *No. 505, declared 5/22/90*

WOOD RESIDENCE SITE

CONSTRUCTION DATE AND ARCHITECT UNKNOWN
(RELOCATED 1920)

4026 Bluff Place
San Pedro

In a somewhat confusing designation, the current site of the historic Wood Residence has been designated, but all improvements thereon have been excluded from the designation. In effect, this means that the Wilbur Wood Residence can be demolished with no further review by the Cultural Heritage Commission. Wood is known for having operated the first successful tuna cannery in America; he developed the method for tuna preservation that continues in use today, and he was one of the founders of the country's largest tuna cannery, Chicken of the Sea. In 1920, he doubled the size of his architecturally undistinguished home with a second-floor addition. He then had it moved to the current (now designated) site, which is the southernmost point of the San Pedro peninsula, on a 150-foot-high bluff overlooking the harbor, Cabrillo Beach, and Santa Catalina Island. *No. 557, declared 4/28/92*

FIRST BAPTIST CHURCH

S.S. CATALINA

BABCOCK AND WILCOX 1924

(RELOCATED)

The Great White Steamship
Currently berthed in Ensenada, Mexico

For more than fifty years, the 301-foot-long S.S. *Catalina*, financed by William Wrigley, carried passengers between San Pedro and Avalon on Santa Catalina Island. Chewing-gum magnate Wrigley had purchased a major interest in the island and developed it as a resort. It has been estimated that more than 25 million people traveled on this vessel, which was the last of a fleet of luxury vessels that served the island and was very significant in the life of Southern California.

Originally, service to Catalina ran from Timms Point in San Pedro to Timms Harbor, now named Avalon. Today, the departing pier for Catalina Island is near the Maritime Museum, although planes and private boats have lessened the need for large passenger ships like the *Catalina*. The listing of movable landmarks like this one raises certain questions regarding the process of approving changes, since its location cannot be controlled. The *Catalina* is listed on the National Register. *No. 213, declared 5/16/79*

FIREBOAT NO. 2, THE RALPH J. SCOTT

1925

FIREHOUSE NO. 112

1925

(DEMOLISHED)

Sixth Street at Harbor Boulevard
(north of Maritime Museum)
San Pedro

Ralph J. Scott was known as one of the most progressive fire chiefs in the nation and served Los Angeles from 1919 to 1940. The fireboat that bears his name is "the grand old lady" of the Fire Department fleet. Beautifully polished and maintained, it is still in service in San Pedro harbor. *No. 154, declared 5/5/76*

ARMY AND NAVY YMCA

1926

Harbor View House
921 Beacon Street
San Pedro

This five-story Spanish Colonial Revival structure is among the largest in San Pedro. It was built to serve as a recreational center for servicemen, and today it is a residential mental-health facility. Minor alterations have taken place at the street-level windows, but its general appearance is much the same as when it was built. *No. 252, declared 8/25/82*

SILVER LAKE

FIRE STATION NO.56

LOS ANGELES BUREAU OF ARCHITECTURE 1924

2838 Rowena Avenue
Silver Lake

This modest fire station is one of the few remaining institutional structures built to harmonize with the communities in which

FIREBOAT NO. 2,
THE RALPH J. SCOTT

they were located. In this case, the modest Mediterranean Revival style building could easily be mistaken for a residence, and consequently, it blends nicely into its residential setting. It is currently boarded and vacant, awaiting, one hopes, a residential conversion. *No. 337, declared 1/12/88*

FRANKLIN AVENUE BRIDGE

ENGINEER J. C. WRIGHT 1924-26

"Shakespeare Bridge"
Between St. George Street and Myra Avenue
Silver Lake

From below, this is a graceful Gothic span that provides a background for the small school campus built in the lower canyon. From above, the perception of the bridge is that someone has left some giant chess pieces lying about; an altogether charming and unique experience in a city with many unique bridges. The appellation "Shakespeare Bridge" is unexplained. *No. 126, declared 4/17/74*

CANFIELD-MORENO RESIDENCE AND COMPLEX

ROBERT D. FARQUHAR 1922

Franciscan Convent
1923 Micheltorena Street
Silver Lake

Charles Canfield was Edward Doheny's partner and shared the wealth generated by their oil discovery and their other business ventures. His daughter and heiress, Daisy, took as her second husband film star Antonio Moreno (see Moreno Residence, HCM 226), for whom she built this large (22-room) Mediterranean style country villa with extensive grounds, patios, terraces, swimming pool, detached cottages, and a nine-car garage. The Morenos lived and entertained here until 1929, when they converted the estate into a training school for girls which

FIREHOUSE NO. 30

was named for Daisy's mother, Chloe Canfield. In 1953 the property was acquired by the Franciscan Sisters for use as a convent and school. Today the complex is closed to the public and only partially visible from outside the wrought-iron gates. The complex has been empty, except for a caretaker, since it suffered minor damage during the 1987 earthquake, and it is currently on the market for $3.9 million. *No. 391, declared 10/4/88*

SOUTH CENTRAL

SILLS RESIDENCE

GEORGE SILLS 1910

1207 East Fifty-fifth Street
South Central

This two-story masonry home, built by the bricklayer and architect as his own residence, was converted into a duplex in 1928. *No. 518, declared 12/7/90*

FIRE STATION NO.30

JAMES J. BACKUS 1913

1401 South Central Avenue
South Central

This station was the city's first all-black firehouse, a segregated condition that prevailed until 1967. The Los Angeles Fire Department had been integrated until 1923, when the increasing number of black recruits began to be routinely assigned to Station No. 30. Originally a Craftsman building, successive remodelings have left a white, stucco-covered masonry shell, which is currently vacant and derelict, having ironically suffered a fire. Its signage plaques have been ripped from the walls, leaving two gaping holes in the simple front elevation. Included in the designation are a 1941 cook house and a 1947 handball court. *No. 289, declared 2/15/85*

BAIRD RESIDENCE

BUNCHE RESIDENCE

BEFORE 1919

1221 East Fortieth Place
South Central

Nobel Peace Prize winner Dr. Ralph J. Bunche, called the "most prestigious alumnus" of the University of California at Los Angeles, lived in this house while he attended nearby schools. Between 1919 and 1927, this modest building—part of a row of similar buildings in a blue-collar development—was his family's home. Members of the Bunche family continued to reside here until 1975. In an example of how the historic designation process can occasionally work against saving a building, Dr. Bunche's home is the only one in the row that is boarded up and uninhabited, presumably awaiting funding as a house museum. *No. 159, declared 7/27/76*

WAREHOUSES

1920s

ALTERED 1941, ROBERT V. DERRAH

Coca-Cola Bottling Company
1334 South Central Avenue
South Central

Le Corbusier's question, "Why shouldn't a house look like a ship?" failed to anticipate answers such as this! Not really a Streamline Moderne structure at all, this building was formerly a group of four 1920s Spanish Colonial Revival warehouses that have been concealed behind a concrete façade detailed in an all-too-literal fashion (Derrah's specialty) to resemble a ship (see Crossroads of the World, HCM 134). The architect utilized actual portholes, a catwalk, and cargo doors, all topped by a ship's bridge—reflecting an interest in boating on the part of the owner. Appealing as this building may be, designations like this drive some preservationists mad, especially when the popularity of the new façade exceeds that of the original building, which may still exist behind it. *No. 138, declared 2/5/75*

SUMMERVILLE HOTEL

1928

Dunbar Hotel Black Cultural Museum
4225 South Central Avenue
South Central

Named for its builder, Jamaican John Alexander Summerville, who was a pioneer black businessman and cultural leader and the first black graduate of the University of Southern California, the hotel was built specifically to serve black Americans who at the time were systematically denied lodgings throughout the country. An immediate success, the Summerville hosted the first national convention of the NAACP and became a popular hotel for prominent African-Americans in the entertainment and sports world. In the 1930s, the hotel was purchased by Lucius Lomax and renamed the Dunbar. Today the building has suffered unkind alterations, and its original Spanish Colonial Revival detailing has disappeared. But still it remains as a symbol of the beginnings of empowerment in the African-American community. The Summerville Hotel is listed on the National Register. *No. 131, declared 9/4/74*

TUJUNGA

LITTLE LANDERS' CLUBHOUSE

GEORGE HARRIS 1913

Bolton Hall
10110 Commerce Avenue
Tujunga

Built of stone quarried in the area, this one-story structure, with a square tower and extraordinary wooden beamed ceiling, was a community center for the "Little Landers"— owners of small plots of land in the Tujunga subdivision. Later renamed for author, reformer, and philosopher George Bolton, the building served as Tujunga City Hall. Following the annexation of Tujunga to Los Angeles, the building served as a City

Council field office until 1957. After a period of neglect, Bolton Hall was restored in 1980. Additions include some overly elaborate handicap railings. Today, Bolton Hall houses memorabilia from the early days of Tujunga. It is open to the public. *No. 2, declared 8/6/62*

MCGROARTY RESIDENCE

ARTHUR B. BENTON 1923

Rancho Chupa Rosa
7570 McGroarty Terrace
Tujunga

John Steven McGroarty, a congressman, historian, dramatist, and journalist, was also poet laureate of the State of California from 1933 until his death in 1944. McGroarty's fame derives from his long-running *Mission Play*, which was one of Southern California's early tourist attractions. This two-story residence, which replaced an earlier home of his own design, along with its 12-acre site were purchased by the City of Los Angeles in 1953. It is now used as a meeting place for cultural and civic groups. However, the site is fenced and often locked, and access is unpredictable. *No. 63, declared 4/15/70*

VAN NUYS

BAIRD RESIDENCE

1921

Volunteer League Community Centre
14603 Hamlin Street
Van Nuys

This bungalow was first owned by Robert Baird, who was the owner of the Van Nuys Nursery Company. A seductively beautiful building, with the mature plantings it becomes incomparable. *No. 203, declared 10/18/78*

VAN NUYS WOMAN'S CLUB BUILDING

1917

14836 Sylvan Street
Van Nuys

Originally founded in 1912, this whitewashed Craftsman building houses one of the oldest social institutions in the San Fernando Valley. *No. 201, declared 10/18/78*

PICOVER STATION

1917; ALTERED 1932

(DESTROYED BY FIRE 1990)

16710 Sherman Way
Van Nuys

Built as a remote train station combining passenger and freight service, the original structure was about 20 by 40 feet. Later, a larger galvanized sheet-metal structure was added as the area developed and more space was needed. This is another of those preservation attempts that ultimately ended with the building being destroyed in a mysterious fire shortly after designation. *No. 405, declared 1/11/89*

VENICE

PIERCE BROTHERS MORTUARY

MEYER AND HOLLER 1923

714 West Washington Boulevard
Venice

Built for a family with a long-time commitment to the mortuary business, Pierce Brothers' Spanish Colonial Revival building was developed by the family who still maintains an interest in the business. *No. 574, declared 2/9/93*

VERMONT / SLAUSON

DALTON RESIDENCE

E. A. EASTMAN 1911

1100 West Fifty-fifth Street
Vermont / Slauson

This two-story Craftsman residence was built for Frederick Dalton, a well-known landowner in Los Angeles during this period. *No. 511, declared 11/5/90*

DALTON RESIDENCE

WAREHOUSES
(COCA-COLA BOTTLING COMPANY)

EDMISTON RESIDENCE

1913

1157 West Fifty-fifth Street
Vermont / Slauson

Owner/contractor Fred W. Edmiston built this Craftsman residence for his own family. It is substantially larger than most of the other residential structures that he developed in the neighborhood. *No. 510, declared 11/5/90*

WATTS

WATTS STATION

CA. 1910

1686 East 103rd Street
Watts

This charming station is one of a handful of similar wooden stations surviving in California. It represents a style of frame construction used in towns clustered around Los Angeles in the early 1900s, when much of the region depended upon the train for interurban transportation. It is fitting that the building continues its use as a train station, this time as part of Los Angeles's growing rapid-transit system. *No. 36, declared 12/3/65*

WATTS TOWERS

SIMON RODIA 1921-54

1765 East 107th Street
Watts

Among the more colorful and poignant stories in Los Angeles is that of Italian immigrant Simon Rodia and his magical towers. A widower in his forties when he arrived in Los Angeles, he began construction of his first tower, which rose to a height of 97 feet. Without scaffolding, and entertaining himself with arias sung in his native language, he assembled three of these structures, which combined reinforcing bars, cement, and all

YOUNG'S MARKET

manner of found objects, including broken tile, china, and soda bottles.

He persevered for over thirty years to complete the work that he dedicated to his homeland. By most accounts a happy man, he was considered by some to be emotionally unstable. In 1954, at the age of eighty-one, Rodia left it all behind, deeding the property to a friend and retiring to the Northern California town of Martinez, where he died in 1965, feeling forgotten and misunderstood.

The tallest tower (over 100 feet) later precipitated a civic conflict because it was constructed without a building permit. Fearing structural instability, attempts were made to have the towers demolished, but ultimately they withstood structural tests. It is likely that Rodia would have been pleased with the recognition ultimately afforded his work, for the towers are now acclaimed internationally, and he is considered a significant folk artist. After a period of decline, the city now restores and protects this civic treasure. But "Sam" would probably object to the insensitive fencing that has been added to protect the towers against vandalism. This alteration significantly diminishes the visitor's experience of this unique structure. *No. 15, declared 3/1/63*

WESTLAKE

FIRST CHURCH OF CHRIST, SCIENTIST

ELMER GREY 1912

Central Spanish Seventh-Day Adventist Church
1366 South Alvarado Street
Westlake

This richly romantic structure, in the Romanesque Revival style, displays a joyous fluidity as it covers, and makes the most of, its difficult, oddly shaped site. It displays curvilinear forms, arcades, a campanile—no architectural element has been omitted in this warmly colored neighborhood jewel. Judging from its date, this is probably the second building constructed for the congregation. *No. 89, declared 7/7/71*

CLARK RESIDENCE HALL OF THE YWCA

ARTHUR B. BENTON 1913

306 Loma Drive
Westlake

A huge building, beautifully sited atop a bluff with views of downtown, this handsome French Colonial Revival building was built as a memorial to William Andrews Clark's mother, Mary (see Clark Memorial Library, HCM 28). Its interior features beautiful woodwork, marble, tile, and art glass. It is considered a tribute to the fine craftsmanship of the early twentieth century. *No. 158, declared 7/7/76*

YOUNG'S MARKET

CHARLES F. PLUMMER 1924

1610 West Seventh Street
Westlake

An interesting example of a Romanesque Revival commercial building, its exterior grillwork, marble, and ceramic polychrome frieze were well executed. Built as the flagship store for a grocery chain, the building's scale and richness attest to its value as an important neighborhood asset. Today, it is the only large building at an intersection that offers only service stations and empty lots for comparison. Badly damaged during the riots following the Rodney King verdict, the ground floor was scheduled to reopen as a swap meet in spring of 1993 with the upper floors scheduled to open later. *No. 113, declared 2/7/73*

ELK'S LODGE BUILDING

ALEXANDER CURLETT AND
CLAUDE BEELMAN 1925

Park Plaza Hotel
607 South Park View Street
Westlake

This monumental structure might have been conceived as a civic building, rather than a privately owned hotel. It is often cast as a civic building when used as a movie set. Its architecture seems to have been influenced by contemporaneous drawings of Bertram Goodhue's Los Angeles Public Library

LA FONDA RESTAURANT BUILDING

(1922-25), but its various architectural trappings have considerable merit in their own right. Particularly noteworthy (and similar to those at the library) are the sculpted figures on the corners of the tower and the bronze entranceway. *No. 267, declared 6/24/83*

LA FONDA RESTAURANT BUILDING

MORGAN, WALLS AND CLEMENTS 1926

2501 Wilshire Boulevard
Westlake

This two-story Spanish Colonial Revival building houses not only the venerable La Fonda Restaurant but also the Vagabond Theater. It represents a most unusual architectural program, beautifully resolved. The building now seems to have fallen on hard times and would benefit from refurbishing, but the elaborate cast-concrete and iron work remain nearly intact. *No. 268, declared 6/24/83*

WATTS STATION

WESTLAKE THEATER

RICHARD D. BATES 1926

636½ South Alvarado Street
Westlake

With an Adams-inspired Period Revival interior, this large (nearly 2,000-seat) neighborhood theater proved to be an ideal "break-in house." Touring theatrical shows could conduct tryouts on the Westlake's deep stage before moving on to East Coast venues. Today, "break-in house" has a very different connotation in this district. Sadly, the Westlake, with its boarded-up windows, will have to await the completion of the MacArthur Park subway station to see if the neighborhood will revive sufficiently so that this once grand auditorium can be reopened. *No. 546, declared 9/24/91*

BULLOCK'S WILSHIRE

DONALD AND JOHN PARKINSON 1928

I. Magnin
3050 Wilshire Boulevard
Westlake

This building has been referred to as an "American version of Parisian Moderne," and "the masterpiece of Los Angeles's golden age of Art Deco" for its striking use of buff terra-cotta, patinaed copper, and glass. It features extraordinary interiors by Eleanor Lemaire and handsome murals that define the period by Herman Sacks. A little-known fact is that the building was never finished. If completed as originally designed, the ten-story structure would have resembled the Parkinson's Guaranty Trust Building (HCM 278) of the same period. As built, Bullock's owes at least part of its architectural success

WATTS TOWERS

WILSHIRE CHRISTIAN CHURCH
BUILDING

to the resultant eccentric massing that emphasizes its tower.

Bullock's was one of a handful of buildings that anticipated the importance of the automobile to retailing. The structure pioneered a design that had a ceremonial entry at the front, but a more important auto entrance and parking lot in the rear. In Bullock's case, a luxurious porte cochere was provided, so chauffeur-driven shoppers could be safely and luxuriously accommodated. Unfortunately, in recent years, this space has been enclosed. Unbelievably, Bullock's is now empty, boarded-up, and disfigured with graffiti. Hopefully, new tenants will soon rescue this important building. *No. 56, declared 6/5/68*

MOTHER TRUST SUPERET CENTER

TRUSDELL AND NEWTON 1922 AND LATER

2512-2516 West Third Street

Westlake

Los Angeles has been, for many years, a place that attracts people whose spiritual directions have been other than mainstream.

HOLMBY HOUSE

Among the better-known spiritual advisors who have been drawn to the city was Aimee Semple McPherson, who built her own house of worship, the Angelus Temple. From the same period, but less well known, is Dr. Josephine DeCroix Trust, a healer and spiritual guide who conceived a religion built around the concept of auras. This philosophy has enjoyed a resurgence of popularity in recent years. The church Dr. Trust founded is called the Holy Superet Light Church. Her work is explained in her many books and published lectures, and has been carried on since her death in 1957 by the Mother Trust Superet Center College.

Mother Trust was the founder and only pastor of this denomination, a position she held for more than thirty years. Beginning with the purchase of the little wooden church in 1926, the complex now includes several structures spread over four building lots, including the eclectic (1941) Georgian Revival style annex (designed by Mother Trust), the Atom Aura Science Billboard, Mother Trust's shrine (her living quarters), and the illuminated prayer garden with its life-size figure of Christ. *No. 555, declared 3/18/92*

WILSHIRE CHRISTIAN CHURCH BUILDING

ROBERT H. ORR 1922-23

634 South Normandie Avenue
Westlake

A handsome example of the Romanesque Revival by one of the outstanding church architects of the period, this richly romantic complex epitomizes twenties Los Angeles church architecture at its best. *No. 209, declared 1/17/79*

WESTWOOD

HOLMBY HOUSE

P. O. LEWIS 1928

1221-1223 Holmby Avenue
Westwood

This large and elaborate Mediterranean Revival duplex, with some interesting Monterey style details, represents a type of residential development that gradually evolved after World War I. Seemingly all of its elements have survived, well maintained and virtually unchanged, except for the wrought-iron security gates that cover all the street-level openings. *No. 318, declared 2/13/87*

WILMINGTON

CAMPHOR TREES

1920s

1200 Lakme Avenue
Wilmington

As is often the case, these surviving mature trees (56 of an original 126) succeed as much as any other factor in defining this

residential neighborhood. This land was once a part of the Banning Estate. *No. 509, declared 12/3/90*

WOODLAND HILLS

PEPPER TREES

1920s

Canoga Avenue from Ventura Boulevard to Saltillo Street
Woodland Hills

The approximately three hundred pepper trees now growing along Canoga Avenue started from a South American *Schinus Molle* seed, germinated at Victor Girard's nursery. Girard headed the Boulevard Land Company, developers of Woodland Hills. The trees now form an arch over the street in many places. *No. 93, declared 1/5/72*

CAMPHOR TREES

BRANCH LIBRARY CONSTRUCTION PROJECTS

Between 1916 and 1930, thirty branch libraries were built in Los Angeles; all were designed by prominent regional architects. In 1986, twenty-four of them were placed on the National Register and thirteen were designated as Historic-Cultural Monuments. Earthquake safety, expansion requirements, and climate control have resulted in the temporary closure of most of these branches, and the eventual abandonment of a few. This situation has caused extreme concern within the preservation community, which, although it recognizes the need to upgrade public buildings, fears the consequences if these buildings are left vacant for too long.

VERMONT SQUARE BRANCH LIBRARY

1913

1201 West Forty-eighth Street
Exposition Park

This was the first permanent branch library building in Los Angeles and the first of six such branches funded by Pittsburgh industrialist and philanthropist Andrew Carnegie. In a park setting, it is simplified Italian Renaissance Revival architecture. *No. 264, declared 6/7/83*

EAGLE ROCK BRANCH LIBRARY

NEWTON AND MURRAY 1914; ALTERED 1927

2225 Colorado Boulevard
Eagle Rock

Substantially altered from its 1914 appearance, the library was built with funds requested by the community from Andrew Carnegie. The current version springs from

BULLOCK'S WILSHIRE

EAGLE ROCK BRANCH LIBRARY

WILMINGTON BRANCH LIBRARY

Spanish ecclesiastical origins. It is a cruci-
form plan with a reading room flanked by the
stacks and illumination supplied by high
clerestory windows. *No. 292, declared
6/18/85*

CAHUENGA BRANCH LIBRARY

CLARENCE H. RUSSELL 1916

4591 West Santa Monica Boulevard
Hollywood

Another of the small but excellent branch
libraries built with Carnegie funds, this
Renaissance Revival "palazzo" is also
boarded up awaiting earthquake stabiliza-
tion. *No. 314, declared 10/24/86*

LINCOLN HEIGHTS BRANCH LIBRARY

HIBBARD AND CODY 1916

2530 Workman Street
Lincoln Heights

Initially a Carnegie-funded library, the
design of this two-story brick and stucco
structure is said to be based upon the
quarter-circular plan and exterior of the Villa
Papa Giulio in Rome. Even in reproduction,
it is a truly handsome building and one of
the neighborhood's more interesting architectural experiences. *No. 261, declared 6/3/83*

JOHN MUIR BRANCH LIBRARY

(DESTROYED BY FIRE 1992)

HENRY F. WITHEY 1920s

1005 West Sixty-fourth Street
Hyde Park

Named for early environmental writer and
activist John Muir, this building was empty
pending rehabilitation under the Library
Reconstruction Project, when it was burned
to the ground following the announcement of

the verdict in the Rodney King beating trial. It was designed in the Renaissance Revival style. Architect Withey is known for his *Biographical Dictionary of American Architects (Deceased)*. *No. 305, declared 6/27/86*

IRVING BRANCH LIBRARY

ALLISON AND ALLISON 1926

1803 South Arlington Avenue
Country Club Park

Named for writer Washington Irving, this Romanesque Revival structure is one of the original branch libraries of the Los Angeles Public Library system. Construction was made possible by a grant from Andrew Carnegie. Although the Library Commission is committed to relocating this library, it has also promised, under pressure from the preservation community, to maintain occupancy at this location until a new tenant can be found, lest the building be allowed to fall into disrepair. *No. 307, declared 6/27/86*

WILMINGTON BRANCH LIBRARY

SYLVANUS MARSTON, GARRETT VAN PELT, AND EDGAR MAYBURY 1927

309 West Opp Street
Wilmington

An architecturally interesting Spanish Colonial Revival edifice, with a relentlessly symmetric front elevation, this boarded-up building will be replaced by a larger facility at a new location. The future of the existing building is not known. *No. 308, declared 6/27/86*

EARHART BRANCH LIBRARY

WESTON AND WESTON 1929

5211 North Tujunga Avenue
North Hollywood

This Spanish Colonial Revival style library, named for pioneer aviatrix Amelia Earhart, derives much of its architectural interest

from the linear quality of its clerestory windows. In 1957, it was enlarged from its original 4,000 square feet to become a regional library of nearly 12,000 square feet. *No. 302, declared 6/27/86*

WILSHIRE BRANCH LIBRARY

ALLAN K. RUOFF 1926

149 North St. Andrews Place
Hancock Park

Named for millionaire socialist and early developer H. Gaylord Wilshire, this is a Romanesque Revival L-shaped library. Its most notable feature is the asymmetric placement of the entrance, which is said to be based on the Porta San Costanzo in Perugia. Allan K. Ruoff was best known for his residential work, mostly in the Mediterranean Revival style. *No. 415, declared 2/1/89*

FRÉMONT BRANCH LIBRARY

MERL LEE BARKER 1927

6121 Melrose Avenue
Hollywood

Named for the conqueror of California and its first United States Senator, Maj. General John Charles Frémont, this beautiful Spanish Colonial Revival library features an L-shaped plan with a cylindrical colonnaded entrance. As is the case with most Los Angeles branch libraries, this one is closed pending earthquake upgrades. *No. 303, declared 6/27/86*

MALABAR BRANCH LIBRARY

WILLIAM LEE WOOLETT 1927

2801 East Wabash Avenue
Boyle Heights

Built with funds from a 1925 bond issue, this charming branch replaces one built on the corner of Wabash and Green streets. Stylistically recalling masonry buildings of rural Latin America, fieldstones were used in

the foundations and the threshold, in a manner suggesting the simple building methods of these people. Restoration work was well under way during the preparation of this manuscript. *No. 304, declared 6/27/86*

FELIPE DE NEVE BRANCH LIBRARY

AUSTIN WHITTLESEY 1929

2820 West Sixth Street
Westlake

Named for Spaniard Felipe de Neve, who governed California from 1776 to 1782, and who directed the 1781 founding of the Pueblo of Los Angeles, this picturesque building with its Spanish Colonial references recalls the period of the founding father. Empty and awaiting restoration, it, too, was vandalized during the riots following the announcement of the verdict in the Rodney King beating trial. *No. 452, declared 10/17/89*

MEMORIAL LIBRARY

ASHLEY AND ASHLEY 1930

4625 Olympic Boulevard
East Los Angeles

A Tudor Revival library, commemorating the World War I deaths of twenty Los Angeles High School alumni, it was built on this site which was purchased by the Alumni Association as a memorial park. *No. 81, declared 4/7/71*

VERNON BRANCH LIBRARY SITE

(DEMOLISHED)

4504 South Central Avenue

The original building on this site housed a collection of books on African-American history. *No. 306, declared 6/27/86.*

PART V / 1929-1939

Now a major metropolitan area, Los Angeles shared with other American cities the misery and labor strife caused by the Great Depression. By the end of the decade, it was able to share, too, in the prosperity that had returned as the United States became "the great arsenal of democracy."

The International Style arrived with a significant impact; Neutra's Health House was completed (1929); Art Deco styles continued to have a strong influence; academic Picturesque and Period Revival styles lost their final vestiges of mainstream intellectual respectability, except in private residential and small commercial projects, where they continue, unabated to this day. Historic Chinatown was demolished to make way for Union Station (1933-39).

PACIFIC COAST STOCK EXCHANGE

CURTISS WRIGHT FLYING SERVICE
HANGAR

AIRPORT

CURTISS WRIGHT FLYING SERVICE

GABLE AND WYANT 1929

Hangar No. 1
5701 West Imperial Highway
Airport

Built to house Los Angeles's first commercial flying service, this building came to be known as Hangar No. 1 after other structures were built at Mines Field, which is now the Los Angeles International Airport. A Spanish Colonial Revival structure, with interesting massing, it has been recently restored and features a beautifully colored and patterned tile-roofed tower. *No. 44, declared 11/16/66*

ATWATER VILLAGE

VAN DE KAMP'S HOLLAND DUTCH BAKERY

J. EDWIN HOPKINS 1930

3016-3020 San Fernando Road
Atwater Village

Only the façade of this Dutch Renaissance Revival commercial building is protected. Not the famous Van De Kamp's Bakery building, which was constructed in the form of a dutch windmill to the picturesque design of Roy Oliver, this building nonetheless represents an old-time Los Angeles business. Designations that protect only façades continue to be controversial; the preservation

community generally rejects them. The practice of demolishing a building while retaining the front elevation is something preservationists refer to as "facadomy." *No. 569, declared 5/12/92*

BEL AIR ESTATES

LUBLIN RESIDENCE

PAUL R. WILLIAMS 1931
(GUTTED BY FIRE)

Nicolosi Residence
414 St. Pierre Road
Bel Air Estates

Recently gutted in a fire, this Period Revival residence built for Swiss émigré John Lublin was later purchased by actress Marion Davies. It featured very elaborate interiors and extensive grounds and landscaping. *No. 485, declared 4/6/90*

MARYMOUNT HIGH SCHOOL

ROSS MONTGOMERY 1932

Administration Building, Chapel, and Auditorium
10643 Sunset Boulevard
Bel Air Estates

This is a beautifully sited high school complex, a late example of the Spanish Colonial Revival style, decorated with handsome tile work, wrought iron, frescoes, and stained glass. Because of its relative youth, the building has the feel of a picturesque stage set. *No. 254, declared 9/28/82*

BOYLE HEIGHTS

FOURTH STREET VIADUCT

LOUIS L. HUNT 1930
ENGINEER, MERRILL BUTLER

At Lorena Street
Boyle Heights

In a jarring displacement, this bridge, with its oddly pointed secondary arches, seems to span houses rather than water. It is the only

double-arch catenary bridge in Los Angeles. Its design included supports for electric cables, which powered the trolley cars that once crossed the bridge. Now unused, these supports are mute reminders of Los Angeles's many lost modes of mass transit. *No. 265, declared 6/7/83*

BRENTWOOD

EASTERN STAR HOME

WILLIAM MOOSER 1931

11725 Sunset Boulevard
Brentwood

The siting of this Spanish Colonial Revival retirement facility may be its most compelling feature. Sprawling along a slope high above Sunset Boulevard, the building appears to be a series of almost unrelated architectural experiences. It is stylistically consistent but gives the impression of having been constructed or expanded over a long period of time. Together with the Santa Barbara Courthouse, this is one of two important Southern California buildings by this second-generation, San Francisco-based architectural firm. The building was used for a key scene in the film *Chinatown*. *No. 440, declared 5/16/89*

SERVICE STATION

RAYMOND A. STOCKDALE 1938

110 South Barrington Avenue
Brentwood

Late, eclectic structures such as this one, which utilize Spanish Colonial motifs to provide suburban residential neighborhood compatibility, were a commonplace occurrence until the introduction of the more institutional-looking stations of the 1950s. Now these are a rare and vanishing breed. In this example, the pumps still work, but the garage space is for rent. *No. 387, declared 9/2/88*

CANOGA PARK

ORCUTT RESIDENCE

CA. 1930

"Rancho Sombra de los Robles"
(Orcutt Ranch Horticulture Center)
23555 Justice Street
Canoga Park

The 23-acre ranch site includes a picturesque complex, which was derived from Spanish Colonial Revival ideals, and a historic grove of oak trees. The residence, reputedly exquisitely designed and furnished, though rarely open to the public, is of historic interest for its associations with its original owner, oil baron W. W. Orcutt. Born in 1869, he was a geologist who recognized

SERVICE STATION
(SOUTH BARRINGTON AVENUE)

ORCUTT RESIDENCE

that the archaeological value of the La Brea tar pits far exceeded their value for petroleum. Legend has it that the historic oaks on this site were stripped to fuel the kilns that produced the adobe bricks for the original San Fernando Mission. Historic scars from the limb removal remain on the oak trees at the ranch. *No. 31, declared 1/22/65*

LEDERER RESIDENCE

1934

23134 Sherman Way

Canoga Park

The handsome film star Francis Lederer (*The Bridge of San Luis Rey*, 1944), a leading man to such stars as Ginger Rogers and Claudette

Colbert, built his home in the fashion employed on movie sets: fake. The case files for this building describe materials that were "painstakingly employed in such a manner as to make them look old." The reasons for inclusion of this building as a monument are unclear. Strongly worded signs forbid entry even to the grounds. Restricted-access designations such as this raise questions about the public benefit of designations. *No. 204, declared 11/15/78*

LEDERER STABLE

1935

Canoga Mission Gallery
23130 Sherman Way
Canoga Park

Prior to the extension of Sherman Way, this site adjoined the Lederer ranch. Living prosperously off real-estate investments in the San Fernando Valley, Lederer built this elaborately false Mission Revival stable from stone quarried on the property. Isolated from the residential property, but highly visible along the main thoroughfare, the stable was later converted into a gift shop that specializes in Mexican folk art and California crafts. *No. 135, declared 12/4/74*

CHATSWORTH

STANWYCK RESIDENCE

PAUL R. WILLIAMS 1937

"Oakridge"
18650 Devonshire Street
Chatsworth

Another publicly inaccessible monument, this one lies behind impenetrable walls. It is an eclectic "English Manor house" originally designed and built for actress Barbara Stanwyck. Within two years of completing the house, she married actor Robert Taylor and moved to a Period Revival home they had built in San Marino. The Chatsworth

LEDERER STABLE

house was sold to comic actor Jack Oakie (*The Great Dictator*) who renamed it Oakridge. The grounds, surrounded on all sides by solid walls, are hidden and inaccessible to the public. At the entrance gate, signs make it clear that uninvited visitors are not welcome. This designation, too, represents a highly questionable use of public time and resources since no public benefit derives from designation. *No. 484, declared 3/23/90*

DOWNTOWN

WOLFER PRINTING COMPANY BUILDING

EDWARD AND ELLIS TAYLOR 1929

416 Wall Street
Downtown

This engagingly picturesque structure was patterned after a nineteenth-century English print shop, and it is an endearing example of Jacobean eclecticism. It is located in a part of the city that was once filled with service-oriented businesses but today is Los Angeles' skid row. *No. 161, declared 9/15/76*

WOLFER PRINTING COMPANY
BUILDING

CALIFORNIA CLUB BUILDING

CALIFORNIA CLUB BUILDING

ROBERT D. FARQUHAR 1929-30

538 South Flower Street

Downtown

An elegant and modestly scaled entrance brings a human scale to this eight-story Renaissance Revival club and hotel building, which is clad in Roman brick and detailed with granite and stone trim. Located near new high rises and the main library, it speaks quietly of old money. *No. 43, declared 11/2/66*

LOS ANGELES THEATER

S. CHARLES LEE WITH S. TILDEN NORTON 1931

615 South Broadway

Downtown

It has been said that S. Charles Lee practically cornered the market on Los Angeles theater design, producing hundreds of these elaborate buildings in the 1930s. Lee was best known for his Art Deco and later Streamline Moderne projects. This building and his Tower Theater must be viewed as belonging to his "Motion-Picture Baroque" period; they were both outside the stream of his contemporary designs. The Los Angeles Theater's rich and flamboyant French Renaissance eclecticism, which was a copy of San Francisco's legendary "lost" Fox Theater, concealed some fancy planning that allowed for retail shops to be integrated into the façade, flanking the entrance to the theater. Street space on Broadway at this period was simply too valuable to be taken up by the bulk generated by an auditorium. Unfortunately, this concept bore with it the seeds of the building's own obliteration. The signage requirements of the shops came to overwhelm the architecture of the whole; detailing on the northern wing, sadly, has almost disappeared. The interior is still as lavish as the exterior once was. *No. 225, declared 8/15/79*

NURSES CLUB

JOHN FRAUENFELDER 1931

245 South Lucas Avenue

Downtown

Institutional housing is a rare commodity outside of religious institutions. Indeed, this subdued structure is believed to be the first and only remaining example of this type of social/architectural engineering in Los Angeles. The Nurses Club provided professional women with not only housing but also an entire support network complemented by a "club" building and atmosphere that addressed the inhabitants' social and recreational needs. Amenities included an auditorium and a sewing room. *No. 352, declared 4/8/88*

ROXIE THEATER BUILDING

JOHN M. COOPER 1931

512-524 South Broadway

Downtown

The last theater built downtown until the 1960s, this modest Art Deco auditorium marked the end of the evolution of theater design from the earliest vaudeville houses, through the beginnings of the silent film industry, and finally to "talkies." Both this theater and the Los Angeles (HCM 225) were designed specifically for talkies. The Roxie derives its significance, at least partially, from its role in reversing the trend toward traditional, highly ornamental, overly decorated theaters, not necessarily a trend to be celebrated. As is the case with at least two other theaters on Broadway, the auditorium is without access, as the lobby is currently in retail use. *No. 526, declared 2/26/91*

LOS ANGELES THEATER

EASTERN-COLUMBIA BUILDING

CLAUDE BEELMAN 1929

849 South Broadway
Downtown

Beelman's masterpiece, this is among the best Art Deco buildings downtown since Clement Stiles's black and gold Richfield Tower was demolished. A thirteen-story Zigzag Moderne retail block, in blue-green and gold terra-cotta, it was constructed for Adolph Sieroty's Columbia Home Furnishings and the Eastern Outfitting Company. It was converted to office use in 1956, and the street level now houses a fast-food operation. The roof-tower clock is original and was designed to chime every quarter hour. *No. 294, declared 6/28/85*

TITLE GUARANTEE AND TRUST COMPANY BUILDING

DONALD AND JOHN PARKINSON 1931

401 West Fifth Street
Downtown

Following on the success of their earlier project for Bullock's Wilshire, the Parkinsons again essayed Art Deco, this time with considerably less pizzazz. While the massing here echoes Bullock's, the pierced and filigreed corner tower is painfully emasculated. The simpler palette of materials has resulted in a building that might be thought of as "Background" Deco. However, when combined with the retro-Deco Philharmonic Hall, which once sat on the adjacent site, these two buildings complemented one another handsomely. They must have provided a nice wall for the urban living room that Pershing Square once was. *No. 278, declared 7/11/84*

PACIFIC COAST STOCK EXCHANGE BUILDING

LUNDEN, PARKINSON AND PARKINSON 1931

618 South Spring Street
Downtown

An interesting design solution gives the Stock Exchange a resemblance to a small-scale banking temple at the property line, while diffusing the impact of the attached office block sitting behind it. This outstanding Art Deco building with its classical detailing undoubtedly assured investors. Fine bas-relief work on the exterior (by Salvatore Scarpitta) is echoed by Wilson Studio sculpture inside. Special attention is given to the interior finishes of the building, which originally featured high-quality materials, including bronze doors, cove lighting, and ceiling murals. After recent use as a discotheque, the building is now unoccupied and currently on the market. *No. 205, declared 1/3/79*

UNION STATION

DONALD AND JOHN PARKINSON 1933

800 North Alameda Street
Downtown

Three of the nation's major railroads—Southern Pacific, Santa Fe, and Union Pacific—pooled their resources to construct this station. For even the most sophisticated traveler, the typically Californian terminal, with its hybrid Spanish Colonial/Art Deco style, is likely to evoke some of the excitement and nostalgia of days gone by. It was the last of the large train stations to be built in the United States; the handwriting was already on the wall regarding the future of rail travel. This massive project was undertaken in the same year as the completion of the Arroyo-Seco Parkway, signaling the beginning of Los Angeles' increasing reliance on the automobile. Used often as a movie background, most memorably in *The Way We Were*, its lush and beautiful landscaping was created by landscape architect Tommy Tomson.

A preservation irony, this distinguished building was constructed on the site of Los Angeles' original and historic Chinatown, whose demise was a major loss to the understanding of the city's history. Chinatown disappeared long before there was organized opposition to such change in Los Angeles. The building has come alive again with the arrival of the subway. *No. 101, declared 8/2/72*

SOUTHERN CALIFORNIA EDISON BUILDING

ALLISON AND ALLISON 1934

One Bunker Hill Building
601 West Fifth Street
Downtown

This was one of the first all-electric buildings constructed in the West, an act of enlightened self-interest on the part of the owner. Its Art Deco styling is among the best in the city, with important murals and sculpture included in this handsome, fourteen-story, steel-framed building. Pioneering too in the use of exterior illumination, the building is a beacon at night on its hillside site. *No. 347, declared 3/25/88*

ECHO PARK

RESIDENCE

JOHN VICTOR MACKA 1937

817 North Glendale Boulevard
Echo Park

This is a largish, well-sited, but otherwise unremarkable Mediterranean Revival residence that overlooks Echo Park Lake. *No. 257, declared 11/5/82*

ELYSIAN PARK

LOS ANGELES POLICE ACADEMY AND ROCK GARDEN

FRANÇOIS SCOTTI 1937

Academy Way
Elysian Park

The buildings of the academy supply little that is of unusual architectural interest, but a certain restless energy provided by the members themselves makes for an interesting and memorable visit. As for the Rock Garden, a landscape artist was employed to design and build it. The result has a quasi-folk-art feel, with its series of four pools, cascades, a small amphitheater for band and stage settings, and an outdoor dining area. A large patio, a barbecue pit, stairways, walks, and recessed stone seats are also included. It was developed by the Los Angeles Police Revolver and Athletic Club. The Academy was the location for the farewell party for controversial outgoing Police Chief Darryl Gates in June 1992. *No. 110, declared 1/17/73*

EXPOSITION PARK

KOREAN INDEPENDENCE MEMORIAL BUILDING

1937

1368 West Jefferson Boulevard
Exposition Park

This modest one-story, bungalow-style wood and masonry meeting hall was built to house the United States headquarters of the Korean independence movement (from Japanese occupation) between 1937 and 1945; the *New Korea* newspaper was published here. It is the oldest of the many Korean-identified structures in this neighborhood. *No. 548, declared 10/2/91*

GRANADA HILLS

DEODAR TREES

1932

White Oak Avenue
Granada Hills

The 144 trees (located on both sides of White Oak Avenue between San Fernando Mission Boulevard and San Jose Street) are a source of great pride to Granada Hills residents. These deodar trees (*Cedrus deodara*) were planted at the direction of John Orcutt, superintendent of "Sunshine Ranch," who was responsible for the care and maintenance of extensive citrus groves in the area. Orcutt had an eye for beauty and decided that the avenue needed attention. He purchased the trees from a prominent nursery and had them planted by his crew of orchard workers.

The trees, native to the Himalayas, are valued for their size, beauty, and timber. They have a mountain grace and are pyramid shaped, 50 to 100 feet high, with long, horizontally spreading branches. They are a rather odd choice for a street tree since they require such a large setback. *No. 41, declared 8/3/66*

EASTERN-COLUMBIA BUILDING

HANCOCK PARK

CHAPMAN PARK STUDIO BUILDING

MORGAN, WALLS AND CLEMENTS 1929

3501 West Sixth Street
Hancock Park

A steel-frame structure with masonry veneer, this richly detailed Mediterranean Revival building remains a neighborhood favorite. With shops at the street level and parking behind, the Chapman Park offers beautiful maisonettes above, and sets a standard against which more recently constructed "strip-centers" might well be judged. The architects designed well over a dozen buildings in this style around town. They were all variations on the "decorated stucco box" with Spanish/Mexican/Portuguese decorations in cast concrete or plaster. Comparing it to the four thousand new strip centers, one can only wish these early architects had been even more prolific. *No. 280, declared 7/24/84*

CHAPMAN PARK STUDIO BUILDING

UNION STATION

FIRST UNITED METHODIST CHURCH
OF HOLLYWOOD

CHAPMAN PARK MARKET BUILDING

MORGAN, WALLS AND CLEMENTS 1929

3451 West Sixth Street
Hancock Park

A companion piece to its neighbor, the Chapman Park Studio Building (HCM 280), this, too, is an early, auto-oriented shopping center covering an entire block and detailed in the Churrigueresque style popularized largely by this firm. In this instance, the central court was for parking. *No. 386, declared 8/30/88*

SELIG BUILDING

ARTHUR E. HARVEY 1931

273 South Western Avenue
Hancock Park

This slightly wilted little gem is one of two remaining black and gold terra-cotta Art Deco buildings in Los Angeles. It sports a curved glass-block corner entrance, which may be a later, but not inappropriate alteration, and a façade that features highly decorative pilaster capitals and a frieze and cornice of stylized plant forms. Built originally as an elegant haberdashery, after serving a stint as a bank and later a disco, it currently houses a new generation of retail tenants, including a video store. *No. 298, declared 9/20/85*

HOLLYWOOD

LITTLE COUNTRY CHURCH OF HOLLYWOOD

PAUL KINGSBURY 1934

1750 North Argyle Avenue
Hollywood

This Period Revival church on a Hollywood side street was a radio ministry before World War II. *No. 567, declared 10/2/92*

FIRST UNITED METHODIST CHURCH OF HOLLYWOOD

THOMAS B. BARBER 1929

(RECONSTRUCTED 1936)

6817 Franklin Avenue

Hollywood

This is one of two Methodist churches designed by Barber in the 1920s in the Los Angeles area (the other is in Pasadena). The sanctuary sports a hammer-beam roof ceiling within a steel-frame English Gothic Revival structure. With its elaborate corner tower, and its location on busy Franklin Avenue, it is among the best-known buildings in Hollywood. Destroyed by fire shortly after it was built, it was immediately rebuilt, the second time by architects McLellan and McGill. *No. 248, declared 12/4/81*

FALCON STUDIOS

1929

5524 Hollywood Boulevard

Hollywood

In film histories, actor, athlete, swordsman, teacher, and Falcon Studio founder Ralph B. Faulkner rates little more than a footnote. His claim to immortality is inextricably tied to his work as a fencing coach to Douglas Fairbanks and Ronald Colman in *The Prisoner of Zenda*, which earned him the nickname "Swashbuckler to the Stars." Similarly, the distinction of this studio "complex" makes it more or less the common man's Grauman's: found within the garden are concrete squares bearing the handprints and signatures of John Barrymore, Jr., Basil Rathbone, and others. *No. 382, declared 7/26/88*

AMERICAN LEGION POST NO. 43

WESTON AND WESTON 1929

2035 North Highland Avenue

Hollywood

Considered possibly the best work by these prestigious architects, this structure is an interesting example of the second Egyptian Revival style, popularized after the opening of King Tut's tomb in 1922. Its front façade is a highly visible local landmark that capitalizes on this well-known social and philanthropic organization's penchant for Egyptian symbolism. *No. 462, declared 11/3/89*

AMERICAN LEGION POST NO. 43

ST. MARY OF THE ANGELS CHURCH

CARLETON WINSLOW 1930

4510 Finley Avenue
Hollywood

Its distinctive Mediterranean Revival exterior, simple Mexican chapel, and impressive Renaissance Revival entrance have caused this eclectic church to be described as a "little jewel of architecture." Its altar, dedicated to St. Genesius (the patron saint of actors), is located at the east transept wall near the pulpit. For many years it was used to celebrate masses for departed members of the acting profession. *No. 136, declared 12/4/74*

ARZNER / MORGAN RESIDENCE

W. C. TANNER 1931

2249 Mountain Oak Drive
Hollywood

This house was built for pioneering woman film director (*Dance, Girl, Dance*, 1940) Dorothy Arzner and her domestic partner, avant-garde dancer Marian Morgan. The beautifully sited eclectic residence features a second-floor Doric-colonnaded loggia suggesting a Greek architectural heritage, but it is surmounted with a sleeping porch on the floor above that is pure California. Nonetheless, this is a most interesting and unusual building. *No. 301, declared 10/29/86*

EDWARDS RESIDENCE

GREGORY AIN 1936

2642 Holly Oak Drive
Hollywood Hills

Originating in the fertile imagination of second-generation modernist Gregory Ain—whose principal concern was affordable, quality housing—this modest International Style house was named "House of the Year" for 1938 by *House Beautiful*. It was also listed as one of the best small houses in America in *Architectural Forum* in 1940. It features a trellised garden leading from each of the two small bedrooms to the swimming pool. *No. 260, declared 5/17/83*

PANTAGES THEATER

B. MARCUS PRITECA 1929
INTERIORS: ANTHONY B. HEINSBERGEN

6233 Hollywood Boulevard
Hollywood

The last of three Pantages theaters built in Los Angeles, this one is an exceptional example of Art Deco interior architecture. Pantages was a legendary vaudeville showman and theater owner. This technically correct, but unremarkable Art Deco exterior does little to prepare the visitor for what is to come. There is simply no adequate preface for the High Deco extravaganza happening within, which has been called the most magnificent example of a theater interior ever built. For many years, this Pantages hosted the annual Academy Awards presentations because it was inarguably the most glamorous place in Hollywood. The lobby and the women's rest rooms are particularly spectacular. Seating 2,800 people, the Pantages is now used for live theater. *No. 193, declared 7/5/78*

SELIG BUILDING

CROSSROADS OF THE WORLD

ROBERT V. DERRAH 1937

6671 Sunset Boulevard

Hollywood

It is impossible not to be charmed by this astonishingly picturesque amalgamation, which resembles a ship docked in some miniature European locale. Only if it had been designed as the headquarters for a cruise line could its programmatic excesses be forgiven. As seductive as it may be, it is also a remarkable celebration of the absolutely fake. Originally a group of small shops, today the complex has become a group of small offices; it may be that the anticipated tourists tired of a midway wannabe that offered no rides. What is most frustrating about Robert Derrah's excursion into marine kitsch is the missed opportunity of his all-too-literal ship shapes. With a little restraint the result might have been true International Style for the masses; by leaving the impression of a marine architect run aground, the joke is on him. *No. 134, declared 12/4/74*

MELROSE HILL HISTORIC PRESERVATION OVERLAY ZONE

Includes an area bounded by North Oxford Avenue, North Hobart Boulevard, Marathon Street, and North and West Melrose Hill streets. *Declared October 1983*

HYDE PARK

MT. CARMEL HIGH SCHOOL

1934

(DESTROYED BY FIRE 1982)

7011 South Hoover Street

Hyde Park

On a site now owned by the Recreation and Parks Department, this is where the first school specifically designed to meet California's upgraded earthquake standards was built. It was an excellent, if late, example of the Spanish Colonial Revival style being used for California schools of this period because the open courtyards and simple but durable materials and shady arcades offered new approaches to educational architecture. *No. 214, declared 6/6/79*

KOREATOWN

PELLISIER BUILDING / WILTERN THEATER

MORGAN, WALLS AND CLEMENTS 1930

Warner Bros. Western Theater

3780 Wilshire Boulevard

Koreatown

The blue-green terra-cotta-covered twelve-story tower, in the Zigzag Moderne style, houses the ornate Wiltern Theater with its elaborate pipe organ, among the largest in the country. The delicious and virtually intact theater interior, coupled with the exquisitely resolved miniature office tower, provide a large architectural statement along Wilshire inversely proportional to its modest size. *No. 118, declared 5/16/73*

LINCOLN HEIGHTS

MUNICIPAL LIGHT, WATER, AND POWER OFFICE BUILDING

S. CHARLES LEE

CA. 1937

2417 Daly Street

Lincoln Heights

This building bears remarkable similarity to one created by architect Lee on Brand Boulevard in San Fernando, although that one appears to have been built new, while this one is said to be a remodel. There is no information about the original building, but this charming alteration packs a lot of superior Art Deco design into its small, convex façade. It continued to serve the utility until fairly recently, but today it is empty and overrun by graffiti and neglect. *No. 384, declared 8/5/88*

LOS FELIZ

GLENDALE-HYPERION BRIDGE

LANGE AND BERGSTROM 1929

*Los Feliz where it spans Riverside Drive,
Interstate 5, and the Los Angeles River*
Los Feliz / Atwater Village

Constructed of reinforced concrete in a traditional design, this bridge is actually a series
of spans totaling 1,379 feet in length. The
bridge memorializes those who died in World
War I, and although it bears a bronze plaque,
the speed, dexterity, and adventurousness
required to negotiate this complex roadway
prevent appreciation of the tribute. The
curved arch spanning the Golden State
Freeway is the most interesting part from an
engineering standpoint. *No. 164, declared
10/20/76*

MUNICIPAL LIGHT, WATER, AND
POWER OFFICE BUILDING

LOVELL RESIDENCE

RICHARD NEUTRA 1929

Health House
4616 Dundee Drive
Los Feliz / Griffith Park

This is unquestionably the most influential and significant building of the International Style to be built in Los Angeles or, perhaps, the United States, and it is Vienna-born architect Richard Neutra's most important work. Haunted by the mistaken perception that he had stolen the commission from his partner, Rudolf Schindler (who introduced Lovell to Neutra), the architect was still trying to clear his reputation forty years later! This imagined blight on his professionalism apparently took the edge off Neutra's satisfaction that, with this project, he had attained a significant place in architectural history.

A most unusual client even in the Roaring Twenties, Lovell was an early practitioner of holistic medicine. A vegetarian and exercise buff, he also espoused the health benefits of nude sunbathing. In his *Los Angeles Times* newspaper column he promoted a life-style that today seems prescient, and in its casting off of the cultural bonds of the previous generation, it epitomized the 1920s. The "health" house accommodated his progressive life-style with its elaborate kitchen, gymnasium, pool, sun decks, and exterior sleeping porches. It caused a sensation when it was completed, receiving more than fifteen thousand visitors in its first few weeks and catapulting Neutra to international recognition.

Recently restored by its second owner to pristine condition in time for the centennial of Neutra's birth, the only criticism that seems appropriate, even now, is that Neutra seemed unable to appreciate the potential for California vegetation to overwhelm his beautifully sited but overplanted masterpiece. Today, one must rely on older photographs to perceive clearly what was accomplished here. Like some Hollywood beauties, the famous rear of this building can no longer be seen from its best angles. The Lovell Residence is listed on the National Register. *No. 123, declared 3/20/74*

GRIFFITH OBSERVATORY

JOHN C. AUSTIN AND FREDERIC M. ASHLEY 1935

2800 East Observatory Road
Los Feliz / Griffith Park

This structure is one of the finest examples not only of exquisite Art Deco design but of brilliant formalist site planning that rivals the châteaux of France. Like the 3,000-acre Griffith Park, which was given to the city in 1896, the funds for an observatory were also a bequest (this time posthumously in 1919) of self-made millionaire Colonel Griffith J. Griffith. The colonel felt that residents and visitors to Los Angeles should have access to the cosmic discoveries of astronomy and modern science. It is theorized that this gift from Griffith's estate was one of atonement; he had served a prison sentence for shooting his wife, whom he accused of diverting his money to the Catholic Church.

Though filled with extraordinary experiences within, it is the views of the Los Angeles basin as seen from the building's roof terraces that continue to draw huge crowds. The observatory has been featured in many films, most notably *Rebel Without a Cause*, starring James Dean, who is memorialized by a bronze sculpture near the west end of the building. *No. 168, declared 11/17/76*

THE LITTLE NUGGET

INTERIOR, WALT KUHN 1937

Travel Town (Railroad) Museum
Los Feliz / Griffith Park

In a bizarre quirk, even for the often quirky preservation movement, the designer of this 85-foot-long, 1930s Streamline style car remains uncredited, while its stage-set lounge interior, done in the style of an 1880s dance hall, has become the object of preservationist veneration. The boldly colored "Armor Yellow" car, manufactured by the Pullman-Standard Manufacturing Company, originally served the Los Angeles/Chicago rail line. It was donated to the city by the Union Pacific Railroad Company, and its interior is currently undergoing restoration by members of the American Southwestern Railway Association. Consequently, it is not yet open to the public. A similar car, with a different interior, may be seen on Sunset Boulevard, where it has been transformed into Carney's Diner. *No. 474, declared 1/26/90*

MID CITY

WILSHIRE WARD CHAPEL

HAROLD W. BURTON 1929

Church of Jesus Christ of Latter Day Saints
1209 South Manhattan Place
Mid City

This is the oldest Mormon church in Los Angeles. Burton was the official architect of the church and completed many other Mormon buildings, including temples in Hawaii and Canada. The reinforced concrete structure is in a Classical Art Deco style with allusions to Spanish Colonial works; some consider it stylistically related to works of Bertram Goodhue. Today, the building serves a largely Korean congregation. *No. 531, declared 5/10/91*

WILSHIRE WARD CHAPEL

LOVELL RESIDENCE

GRIFFITH OBSERVATORY

HOWARD RESIDENCE

BUCK RESIDENCE

RUDOLF M. SCHINDLER 1934

805 Genesee Avenue South
Mid City

A beautifully composed, relatively window-less front elevation with an open-air entry only hints at the house's orientation toward the rear, south garden. Quirky, upturned roof planes give way to an intellectual exercise in receding and advancing white stucco planes, which only partially succeeds. The voids that are windows cannot compete with the voids that are not. Still, for many, this is Schindler's best work, and it is beautifully maintained. One could quibble with the choice of plants in the raised planter next to the garage; surely this was meant for plant-ings that would spill over, not conceal, the architecture. *No. 122, declared 3/20/74*

SOUTH CARTHAY HISTORIC PRESERVATION OVERLAY ZONE

This neighborhood contains a high concentration of eclectic Spanish Colonial Revival, single-family residential structures in an area bounded by Olympic Boulevard on the north, Crescent Heights Boulevard on the east, Pico Boulevard on the south, and Alfred Street on the west. Developed in the 1930s by a builder named Ponti, it is, according to Robert Winter, "remarkable only for its consistent good design"—one is tempted to add, its high-quality construction, uniformity, and romantic imagery. *Declared 7/2/85*

MIRACLE MILE

MIRACLE MILE HISTORIC PRESERVATION OVERLAY ZONE

Although Los Angeles' "Miracle Mile" was named for the mile-long stretch of luxury shops and taller Art Deco buildings along Wilshire Boulevard near La Brea, there also exists a residential extension of that area that is another of those remarkably intact residential enclaves that is gradually giving way to newer development. Divided by Third Street into two sections, it may be described as the neighborhood immediately east of the giant Park La Brea Housing Complex. The area is characterized by a high concentration of contributing residential structures, including the Howard Residence (HCM 436). *Declared 11/16/88*

HOWARD RESIDENCE
PAUL R. WILLIAMS 1929
146 South Fuller Avenue
Miracle Mile

This eclectic, English-inspired red-brick, wood, and stucco residence was built for Roland Howard. Howard was of relatively modest means, but he admired Paul Williams's work and commissioned this small but seductively pretty house. Williams was better known for his larger residential work for movie stars, but in his long and distinguished career, which included residential subdivisions, he is known to have designed more than three thousand homes. Even the most modest of Williams's projects received the attention to detail upon which his career was based, and the Howard residence is no exception. *No. 436, declared 5/19/89*

FARMER'S MARKET
JAMES DOLENA 1934
Third Street at Fairfax
Miracle Mile

The Farmer's Market, important both to locals and as a tourist destination, began life as a Depression-era outdoor marketplace for farmers whose produce was grown nearby.

Oil fortune heir Earl Gilmore, who owned the land, was compelled by real-estate promoter Roger Dahljolm to develop this site into a permanent showplace for California produce. The complex has evolved over time, including the replacement of the original (farmer's) windmill with a clock tower in the 1950s; later, a second clock tower was built. The architectural style encompasses high kitsch of both the Anglo and Spanish Colonial varieties. The entire experience of Farmer's Market is quintessential Los Angeles. *No. 543-B, declared 3/6/91*

GILMORE SERVICE STATION
ENGINEER: R. J. KADOW 1935
Auto Repair and Snack Shop
859 Highland Avenue
Miracle Mile

Although the pumps are gone, this former service station still exudes all the confidence of the Art Deco styling it demonstrates. Streamlined cantilevered roof forms that extend from the garage once provided shelter for the gas pumps. Today, the building is often used for its period atmosphere in print ads, music videos, commercials, and films. Most recently, it appeared in Steve Martin's *L. A. Story. No. 508, declared 11/2/90*

BUCK RESIDENCE

PAN PACIFIC AUDITORIUM

WEST FAÇADE OF THE PAN PACIFIC AUDITORIUM

PLUMMER, WURDEMAN AND BECKET 1935

(DEMOLISHED 1992)

7600 Beverly Boulevard
Miracle Mile

The site of this premier example of Streamline Moderne architecture has been acquired by the state and developed as a park. It was built for the 1935 National Housing Exposition, which took place in Los Angeles. The building epitomized the "decorated box" school of architecture, and while dozens of photos of it exist, few illustrate anything but the front; the auditorium itself remains a phantom. Consequently, the whole auditorium was demolished many years ago, while the front façade was retained for a new use in the park. Unfortunately, it too was destroyed (by fire) in the late 1980s, and the site was finally cleared by a demolition crew in May 1992.

This building, as much as any, may be said to have defined the thirties in Los Angeles. Perhaps second only to the Hollywood sign, it has become (posthumously) an international symbol of the region. A computer recreation of the front appeared recently in a television commercial. *No. 183, declared 3/1/78*

EL GRECO APARTMENTS

CLARA BARTAM HUMPHREY 1929

(RELOCATED)

817 Hayworth Avenue North
Miracle Mile

Few traces of this two-story Spanish Colonial Revival apartment complex remain. It was originally located at 1028 Tiverton Avenue in Westlake, where it was designed for compatibility with the character and architecture that give that district its special charm. *No. 231, declared 4/9/81*

MAY COMPANY / WILSHIRE BOULEVARD

A. C. MARTIN AND SAMUEL A. MARX 1939

6767 Wilshire Boulevard
Miracle Mile

After Bullock's Wilshire, this may be the Los Angeles shopper's favorite historic building. Although recently it was threatened by demolition, it has now been decided to retain this seductive Art Deco gem and to include it in a larger new development. Its flagship gold mosaic tile cylinder with a black semicircular surround has served as a beacon to neighborhood consumers for more than fifty years, and there is still life left in this forward-looking architectural treatment. A large shopping center is proposed for the remainder of the block. *No. 566, declared 9/30/92*

MT. OLYMPUS

SUNSET PLAZA APARTMENTS

PAUL R. WILLIAMS 1934

(DEMOLISHED 1987)

1220 Sunset Plaza Drive
Mt. Olympus

A protracted battle for the preservation of this eclectic Neo-Georgian 21-unit apartment complex pitted the Laura Investment Company against an organized neighborhood group that cited the building's significance to the film community. Former tenants here included Katharine Hepburn, Mitzi Gaynor, and James Dean. It was also the home of Richard Gere's *American Gigolo* character, whose profession suggests that the building was then in decline. An excellent example of prominent architect Williams's multifamily work, the units were described as giving the appearance of private homes on the grounds of an estate. This complex featured many of the details of his more luxurious single-family residences. *No. 233, declared 10/9/80*

NORTH HOLLYWOOD

DEPARTMENT OF WATER AND POWER BUILDING

ATTRIB. S. CHARLES LEE

CA. 1939

5108 Lankershim Boulevard
North Hollywood

In an area whose architecture is best characterized as bland, this stark and somewhat fragile-appearing Streamline Moderne structure has been adapted for reuse as a neighborhood art center. A subtly out-of-square site contributes to the building's surreal impact. Minor refurbishment would return this vintage gem to pristine condition. *No. 232, declared 7/14/80*

PARK LA BREA

MORGAN RESIDENCE

OCTAVIUS MORGAN, JR. 1929

181 South Alta Vista Street
Park La Brea

Second-generation architect Octavius Morgan, Jr. built this Spanish Colonial Revival home for himself and his family at a time when his firm had already discovered new directions in architecture. It is a low-key design, now nearly overwhelmed by mature landscaping. The parent firm, Morgan and Walls, had achieved major success in Los Angeles, and following the senior Morgan's death in 1922, the firm was joined by Stiles O. Clements. As Morgan, Walls and Clements, they became one of the city's trend-setting firms, designing several of Los Angeles's most important buildings, including the Mayan, Belasco, and El Capitan theaters, and the demolished black and gold Art Deco Richfield Building. The firm is not known for residential structures, making this house most likely Morgan's personal architectural expression. *No. 444, declared 6/20/89*

DEPARTMENT OF WATER AND
POWER BUILDING

EL REY THEATER BUILDING

CLIFFORD BALCH

LATE 1920s

El Rey Restaurant / Nightclub
5515-5519 Wilshire Boulevard
Park La Brea

A superior example of the Zigzag Moderne
style, most of the building's stylistic achievements remain intact, including the marquee,
which ascends through a series of stepped
forms to become a vertical neon fin sur-
mounting the roof line. Original terrazzo
flooring and signage also remain. *No. 520,*
declared 2/26/91

DESMOND'S DEPARTMENT STORE

GILBERT STANLEY UNDERWOOD 1929

Wilshire Tower
5514 Wilshire Boulevard
Park La Brea

The first of the "Miracle Mile" high rises,
this one centered in an elegant eight-story
tower on a curvilinear two-story base in the
Streamline Moderne style. The building
appeared at the same time as many other Art
Deco designs in the immediate neighborhood
and helped set the standard for what was to

become a new architectural solution. This "signpost" building provided a "front" for pedestrians and a second "front" at the rear for access from the parking lot. This concept was also used for stores like Bullock's and the May Company when Los Angeles's reliance on the automobile became understood. Today, much of Los Angeles's newer architecture continues to utilize the same principle. *No. 332, declared 12/8/87*

THE DARKROOM CAMERA SHOP

MARCUS MILLER 1938

5370 Wilshire Boulevard
Park La Brea

One of the few programmatic storefronts to receive official recognition, this unusual camera shop façade resembles a 9-foot-tall Argus 35mm camera. The design, executed in black Vitrolite (a material created in the 1930s), was conceived by shop owner Sigmond Diamond. It included a small projector that would play newsreels in the "lens" of the camera to entertain pedestrians. It is no accident that these programmatic structures would come to be associated with Los Angeles. The concept was, more or less, to build a super-size object, whether it be camera, hot dog, or bagel, which would announce to a quickly passing motorist, the contents offered within. *No. 451, declared 8/1/89*

SAN PEDRO

WARNER BROS. THEATER

B. MARCUS PRITECA 1931

Juarez Theater
478 West Sixth Street
San Pedro

An Art Deco extravaganza on a neighborhood scale, the interior features original murals and furnishings. *No. 251, declared 8/25/82*

CABRILLO BEACH BATH HOUSE

ENGINEER: DAVID BERNIKER 1932

3720 Stephen White Drive
San Pedro

This modest Mediterranean Revival building was the last public bath house to be built in Los Angeles. *No. 571, declared 12/23/92*

SHERMAN OAKS

HIRCHBERG RESIDENCE

1930

The Magnolia
13242 Magnolia Boulevard
Sherman Oaks

The picturesque Magnolia—a large, set-back, late Spanish Colonial Revival style residence, with detached garage and chauffeur's quarters—was built for businessman Theodore B. Hirchberg, Sr. who made this hand-wrought eclectic extravaganza his home for fifteen years. The extensive grounds have received a landscape-restoration award. *No. 293, declared 6/18/85*

LA REINA THEATER

S. CHARLES LEE 1938

14626 Ventura Boulevard
Sherman Oaks

This 875-seat, one-story Streamline Moderne theater façade and lobby were recently incorporated into a shopping complex with some mixed but interesting results. The lobby has been converted into a retail clothing store, which retains the ceiling and some of the original lobby atmosphere. The theater marquee even advertises the shops within. The architects have achieved a bland harmony with the existing theater façade which has become merely a small incident on a neutral business block. Lee's original and compelling work deserves better treatment. *No. 290, declared 2/15/85*

SILVER LAKE

SUNSET BOULEVARD BRIDGE

LOS ANGELES BUREAU OF ENGINEERING 1934

At Silver Lake Boulevard
Silver Lake

Passing over or under this bridge is such a commonplace experience in this neighborhood that the bridge—which is noted for its muted Romanesque Revival arches and detailing—generally remains unnoticed. It is a single span, some 97 feet wide and 62 feet long. It features pedestrian tunnels decorated with the seal of the City of Los Angeles. *No. 236, declared 4/9/81*

SUN VALLEY

STONEHURST RECREATION CENTER BUILDING

MANTELANGO

CA. 1930

9901 Dronfield
Sun Valley

This unique Depression-era structure was built by Mantelango, a Native American stonemason, who, with his helpers, employed the round and smooth rock indigenous to the area. Many other homes and public buildings in the area also use this stone. *No. 172, declared 3/9/77*

VAN NUYS

VAN NUYS CITY HALL

P. K. SCHABARUM 1932

Valley Municipal Building
14410 Sylvan Street
Van Nuys

An impressive visual landmark for the area, this is a good example of Zigzag Moderne styling. Responsible also for the Renaissance Revival Fire Station No. 27 (HCM 127) some two years earlier, Schabarum seems to have been amenable to stylistic transformation as requested by the client. What he may have

STONEHURST RECREATION
CENTER BUILDING

SOUTHERN CALIFORNIA EDISON.
SUBSTATION

lacked in conviction, he made up for in academics; neither building is inspired, but both represent a solid expression of the craft of building. *No. 202, declared 10/18/78*

WATTS

SOUTHERN CALIFORNIA EDISON SUBSTATION
LOS ANGELES DEPARTMENT OF WATER
AND POWER 1931

615 East 108th Street
Watts

Another derelict and neglected building, this chaste gem has all the stylistic hallmarks of buildings many times its size. Its formal Mediterranean Revival design features a cast-stone base, warm-colored masonry with three contrasting belt courses, and red tile roof. Symmetric placement of doors and windows complete this modest exercise in formality. *No. 513, declared 11/1/90*

WESTLAKE

CHOUINARD INSTITUTE OF THE ARTS
MORGAN, WALLS AND CLEMENTS 1929

743 South Grandview Street
Westlake

Double-checking the address will not prove helpful; this really is the building that once housed the Chouinard Institute. In its day it was described as having "an industrial brusqueness and severity about the design." That severity is all that remains today. Original black-marble pilasters were removed in 1934, resulting in a building that now displays the ever-popular bunker aesthetic. Nelbert Chouinard, who was considered a brilliant arts educator, commissioned this early modernist work. Chouinard's repu-

tation and that of the architects have survived in better shape than the building that was their collaboration. Oscar-winning costume designer Rennie (Irene Brouillet) received her training here. *No. 454, declared 10/24/89*

SHERATON TOWNE HOUSE
NORMAN ALPAUGH 1929

2959-2973 Wilshire Boulevard
Westlake

Even the neon signage atop this Neoclassical Revival hotel structure has been noted for protection in this bitterly contested nomination, which saw the City Council extend protection to the building after the Cultural Heritage Commission declined to nominate it. *No. 576, declared 4/7/93*

I.MAGNIN AND CO. BUILDING
HUNT AND CHAMBERS 1939

3240 Wilshire Boulevard at New Hampshire Avenue
Westlake

Originating as a group of women's high-fashion shops located in prestigious hotels, I. Magnin Co. commissioned its first free-standing store building in Los Angeles at this location. With interiors done by legendary San Francisco architect Timothy Pflueger, the building's design is seen as something between the coolish International Style and the more popular and fashionable Art Deco. The exterior of this six-story building is faced in white Colorado yule marble resting on a base of polished black granite. Today, this building is vacant. *No. 534, declared 6/11/91*

RALPH'S MARKET

WESTWOOD

RALPH'S MARKET

RUSS COLLINS 1929

Bratskeller / Egyptian Theater
1142-1154 Westwood Boulevard
Westwood

Among the first half-dozen or so buildings to
be constructed in the design-controlled
village, this early supermarket, in the mandated Mediterranean Revival style, remains
a focal point for all who enter the area from
the south. A red clay tile roof atop a cylindrical tower terminates wings dominated by
beautifully proportioned arched windows. All
of this is surfaced in a stone-like material
that exploits the shadow play on its surfaces
and forms. Aside from a somewhat clumsy
marquee, the conversion of a portion of the
building to theater use has had little negative
impact on this handsome edifice. *No. 360,*
declared 6/12/88

JANSS INVESTMENT COMPANY BUILDING

ALLISON AND ALLISON 1929

1045-1099 Westwood Boulevard
Westwood

Designed as a flagship for the development
of Westwood, this headquarters building for
the offices of the developers continues to be
the visual center of the village. Its colorful
Moorish tile, with its zigzag pattern and
unique rotunda, set it apart from the other
buildings and imply a role as a civic building. The dome-top lantern is a later addition.
The building's architects were also retained
by the nearby University of California to
design many campus buildings. *No. 364,*
declared 6/21/88

JANSS INVESTMENT COMPANY
BUILDING

PART V / 1929–1939

235

FOX THEATER

P. O. LEWIS 1931

Westwood Village Theater
945 Broxton Avenue
Westwood

This was the first theater built in Westwood, a district that subsequently became famous for the quality and quantity of its theaters. Its soaring, towered spire signaled its location and attracted customers from nearby Wilshire Boulevard. The Fox was one of a group of Depression-era Spanish Colonial Revival/Art Deco style theaters built by Twentieth Century Fox. *No. 362, declared 6/21/88*

BRUIN THEATER

S. CHARLES LEE 1937

926 Broxton Avenue
Westwood

The Bruin stems from the fertile imagination of a theater designer who produced more than four hundred different theaters. This Streamline Moderne structure contrasts effectively with the Fox Theater on the opposite corner. The concave entryway, with its cylindrical neon marquee, is among the most memorable in Los Angeles. *No. 361, declared 6/21/88*

GROVE APARTMENTS

ALLEN SIPLE 1934

ADDITIONS 1940, ELDA MUIR

The Grove at Atria West
10569-10583 Santa Monica Boulevard
Westwood

Recently converted to retail use, these cottages were among the few remaining courtyard dwellings by this architect, known primarily for his work with the Janss Development Company. Later loft additions by Elda Muir were made part of this Chalet style complex. This is an interesting, if slightly too fresh, adaptive reuse. *No. 319, declared 3/11/87*

LINDBROOK APARTMENTS

ENGINEER: CLYDE DIRLAM 1935

10800-10808 Lindbrook Drive
Westwood

The Lindbrook is an oddly eclectic Period Revival courtyard apartment complex with upturned roof eaves that create a vaguely Asian architectural sensibility. Apartments of this style and period are associated with the development of Westwood. *No. 324, declared 8/14/87*

THE FOX AND
BRUIN THEATERS

COURTYARD APARTMENTS

LANDFAIR APARTMENTS

RICHARD NEUTRA 1937

10940-10954 Ophir Drive
Westwood

A sensation in their day, these daring
International Style apartments have been
owned and occupied for many years by the
University of California Cooperative Housing
Association. Although the building itself is
virtually intact, handicap-accommodation
overkill has provided overly elaborate pipe
rails. Combined with new landscaping in a
rustic style, the impact of this early trend-
setter has been diminished. *No. 320,*
declared 5/20/87

STRATHMORE APARTMENTS

RICHARD NEUTRA 1937

11005-11013½ Strathmore Drive
Westwood

This updated bungalow court project provides interesting insights into Neutra's work
and life. Less visually compelling than his
earlier work, the Strathmore's conservative
design may be attributed to Neutra's own
financial stake in the project. Then again, it
may just reflect his maturity. After a slow
start in renting the eight units (evidently
many prospective tenants balked at the perceived "coldness" of the design), the court-
yarded International Style complex
ultimately became very popular with the
movie colony. Residents at various times
included Dolores Del Rio, Orson Welles,
Clifford Odets, and Luise Rainer. Charles
and Ray Eames are said to have created the
first of their famous chairs during their
tenancy here. Richard Neutra's biographer
Thomas Hines lived here in the 1970s.
No. 351, declared 4/8/88

COURTYARD APARTMENTS

FREDERIC CLARK 1939

11830 Lindbrook Drive
Westwood

These stylish apartment compounds were
built with a picturesque Monterey Revival
quality to them. Upper balconies open onto
richly landscaped courtyards. While clearly
not in the vanguard of architectural design
for the period, they nonetheless provide
quality living space while serving as a handsome transition to the neighboring commercial area. *Nos. 446 and 447, declared 8/1/89*

LANDFAIR APARTMENTS

PART VI / 1940 TO THE PRESENT

By 1940, Los Angeles had become the fifth-largest city in the United States, and both its industry and its population grew as the nation went to war. Following the attack on Pearl Harbor, fear fueled by bigotry excited sentiment against California's large Japanese population, and President Franklin Roosevelt ordered most of them interned for the duration. Peace brought even more people to Los Angeles, and as freeways and housing developments were built, agricultural lands disappeared.

A large Korean immigration followed the end of the Korean conflict in 1953. Precariously poised both geographically and socially, Los Angeles endured the Watts riots in 1965 and a major earthquake in 1971.

During this period Los Angeles saw both the preservation and restoration of older sites and buildings and the construction of many new and important buildings.

EAMES STUDIO COMPOUND

BRENTWOOD

CORAL TREES

1966

San Vicente Boulevard between Twentieth-sixth Street
and Bringham Avenue
Brentwood

It was the coral tree, not the ubiquitous palm tree, that was chosen in 1966 as the official tree of the City of Los Angeles. With its characteristic reddish trunk and waxen dark green leaves, *Erythrina caffra* is an unusually elegant choice. As a neighborhood beautification project, a large grouping of these trees was planted down the median of San Vicente Boulevard. Today these mature trees provide a memorable experience. *No. 148, declared 3/3/76*

COUNTRY CLUB PARK

WILLIAMS RESIDENCE

PAUL R. WILLIAMS 1952

1690 Victoria Avenue
Country Club Park

Paul R. Williams earned renown as a designer of thousands of private residences throughout the United States and South

America. He created homes for such celebrities as Frank Sinatra, Danny Thomas, and Cary Grant. His outstanding commissions include the Music Corporation of America's office building in Beverly Hills and the Los Angeles Court House. His firm was also responsible for three buildings on the Los Angeles campus of the University of California and the Polo Lounge of the Beverly Hills Hotel.

His best work, as indicated by this home, which he designed for his own family, was in the early modern vein. However, his clients seemed to prefer a more genteel and traditional/classicist approach, and it was work in this style that became the basis of his reputation. His success is particularly remarkable in that he was a black man working in a wealthy white man's profession in a society that was still largely segregated. *No. 170, declared 12/1/76*

DOWNTOWN

SAN ANTONIO WINERY

O'LEARY AND TEMESAWA 1968

737 Lamar Street
Downtown

The last remaining winery in the city, San Antonio was founded in 1917. The original buildings have all been demolished, so this recognition relates only to the company's place in the history of the city. *No. 42, declared 9/14/66*

EAGLE ROCK

EAGLE ROCK PLAYGROUND CLUBHOUSE

RICHARD NEUTRA 1953

1100 Eagle Vista Drive
Eagle Rock

This mature International Style structure, with its views of the Eagle Rock itself, was built as a community center and a venue for neighborhood athletic events. The clubhouse is the only nonresidential Neutra design to be designated as a Los Angeles monument. It is unlikely that those who use the park today recognize the architectural significance of this modern jewel. *No. 536, declared 6/11/91*

EXPOSITION PARK

HANCOCK MEMORIAL MUSEUM

JOHNSON AND LUNDEN 1940

Within the Hancock Foundation Building
University Avenue at Childs Way
Exposition Park

Incorporated within this Institutional Moderne structure are four formal rooms and a foyer that originally were part of the 23-room turn-of-the-century mansion built for the Hancock family at the northeast corner of Vermont and Wilshire. Yankee patriarch Henry Hancock came to California in the 1850s and purchased much of the Rancho

EAGLE ROCK PLAYGROUND
CLUBHOUSE

La Brea. Following the discovery of oil, the family became fabulously wealthy. After the oil was depleted, they continued to enlarge their fortune by selling off the ranch lands for development. The Hancocks were an important early Los Angeles family, and it is sad that their imposing home has been reduced to these few richly decorated rooms. *No. 128, declared 5/15/74*

HOLLYWOOD

SHULMAN RESIDENCE

RAPHAEL SORIANO 1950

7875 Woodrow Wilson Drive
Hollywood Hills

Soriano was a talented and colorful architect who apprenticed in the International Style under Richard Neutra. For this project, he continued his exploration of twentieth-century technology. Even as late as the 1950s, these architectural pioneers were creating residences using materials they hoped would facilitate the mass production of domestic architecture. While many important advances were made during the period, particularly by graduates of the Neutra office, residential construction remains basically a custom industry to this day.

This residence, owned by legendary architectural photographer Julius Shulman, is said to be the only remaining Los Angeles project of Soriano's still in its original state. Shulman is one of the world's preeminent architectural photographers, and he is also a remarkable friend to the Los Angeles preservation community. *No. 325, declared 8/26/87*

WILLIAMS RESIDENCE

HOLLYWOOD WALK OF FAME

HOLLYWOOD CHAMBER OF COMMERCE 1960

*Hollywood Boulevard between Gower Street
and Sycamore Avenue*
*Vine Street between Yucca Street and
Sunset Boulevard*
Hollywood

Originally conceived by the Hollywood Chamber of Commerce, these commemorative sidewalk markers were intended to honor Hollywood greats and publicize the neighborhood. Each of the regularly spaced pink terrazzo stars contains a bronze marker dedicated to a particular film, radio, television, or recording personality. The walk now contains over 2,500 markers, although one individual may be cited with as many as four markers if he excels in each field. It is occasionally difficult to understand why certain honorees were included, since their principal claim to fame seems to be their inclusion on the walk.

Like the Hollywood sign, the walk is maintained by the Chamber of Commerce, which also selects the inductees. Costs associated with the program ultimately led to charging the honoree $4,800 for each star. This in turn led to charges that the honor was being bought. This circumstance, coupled with charges of fiduciary malfeasance, were settled by the attorney general in early 1992 with the establishment of a nine-member board of trustees that will now oversee both the Walk and the Hollywood sign. *No. 194, declared 7/5/78*

HYDE PARK

COMMERCIAL BUILDING

Institute of Musical Art
3210 West Fifty-fourth Street
Hyde Park

Howard University graduate space engineers Ray Clark and Oliver Brown designed and built these recording studios in 1970, inside an existing undistinguished stucco building with a red clay tile roof. Many works important to black musical history have been recorded here. *No. 344, declared 2/23/88*

INYO COUNTY

MANZANAR WAR RELOCATION CENTER

1942

(DEMOLISHED)

Highway 395
Inyo County

On February 19, 1942, President Franklin D. Roosevelt signed Executive Order No. 9066, ordering the detention of more than 114,000 Japanese-Americans living on the West Coast. Initially reluctant, the government was ultimately coerced into taking this action by a groundswell of post-Pearl Harbor hysteria fueled by the press. Two-thirds of those detained were American citizens; the rest were resident aliens, specifically barred

from applying for American citizenship because they were Japanese.

Located 225 miles northeast of Los Angeles, Manzanar was the first of ten War Relocation Centers created to house the Japanese. The 560-acre main camp housed 10,200 people, in 9 wards of 4 city blocks each. A block contained 16 buildings, measuring 20 by 100 feet each, built of simple framing and covered only in tar paper. The camp was surrounded by guard towers and barbed wire. Manzanar's Owens Valley acreage, owned by the City of Los Angeles Department of Water and Power, was leased to the federal government for this purpose, and 70 percent of the Los Angeles Japanese-American community was relocated to Manzanar.

Today, little remains of the camp except an auditorium, a cemetery with a monument to those who are buried there, and some foundations of the buildings. The designation of Manzanar memorializes those who *lived* there. *No. 160, declared 9/15/76*

MANZANAR WAR RELOCATION
CENTER AND MONUMENT
PHOTOGRAPHED BY ANSEL ADAMS

KOREATOWN

FIRE STATION NO. 1
WORKS PROGRESS ADMINISTRATION 1940
2230 Pasadena Avenue Koreatown

A sleek example of Streamline Moderne architecture, with no significant alterations to its exterior, this fire station evokes memories of an American period of progress and optimism. Gleaming and well maintained, it could benefit by the removal of paint from the interior of the upper windows so the original design could be read as intended. Many similar stations were designed during this period, in this style and color, but none is more fully realized. This one is a true architectural gem. *No. 156, declared 7/7/76*

LOS FELIZ

MULHOLLAND MEMORIAL FOUNTAIN
WALTER CLABERG 1940
Los Feliz at Riverside Drive
Los Feliz / Griffith Park

Built with funds donated after William Mulholland's death, this fountain was conceived as a ring of miniature spillways, as if it were a dam itself. It is one of many tributes around the city to "the father of the Municipal Water System" for his pioneering achievement in the creation of the Owens River Aqueduct, which transports water 238 miles from the Sierra watershed to Los Angeles. Today, Mulholland is considered a visionary by some, but is vilified by the environmental community for what has been called "the rape of Owens Valley." When combined with other dark moments in Mulholland's career, including the collapse of the (Mulholland-designed) San Francisquito Dam in 1928 that took the lives of more than four hundred people, these various honors now seem dubious. *No. 162, declared 10/6/76*

MID CITY

BALDWIN HILLS VILLAGE
REGINALD D. JOHNSON WITH WILSON, MERRILL AND ALEXANDER 1939-41
SITE PLANNING: CLARENCE STEIN
LANDSCAPE: BARLOW AND EDMUSON
5112-5595 Village Green
Mid City

These lands have a good California pedigree. They were part of the Rancho Ciénaga Paso de la Tijera (named for a scissor-shaped pass or canyon), which featured natural springs and marshlands. The title is traced from original owner Vicente Sanchez, and the land was ultimately acquired and named for American mining legend "Lucky" Baldwin. The ranch lands were gradually subdivided and developed by a syndicate that included Baldwin's daughter and grandson. In the late 1930s planning began on what was to be a unique residential project, the likes of which will not be seen again. The resulting 88-acre super-block supports 627 units, located in one- and two-story structures. With only a 15 percent site coverage, there is considerable open space. At 7.3 units per acre, there is actually slightly less open space than the 7 units per acre found on adjacent conventional housing. But it has been put to good use, maximizing the scale of the open space and providing private full-scale parks for the use of its residents. This contrasts with the conventional but largely useless front and back yards of the neighboring development.

Occupant and visitor parking is relegated to the perimeter of the site, creating in the interior a wonderfully tranquil, automobile-free experience. This resultant serenity, coupled with exquisite mature landscaping and an appropriately bland architectural style, was given an AIA Award of Excellence in 1972, twenty-five years after the original construction. Theorists suggest the architecture's greatest asset is its timelessness; many styles have come and gone since the village was built, but there is no sense here of being in a particularly dated environment. By today's standards, the architecture is rather quiet, but the landscaping has matured in such a way as to offer an unprecedented lifestyle in Los Angeles. Today, the beautifully maintained complex still has 100 percent occupancy, and a lengthy waiting list. Most remarkably, it retains a sense of community and civic pride. There are important lessons to be learned here. *No. 174, declared 5/4/77*

SAINT SOPHIA CATHEDRAL

KALIONZES, KLINGERMAN AND WALKER 1948

1324 South Normandie Avenue
Mid City

In keeping with Byzantine tradition, this discreet cathedral is almost totally devoid of exterior decoration, although it boasts a richly decorated interior. The overt symmetry of the front façade does not prepare the visitor for the surprise of the beautifully decorated dome at the rear. Dedicated in 1952, this forty-year-old building seems to reject both eclecticism and modernism in favor of something that might now be viewed as prescient Postmodernism. *No. 120, declared 6/6/73*

HEADLEY / HANDLEY RESIDENCE

LLOYD WRIGHT 1945

(ALTERED 1966)

3003 Runyon Canyon Road
Mt. Olympus

This mature Lloyd Wright design features a two-story pyramidal roof over the living room; low fieldstone walls enclose the bedroom wings. *No. 563, declared 7/14/92*

FIRE STATION NO. 1

MT. WASHINGTON

MAUER RESIDENCE

JOHN LAUTNER 1947

932 Rome Drive

Mt. Washington

Currently inhabited by the second generation of Mauers, this home is typical of the regional idiosyncracy into which Lautner's work evolved, but it is somewhat unique for Lautner in its absence of curvilinear forms. Perhaps some recognition of Wright's

Usonian houses has found its way into the project, but it could never be mistaken for a Wrightian building. Consciously integrated into the site, the home speaks as well as any about a time when the new and modern were also warm and inviting. Architectural features include an interesting blurring of interior and exterior spaces. Today, the building is secured behind unsympathetic chain-link fencing and is not visible from the public thoroughfare. *No. 481, declared 2/26/90*

NORTH HOLLYWOOD

LAURELWOOD APARTMENTS

RUDOLF M. SCHINDLER 1948

11833-11837 Laurelwood Drive
North Hollywood

Like much of Schindler's work, these apartments offer a glimpse into "early modern" life-styles. Secluded behind the blank walls of the building's garage, the complex focuses on a narrow landscaped court that steps up a gentle incline, allowing the units to be stacked while providing some small roof decks. The units are modest in size, but with the characteristic spareness of Schindler's work, they seem relatively spacious. *No. 228, declared 4/22/80*

LAURELWOOD APARTMENTS

FAMILIAN CHAPEL OF TEMPLE ADAT ARI EL

1949

5540 Laurel Canyon Boulevard
North Hollywood

This chapel, named for David Familian and built by a congregation dating from 1938, was the first synagogue constructed in the San Fernando Valley. *No. 199, declared 9/20/78*

PACIFIC PALISADES

CAMP JOSEPHO MALIBU LODGE

ENGINEER: GEORGE J. FOSDYKE 1941

3000 Rustic Road, in Rustic Canyon Park
Pacific Palisades

This vernacular frame lodge structure is located deep in Rustic Canyon at the end of a narrow, rather perilous road. It is surrounded on two sides by state park lands and on the upstream side by county sanitation landfill. Unless one is accompanied by a guide with the skills of an Eagle Scout, the building is hard to find. The land was donated to the Boy Scouts in 1940 by Russian émigré and successful businessman Anatol Josepho. (Among his numerous inventions was the Photomaton, the coin-operated booth in which a picture can be taken and developed instantly.) The interior is replete with paraphernalia from bygone scouting days, including plaques, charts, photographs, and knotting boards. It has been described as the "attic of westside Scouting." *No. 547, declared 10/2/91*

EAMES STUDIO COMPOUND

CHARLES EAMES 1947

203 Chatauqua Boulevard
Pacific Palisades

One of the seminal California Modern residential complexes—designed and built as part of the influential and innovative Case Study Program (see Entenza Residence, HCM 530)—this home and studio, connected by a small garden, has achieved mythic status among architects concerned with contemporary residential design issues. The house is known for its use of industrial parts (like its predecessor, New York's 1931 Aluminaire House), and many of its components were available from parts catalogues. In a remarkable demonstration of the flexibility of his design concept, Eames simplified the original plan by redesigning the home *after* the parts arrived on the site. Unusual also for its use of color and its spectacular siting overlooking an open meadow, it remains, in spite of its hopeful but ultimately unsuccessful attempt to address postwar housing, a singular and extraordinary home of international significance. The buildings are currently inhabited by the third and fourth generations of the Eames family. *No. 381, declared 7/15/88*

ENTENZA RESIDENCE

EERO SAARINEN, CHARLES EAMES 1949

Case Study House No. 9
205 Chatauqua Boulevard
Pacific Palisades

John Entenza created the Case Study House program, which he promoted in his magazine *Arts and Architecture*. The program was conceived to promote new residential design forms and materials, and this house, built near Eames's own residence, was among the first steel-frame houses ever built. It was originally conceived as a simple rectangular form, but it is difficult to recognize the current building when comparing it to the original drawings. It has received many additions over the years, and it has weathered poorly. Sitting vacant, with its gardens in ruins, it may be a blessing that architectural visionary Saarinen's only West Coast home is no longer visible from the public roadway, which serves as a driveway to not one, but two significant achievements of the modern movement. *No. 530, declared 4/8/91*

SAN PEDRO

MUNICIPAL FERRY BUILDING

PUBLIC WORKS ADMINISTRATION 1941

Maritime History Museum
Sixth Street at Harbor Boulevard
San Pedro

Built to accommodate ferryboats carrying workers from San Pedro to Terminal Island, this Streamline Moderne building became obsolete and was transferred to city use following the completion of the Vincent Thomas Bridge in 1968. *No. 146, declared 9/17/75*

KOREAN BELL AND BELFRY OF FRIENDSHIP

1976

Angel's Gate Park
3700 Gaffey Street
San Pedro

Among the few Los Angeles monuments to be built in recent years, this unusual structure was a gift from the people of the Republic of Korea in commemoration of the American Bicentennial. It is patterned after

MUNICIPAL FERRY BUILDING

the historic bronze bell of King Songdok, which is among the world's largest. The siting of this interesting, traditionally styled structure, overlooking the southern tip of Los Angeles, makes it one of the treasures of the city. *No. 187, declared 5/3/78*

USS LOS ANGELES NAVAL MONUMENT

1977

John S. Gibson, Jr. Park
Harbor Boulevard at Sixth Street
San Pedro

Featuring a 70-foot concrete platform housing the heavy cruiser *Los Angeles*'s mainmast, bow, anchor, bollards, and capstan cover, this monument also features a black granite surround that echoes the Viet Nam War Monument in Washington. It is dedicated to the men and ships of the United States Navy. *No. 188, declared 5/3/78*

SILVER LAKE

TIGERMAN RESIDENCE

GREGORY AIN 1940

2323 Micheltorena Street
Silver Lake

The Vienna-born American master Gregory Ain did his apprenticeship in countryman Richard Neutra's office. There he refined not only his understanding of style but also his professionalism. This delightful home, which derives its design from International Style concepts, is significant as an example of a small, affordable, but rigorously refined, architect-designed house. Ain was the recipient of a Guggenheim Fellowship to study low-cost housing. *No. 124, declared 4/3/74*

KOREAN BELL AND
BELFRY OF FRIENDSHIP

LOS FELIZ SCHOOL

LOS FELIZ SCHOOL

JOHN LAUTNER 1960

Lycée International de Los Angeles
4155 Russell Avenue
Silver Lake

This complex was a small and visionary private elementary school campus, comprised of four pavilion-type structures, designed by innovative architect John Lautner. The podlike buildings, on their 8-acre site, featured a reduced scale and simplicity thought to be conducive to the education of children. Although other buildings have been added over time, and the school has changed ownership, these four original buildings remain, remarkably intact in spite of being constructed of fairly delicate materials. *No. 553, declared 3/18/93*

VAN NUYS

TOWER OF WOODEN PALLETS

DANIEL VAN METER 1951

15357 Magnolia Boulevard
Van Nuys

Among the most unusual designations in the annals of historic preservation, this structure lurks near the rear of a private salvage yard. With a base that is 22 feet in diameter, the tower allegedly covers the grave of a child who was buried here in 1869. It is comprised of approximately two thousand 3-foot-by-3-foot wooden pallets stacked in a spiral configuration. Inside, an ersatz shrine of rusting patio furniture is complemented by a variety of kitsch accoutrements. Outside the structure, chickens cackle and peck their way through an eerie landscape of society's discards. The unforgettable Tower of Wooden Pallets is the architectural equivalent of a hand-painted Elvis, cast in plaster. *No. 184, declared 4/19/78*

WESTCHESTER

LOYOLA THEATER

CLARENCE J. SMALE 1948

8610 South Sepulveda Boulevard
Westchester

It was said that this building's bizarre front elevation *was* the building—a prophetic statement considering that the auditorium portion has been lost to office conversion. Not a particularly appropriate use for this large, windowless volume, one can still be grateful that the original 60-foot neon-decked sign tower, etched glass doors, and the ticket booth of this "Baroque-moderne" extravaganza remain as a reminder of the days of the Deco movie palace. *No. 259, declared 12/17/82*

AIRPORT THEME BUILDING

CHARLES LUCKMAN, WILLIAM PIERERA,
WELTON BECKET, AND PAUL WILLIAMS 1960

201 Center Way

Westchester

It is remarkable that this collaboration—by a team comprising most of the design talent in Los Angeles during the period—could have achieved anything as cohesive as this remarkably light and fanciful structure. Resembling a large Alexander Calder sta-bile, it is among the city's definitive architectural statements and could easily serve as a logo for Los Angeles. Its 85-foot-tall "Futurist" structural expressionism is unique in American architectural experience. The continuing development at the Los Angeles Airport crowds but does not diminish the unfettered optimism and glamour associated with jet travel in the 1960s, which is projected by this building. *No. 570, declared 12/18/92*

AIRPORT THEME BUILDING

WESTWOOD

GAYLEY TERRACE APARTMENTS

LAURENCE CLAPP 1940

959 Gayley Terrace
Westwood

A late Period Revival apartment complex, which arranges itself on its site like a small Mediterranean hill town, this structure is stylistically consistent with the Westwood design guidelines, but woefully out of touch with architectural evolution. Since first constructed, it has become one of the best-known residential buildings in the area. *No. 363, declared 6/21/88*

KELTON APARTMENTS

RICHARD NEUTRA 1942

644 Kelton Avenue
Westwood

Like the earlier Strathmore Apartments, this complex continued Neutra's work as both architect and developer. This time there are five units in each of two buildings. Still evolving his work in the International Style, while developing a minimalist sensibility, Neutra designed this building in a more confident and assured mood than some of the more daring, earlier works. *No. 365, declared 6/21/88*

SHEETS APARTMENTS

ELKAY APARTMENTS

RICHARD NEUTRA 1948

638 Kelton Avenue

Westwood

This was the last of Neutra's International Style postwar multifamily housing projects to be built in Westwood, and it is his most refined expression of a California regionalism. Still rigorous in its architectural discipline, this building utilizes more exposed wood and richer landscaping, allowing the structure to blend into its site in a way that was uncharacteristic of his earlier work.

No. 368, declared 6/21/88

SHEETS APARTMENTS

JOHN LAUTNER 1949

L'Horizon

10919 Strathmore Drive

Westwood

Among the more adventurous designs in the Westwood area (a statement that can be made anywhere Lautner builds), this unusual apartment complex (empty at this writing) continued Lautner's explorations in curvilinear form and regional futurism. An uncharacteristic break with Westwood's mandated

Mediterranean Revival style, this eight-unit building is cantilevered over the carports on reinforced concrete struts. Each of the units is independent from the others (there are no party walls), and each has its own outdoor space. *No. 367, declared 6/21/88*

TISCHLER RESIDENCE

RUDOLF M. SCHINDLER 1949

175 Greenfield Avenue
Westwood

Among the more solid and dramatic of Schindler's works and one of his last, this project reflects his evolution to a more complex spatial expression and a more personal aesthetic. Here he leaves the International Style behind, substituting a true regional understanding and appreciation, which had been missing or somewhat forced in his earlier works. *No. 506, declared 10/9/90*

LOS ANGELES ARCHITECTURAL STYLES

For many years, Southern California has been considered one of the world leaders in the areas of design and style. When considering historical trends, however, it is important to remember that California was still the frontier long after America's eastern region was considered cosmopolitan. As an example, in 1867 the designers of the sophisticated Brooklyn Bridge would have understood little of California, where settlers had only recently built their first lumber mills and still had to import glass for windowpanes. Early architectural styles reached California somewhat later than they reached the East Coast, and consequently, nationally recognized architectural periods often occur later in the West.

California also saw the development of several regional styles that rarely appear in discussions of style from a national perspective. The authors have relied on several texts for architectural-style information (see Selected Bibliography) and have also attempted to bring a fresh perspective to a few uniquely Southern California architectural expressions.

One factor that characterizes all discussions of style is how little agreement there is among scholars about nomenclature in this field. Unlike clothing fashions, architectural periods are not tidy; it is difficult to state exactly when a certain period ended and another began. Often there are buildings that are stylistically transitional, combining features of fading styles with new, emerging styles. The single philosophical tenet that distinguishes early styles from "modern" ones is that the early styles were all based upon architecture that had gone before; the later styles generated their designs from so-called rational principles regarding function, siting, and new materials.

COLONIAL
1600-1700

This should be called Late Medieval, or English Colonial. It is best understood from the perspective of the colonist from England who constructed buildings based upon recollections of the architecture of the homeland, utilizing locally produced materials. This same concept is true of all colonial styles, only the place of origin differs. The American Colonial style reached maturity and vanished before Los Angeles was even settled. It is included here as a basis for the Colonial Revival, which comes later.

GEORGIAN
1700-1776

Named for the architecture popularized during the reign of the eighteenth-century English sovereigns and ending with the Revolutionary War, American Georgian architecture was found primarily in the eastern United States but has also inspired revivals in the West. Components include rigid symmetry, axial entrances, fanlight windows, and often, hipped roofs. See the Britt Residence.

FEDERAL OR ADAMS
1780-1820

The Adams brothers (Charles and James) were English architects who produced a style that was dominant on the East Coast. It was a variation of the Georgian style. The interior of the Westlake Theater is described as Adams Revival, meaning that it was decorated with details typical of the Adams period.

SPANISH COLONIAL
1565-1850

A few buildings actually remain in California from this period. They were built by Native Americans to the designs of the Spanish missionaries, who brought copies of Vitruvius with them when they colonized California. The best examples were the seventeen Mission complexes, but most have been so altered that some basic components of the style may have disappeared. The few remaining adobe structures in Los Angeles are also from this period and of this style, and one could argue that buildings like Sancta Vibiana Cathedral have direct roots to the Spanish Colonial tradition.

MONTEREY COLONIAL
1834-1860s

This style was created by Bostonian Thomas Larkin, who brought traditional New England practices to the frontier but interpreted them to reflect California's climate and scarcity of building materials. The Leonis Residence, with its adobe walls and sheltering roof and balcony forms, is the best extant example in Los Angeles. The style is said to demonstrate the triumph of Yankee ingenuity over the

adobe builders. The completion of the railroads in 1869 enhanced communication with the styles of the outside world and made available more refined materials, all of which brought architectural change.

GREEK REVIVAL
1820-1860

These are archetypal white wooden structures in a Greek temple form with a front colonnade (often two-story) beneath a triangular pediment. The largest early Greek Revival domestic structure in California is the Banning Residence in Wilmington. Little in this style was ever built in California and less remains.

VICTORIAN-ERA STYLES

During the long reign of Queen Victoria (1837-1901) architecture imitative of many foreign historic styles was revived in England and exported to America, but not necessarily with proper regard for the correctness of proportion, scale, or materials. Generically called "Victorian," there are actually a number of individually recognized styles. Needless to say, the interpretation of these styles for California produced buildings that are quite different from their English antecedents. The Heritage Square Museum has several representative examples. Among the Victorian-era styles are:

GOTHIC REVIVAL 1840-1860: Some consider this to be a Romantic style that preceded the Victorians, but in California the term *Carpenter Gothic* is used to describe many early Victorian-era structures with details derived from Gothic forms but expressed in wood rather than stone. Gables with barge-boards decorated with tracery reminiscent of Gothic forms are characteristic of this style, which is often associated with small, white, clapboard churches with pointed arch windows. See Wilmington's St. John's Episcopal Church or St. Peter's church in San Pedro.

ITALIANATE 1830-1880: In California, the English translation of fifteenth- and sixteenth-century Italian building forms and ornaments into wooden, mostly residential structures is given this name. A horizontal country version, featuring more romantic and eccentric forms, gives a more Italian feel than the urban row-house form. See the Perry Residence at Heritage Square for a definitive California Italianate.

STICK 1860-1890: Evolving out of the Carpenter Gothic style, and known by some as High Victorian Gothic, this style emphasized the "skin" of the building with applied board, or "stick," detailing. This style sometimes featured such colorful additions as the Moorish-inspired horseshoe arch. Some Stick style detailing found its way into the works of Joseph Cather Newsom, but his work belongs more to the Queen Anne style. See the Collins Residence.

EASTLAKE 1870-1880: Actually, this is a modification to the Stick style, but standard discussions of style often omit this variant, which was named for English designer Sir Charles Eastlake, who produced interiors of simplicity, dignity, and "good taste." Details from his furniture designs were applied to California residential construction as a "backlash" to the more ornate Italianate style. No Eastlake style building was considered complete without several curved eave brackets. Sir Charles himself denounced the style as practiced in California. See the Eastlake Inn.

QUEEN ANNE 1880-1900: Derived from the works of important British architect Richard Norman Shaw, this style featured a more fluid, often asymmetric expression of architectural elements. It often included one or more round towers, elaborate shingle work, and ornament drawn from many different architectural antecedents. Its relationship to Queen Anne herself is vague at best: the architecture produced during her reign (1702-14) was in the Renaissance style. See the Morgan residence at Heritage Square.

EXOTIC REVIVALS 1830-1930

SECOND EMPIRE 1852-1870: A variation of French influence, this style derives from those popularized in France during the reign of Napoleon III. Signature features include the use of a Mansard roof. See the Shaw Residence at Heritage Square.

CHÂTEAUESQUE 1860s-1910: As the Queen Anne style matured, variations on château motifs transformed that style into a more stately expression. Examples include the Bernard and Lane residences.

EGYPTIAN REVIVAL 1830-1850 AND 1920-1930: This style first emerged in response to Napoleon's Egyptian Campaign of 1798. Later, in the 1920s, following the discovery of King Tut's tomb, Egyptian forms once again found architectural expression. In Los Angeles, the Shatto Monument in Rosedale Cemetery resulted from this second revival, as did the Nishi Hongwonji Buddhist Temple in Little Tokyo.

ROMANESQUE REVIVAL 1870-1900: Romanesque forms were given a new "spin" in Boston by a gifted practitioner, the Beaux Arts-trained Henry Hobson Richardson, around 1870. Since that time, nearly every building that has a Romanesque arch is considered Richardsonian; but there are a few wonderful buildings in Los Angeles that seem to recognize the difference between California's climate and that of Boston. These probably should be called California Romanesque. A classic example is the Stimson Residence. On a larger scale, see the exterior of the Bradbury Building.

MISSION REVIVAL 1890-1912: Considered ill-fated by some, this style originated in restatements of the few meager themes explored by the Mission designers, hence the name. Ultimately reduced to a decorated box with a ubiquitous but elaborate parapet called an *espadaña*, the style derived from limited artistic and aesthetic resources that were easily exhausted. In very creative hands, the style may be seen as a forerunner of modernism and the International Style, but most often the Mission Revival style was simply prosaic and dead-ended. It had some interesting, if odd flirtations with both the Queen Anne and Craftsman styles, producing some very odd buildings. The best example in Los Angeles may be the Pomeroy Powers Residence.

SPANISH COLONIAL REVIVAL 1915-1930: A successor to the failed Mission Revival style, and most likely the single style for which Southern California is best known—and some feel best-suited—this style owes its revival to the Panama-California Exposition of 1915 held in San Diego, and the talents of Bertram Goodhue, who helped popularize the style. Those very same Spanish Colonial buildings that were first built in California were now being built again, but this time they drew on the full spectrum of romantic Spanish Renaissance architecture. Many consider the Spanish Colonial Revival style to be simply another variation of the "decorated stucco box" school of architecture for which the state is famous. In many ways, that is true. Among the "decorations" of this style are elaborate carvings or castings, usually around doorways or windows, often referred to as *Churrigueresque* for the Spaniard José de Churriguera (1650-1725) who developed this distinctive style. Occasionally one will see the term *Plateresque*, which refers to similar detailing on buildings inspired by Portuguese architecture. The best example of the Spanish Colonial Revival style in Los Angeles may be St. Vincent de Paul Church.

SECOND GOTHIC REVIVAL 1895-1925: In order to recognize this later period, one must recall that the Gothic period of art and architecture extended from the twelfth to the fifteenth century. An early Gothic Revival period occurred between the years 1830 and 1890. The main contribution of Gothic architecture was the pointed arch, which gave buildings an exaggerated sense of height; this is an architectural trick that is still used today. This style was very popular with churches, schools, and hotels of the period. The latest Los Angeles monument in the style is the United Artists Theater.

COLONIAL REVIVAL 1890-1915: This was a phase of late nineteenth-century architecture that revived Georgian plans and forms. An example is the Camp Drum Officers' Quarters. Relating to both the Queen Anne and Shingle styles, the Colonial Revival was stimulated by the Philadelphia Centennial of 1876, which reminded America of her roots. A hybrid "Queen Anne with Colonial Revival detailing" seems to have emerged as a style of its own in Los Angeles.

TUDOR REVIVAL 1900-1925: Another style named for English royalty (in this case the dynasty that reigned during the sixteenth century), Tudor architecture featured, among other details, the extensive use of half-timbering. Revived at the turn of the century, and sometimes relating to Craftsman buildings, the style has proven remarkably durable. "Villa Maria" is a large-scale version of a Tudor Revival residence.

NEOCLASSICAL
1860-1900

A later version of Beaux Arts, which included Edwardian and Renaissance Revival forms, these buildings were expansive, calm, and nostalgic. Major public buildings, as well as large homes for the very rich, were built during this period. These academic designs were often based upon Neoclassical forms. See Giannini Place.

CHICAGO STYLE
1875-1920

This refers to an architectural style originating in Chicago and credited with the development of the steel frame, which subsequently led to the development of the skyscraper. Exterior expression moved toward functionalism and away from historicist modes. Foremost practitioners of the style included Daniel Burnham, Louis Sullivan, and Frank Lloyd Wright. See the Security Trust and Savings Bank.

SHINGLE STYLE
1880-1900

A truly American style, evolving out of the Queen Anne and including some borrowing from England and Japan, the Shingle Style, with its calm broad eaves, horizontal emphasis, and elaborate, dominating roof forms, is a rare style that has never become dated. Early Frank Lloyd Wright homes are in this style, as is the Gilbert Residence on Alvarado Terrace. It is as appropriate a residential style today as it ever has been. These buildings were invariably covered with shingles, hence the name.

BEAUX ARTS
1890-1920

This style is named for the Parisian architectural school, the Ecole des Beaux Arts—which was founded in the seventeenth century during the reign of Louis XIV—that educated California's first generation of trained architects, beginning in the late nineteenth century. Because it emphasizes the logic of plan as an expression of the exterior and is characterized by a careful avoidance of mixed architectural styles on the exterior, some feel that the Beaux Arts style paved the way for early modernism. The style was easily adapted to the design of large commercial buildings. Elaborate at the base for pedestrian appeal, and at the top for visibility and prestige, this style became archetypal for commercial buildings in America. The Irvine/Byrne Building and the Farmers and Merchants Bank are early examples of this style. These buildings and institutions featured grand staircases, monumental arched openings, and sculptural figures—all of which were toned-down for residential versions of the Beaux Arts style, as in the Guasti Residence, for example.

CRAFTSMAN
OR BUNGALOW
1895-1920

This style derives from the bungalow form, which can be traced to India during the British colonial period. The term usually describes one-story homes surrounded by porches. Combined with William Morris's English Arts and Crafts philosophy, which feared the loss of human values through mechanization, an entire movement sprang up around the idea of hand-fashioning one's own environment. California proved to be fertile ground for this movement, and many of the Los Angeles monuments in this style were built by hand by their owners. See the Dalton Residence in Part IV. at 100 55th Street.

PRAIRIE SCHOOL
1900-1920

Related to the early work of Frank Lloyd Wright, this style may be described as sort of an "evolved" or free-style Edwardian. It is considered to be an indigenous American style, and the architects working in it consciously rejected the academic revival styles and sought to create something reflective of the rolling terrain where these structures were built. They were often concerned with symmetric masonry masses and large, overhanging roofs, usually flat or hipped. Tall casement windows and ornament associated with Louis Sullivan were additional characteristics. The achievements of this style are of international significance. The Prairie School formed the philosophical base for the modern movement. Sadly, the American preference for living in new buildings patterned in exotic and historical modes, instead of in the rationalistic buildings being developed, stalled this important movement in its infancy. See the Highland Park Ebell Club.

INTERNATIONAL STYLE
1920-1945

The style was named by Philip Johnson and Henry-Russell Hitchcock in their groundbreaking exhibition, The International Style, Architecture Since 1922. It is characterized by rationalism and a "machine aesthetic" generated by the progressive Bauhaus architectural school in Germany, which hoped to provide buildings for the masses. It spread throughout Europe with the works of architects Le Corbusier, Walter Gropius, and Ludwig Mies van der Rohe. One of America's most famous buildings in the style is Richard Neutra's Lovell Health House; another is Rudolf Schindler's Lovell Beach House. For many, this failed search for affordable housing exemplifies the failure of the style, and the search continues.

ART DECO
1925-1940

Described by one wit as "the International Style in drag," this style does embody many of the characteristics traditionally associated with the "machine-for-living" aesthetic. But because this style was more decorative, it was consequently more approachable. Originating with the 1925 Exposition Internationale des Arts Décoratifs et Industriels Modernes in Paris, the style took Los Angeles by storm. Some examples convey their European roots, such as the Oviatt Building, while others seem to have a distinct American sensibility. Variations of the style include Zigzag Moderne, Streamline Moderne, and Classical Moderne (See I. Magnin). WPA and PWA Moderne were governmental variations on the style produced by civil-servant architects in the Works Progress or the Public Works administrations. Another variation of Art Deco, in the West, is the American Perpendicular, a style that seems to be almost unique to, and highly visible in, downtown Los Angeles. Its vertical, terra-cotta covered columns present a distinct contrast to the earlier horizontal bays created by Beaux Arts buildings. Together, this exchange of vertical and horizontal forms defines a very unusual streetscape on streets like Broadway or Spring.

PROGRAMMATIC ARCHITECTURE 1920s TO THE PRESENT

This style may be characterized by buildings that were intended to resemble that which was being offered within. They are giant cartoons on the landscape, and memorable examples include the Giant Bagel Shop, which indeed resembled a giant bagel; the old Windmill that used to imply a farm at the Farmer's Market; or the Tail O' the Pup stand (relocated, but extant), which purveys hot dogs. Added to this list might be the redoubtable Brown Derby, which was not a hat shop but did proffer expensive food in a dressy atmosphere. Its loss was a dark moment in Los Angeles preservation history. See the Darkroom, a Los Angeles monument.

PICTURESQUE, ECLECTIC, OR PERIOD REVIVALS 1930 TO THE PRESENT

The continuing fashion for the reproduction of historic building styles is evidence of an eclectic spirit, which is willing to accept illusion at the expense of reality. Georgian, Tudor, Norman, Mediterranean, Meso-American, and Native American homes, apartment buildings, theaters, and shops have all been commissioned, designed, built, and loved by Americans. Contemporary Period Revival buildings are an American architectural phenomenon that has occurred outside the recognized progression of world architecture. Cut-rate reminders of the style are being built today in suburban areas of most large American cities. Los Angeles's position as the home of the illusion factory may allow somewhat more leeway for this style; irrelevant as it may be to the history of architecture, its excesses are at least more easily understood when seen as creations of those in the illusion business. See the Heinsbergen Studio.

LEADING LOS ANGELES ARCHITECTS AND FIRMS

AIN, GREGORY (1908–1988): Ain studied at the University of Southern California but did not graduate. He apprenticed in the offices of both Schindler and Neutra. Devoted to inexpensive housing, Ain won many prestigious awards in this field. His most famous project is the Dunsmuir Apartments in Baldwin Hills. Two of his projects are Historic-Cultural Monuments, and he is considered a member of the "Los Angeles School," along with Neutra, Schindler, and Soriano.

ALLISON, JAMES E. (1870–1955) AND DAVID C. (1881–1962): Their best-known works include the First Congregational, the Thirteenth Christian Scientist, the First Unitarian, the Wilshire United Methodist, and the First Baptist churches; the Wilshire Temple; the Irving Branch Library; and several buildings at the University of California at Los Angeles.

AUSTIN, JOHN C. W. (1870–1937) Austin arrived in Los Angeles in 1892 from England. His best-known works include the Griffith Observatory and the Arroyo Seco Bank. On his own, or in partnerships, Austin was also responsible for the Higgins (Verbeck) Residence, the Hollywood Masonic Temple, City Hall, and the Shrine Auditorium.

BECKET, WELTON (1902–1969): Becket founded a partnership in 1933 with Walter Wurdeman and Charles F. Plummer (Young's Market). Their best-known project was the Pan-Pacific Auditorium. Becket formed his own firm in 1949, and it became one of the largest in the United States, with offices throughout the country. Known for projects such as Capitol Records, the Los Angeles Music Center, and the Master Plan for Century City, the firm continues today as Ellerbee-Becket.

BEELMAN, CLAUDE (1889–1963): Beelman established a partnership with Alexander Curlett (1919) and designed some of Los Angeles's most prestigious buildings, including the Eastern-Columbia, Garfield, Roosevelt, and Barker Brothers buildings, and the Elks Temple.

BRYANT, LELAND (1891–1954): After a career designing eclectic apartment buildings like the Afton Arms, he dazzled Los Angeles with his brilliant Art Deco masterpiece, the Sunset Towers (today the St. James Club).

COATE, ROLAND E. (1890–1958): Born in Indiana and educated at Cornell University—whose architectural courses were based on those of the Ecole des Beaux Arts—Coate apprenticed in the prestigious office of Trowbridge and Livingstone in New York. He formed a brief partnership with period revivalists Reginald Johnson and Gordon Kaufmann in 1921. His best-known project from that collaboration was St. Paul's Episcopal Cathedral in Los Angeles (demolished). On his own he designed homes for many people from the movie colony, including David Selznik, Gary Cooper, and Frank Capra.

CURLETT, ALEXANDER (1880–1942): A second-generation architect (he was the son of William Curlett, 1846-1914), the younger Curlett practiced with his father before relocating to Southern California and forming a partnership with Claude Beelman.

EAMES, CHARLES (1907–1978): Born in St. Louis, Eames attained prominence with his wife, Ray, in furniture design and architecture, although he was not licensed. His most famous building is his own home and studio complex in Pacific Palisades. He collaborated with Saarinen on the adjacent Entenza Residence.

EISEN, THEODORE (1852–1924): Eisen arrived in California in 1854 from Cincinnati. He first went to San Francisco, then Los Angeles. He formed many partnerships including one with Sumner Hunt.

FARQUHAR, ROBERT D. (1872–1968): Farquhar graduated from Pascal's atelier at the Ecole des Beaux Arts in 1901, and he also studied at the Massachusetts Institute of Technology. He executed brilliant late Beaux Arts designs, including the California Club, the Canfield-Moreno compound, the Clark Library, and the Clark Mausoleum at the Hollywood Cemetery.

GILL, IRVING (1870–1936): The son of a Syracuse building contractor, Gill received no formal architectural training but apprenticed in the Chicago office of Adler and Sullivan. Unique among his peers, Gill was a hands-on designer and contractor who personally built his often experimental designs. He is best known for his legendary Dodge House (demolished), considered by architectural critics as one of America's best. He worked through the Mission Revival style to become a forerunner of the modern period.

GOODHUE, BERTRAM (1869–1924): Connecticut born, Goodhue apprenticed for the noted New York ecclesiastic architect James Renwick. He learned his classicism in apprenticeship under—and later in partnership with—Ralph Adam Cram, another noted ecclesiastic architect. Goodhue produced many important works, but he is best known for his pioneering Nebraska State House and the Fine Arts and California State Buildings at the 1915 Panama-California Exposition in San Diego, which popularized Spanish Colonial Revival architecture. Goodhue also designed the Los Angeles Main Library.

GREENE, CHARLES SUMNER (1868–1957); AND HENRY MATHER (1870–1954): These brothers studied at the Massachusetts Institute of Technology and practiced together in Pasadena and Los Angeles between 1894 and 1922. Their most famous project was the Gamble Residence in Pasadena. The work of the Greenes is marked by the ideals of the Arts and Crafts movement

HARVEY, EDWARD ARTHUR (?): Known primarily for his historicist apartment buildings and his later Art Deco works, Harvey designed both the Villa Carlotta and the Château Elysée, as well as the Selig Building.

HUNT, SUMNER P. (1865–1938): Hunt arrived from Brooklyn in 1889. In partnership with Theodore Eisen, he designed the Froebel Institute, the Irvine/Byrne Building, and the Owens and Posey residences. Hunt joined with A. Wesley Eager to design the Kinney, Raphael, Arthur Bent, and Phillips residences. In 1908 he formed a partnership with Silas Burns; their projects included the Southwest Museum (1912 and 1920), the Wilshire Ebell Club (1913), the H. Stanley Bent and McKinley residences, the Southern California Automobile Club, and the Highland Park Ebell Club.

JOHNSON, REGINALD (1882–1952): Born to wealth and privilege, Johnson studied in Paris (but not at the Beaux Arts) and at Williams College. He apprenticed in the office of Myron Hunt and Elmer Grey. In 1912 he launched his own Period Revival practice. Johnson created several significant projects in Southern California, beginning with St. Paul's Cathedral (demolished) with Kaufmann and Coate. His own designs include several homes for various heirs to the Baldwin fortune, the Santa Barbara Biltmore, La Valencia Hotel in La Jolla, and St. Savior's Chapel (relocated to Studio City). His most significant Los Angeles project was Baldwin Hills Village.

KAUFMANN, GORDON B. (1888–1949): Kaufmann began as a Los Angeles Period Revival architect ("Greystone," St. Vincent's Hospital), but he went on to create many of the seminal monuments of American modernism, including the Hoover and Grande Coulee dams and the Los Angeles Times Building. He did the master planning for Scripps College, as well as eleven individual buildings for that campus.

KELHAM, GEORGE W. (1871–1936): Kelham studied at Harvard and the Ecole des Beaux Arts. He came to California as an employee of a New York firm to rebuild the Palace Hotel in San Francisco and stayed on to form his own practice. He was responsible for the Standard Oil buildings in both San Francisco and Los Angeles. Later, Kelham was the master planner for the University of California at Los Angeles but was replaced in this position by the firm of Allison and Allison.

KYSOR, EZRA F. (1835–1907): New York born, Kysor arrived in California in 1860 and in Los Angeles in 1868. His early association with W. J. Mathews produced St. Vibiana's Roman Catholic Cathedral in 1861. Later he worked with E. J. Weston and in 1876 with Octavius Morgan. His early and important works, executed with Morgan, include the Pico House hotel, Widney Hall at the University of Southern California, and several buildings that have since been demolished, including the Fort Street Methodist Church and the McDonald and Cardona buildings. He did some alterations to Queen of the Angels Church on the old Plaza and designed the Perry Residence at Heritage Square.

LANSBURGH, G. ALBERT (1876–1969): Lansburgh graduated from Pascal's atelier at the Ecole des Beaux Arts in 1906. He was a San Francisco-based theater-interior designer whose major San Francisco commission was the Opera House. In Los Angeles he designed several projects, including the interiors of the Shrine Auditorium and the Orpheum and El Capitan theaters.

LAUTNER, JOHN E (b. 1911): Lautner apprenticed for six years with Frank Lloyd Wright. He arrived in California in the late 1930s. His first major successes were the Chemosphere House (1960), which demonstrated what to do with unbuildable sites, and Silvertop in Silver Lake, an enormous private residence in the curvilinear style, which relied on gadgets and labor-saving devices. He also designed the Bob Hope Residence in Palm Springs. His Los Angeles Historic-Cultural Monuments include the Sheets Apartments, the Mauer Residence, and the Los Feliz School.

LEE, S. CHARLES (1899–1990): Lee designed over four hundred theaters, including several in Los Angeles. The styles in which he worked range from High Baroque Eclectic to Moderne. Among his major works are the Los Angeles, Bruin, and La Riena theaters. Lee also created the Hollywood Western Building and the Municipal Light, Water and Power building on Daly Street, both of which are Historic-Cultural Monuments.

MARTIN, ALBERT CAREY, JR. (b. 1913): Martin practiced in the firm founded in 1906 by his father that continues to this day. Socially prominent and very successful, the firm boasts some of the best commissions from each of the last several decades. Its early, important works include St. Vincent de Paul Church, the Los Angeles City Hall, the May Company building on Wilshire, and the Department of Water and Power opposite the Music Center.

MORGAN, JULIA (1872–1957): The first woman to graduate in engineering from the University of California, Morgan was also the first woman to graduate in architecture from the Ecole des Beaux Arts in the atelier of Chaussemiche, and she was the first woman architect licensed in California. Morgan completed over seven hundred projects, including numerous buildings for both William Randolph Hearst and the YWCA.

MORGAN, WALLS, AND CLEMENTS [OCTAVIUS MORGAN, J. A. WALLS, STILES O. CLEMENTS, AND LATER O. W. MORGAN, JR.]: Octavius Morgan, Sr. (1850–1922) was from Canterbury, England. He arrived in California in 1874 and formed a partnership with Ezra Kysor, with whom he is usually credited for St. Vibiana's Cathedral (although the case file credits W. J. Mathews). Later he developed a practice with Walls, and still later, he included his son O. W. Morgan. With Walls, Morgan built the Farmers and Merchants Bank, the Van Nuys Hotel, the Bank of Italy, the Title Insurance Company Building, and the Pantages Theater Building on Broadway. When Clements—a prolific designer in the Moderne style—was brought into the firm, he gave it new direction. With him, the partnership produced the 1928 black and gold Richfield Tower (demolished), and they are credited with the development of shopping centers and drive-in supermarkets. Among their important buildings are the Oddfellows Temple; the Vagabond Theater and La Fonda Restaurant Building; the El Capitan,

Belasco, and Mayan theaters; the Pacific National Bank; the Chapman Park Studios and Chapman Park Market; the Pellisier Building; and the Chouinard Art Institute. The junior Morgan's Spanish style home on South Alta Vista is also a Historic-Cultural Monument.

NEUTRA, RICHARD (1892–1970): Born in Vienna, Neutra graduated from the Technical Institute in 1917. He met the pioneer rationalist Adolf Loos and discovered the works of Frank Lloyd Wright, and both influenced Neutra significantly. He apprenticed briefly with Erich Mendelsohn before immigrating to Chicago in 1923 and Los Angeles in 1925. In Los Angeles he worked briefly with Schindler, and then on his own. His most famous building is the Lovell Health House, and other projects include the (demolished) Von Sternberg and Kaufmann (Palm Springs) houses; the Jardinette, Landfair, Kelton, and Elkay apartment buildings; and the Eagle Rock Clubhouse.

NEWSOM, JOSEPH CATHER (1858–1930): Newsom, a Canadian, arrived in California with his brother, Samuel, in about 1855. Samuel maintained a Northern California practice (1870-1907), while Joseph opened offices in Los Angeles. Joseph popularized his California ideas in several large Victorian-era homes in Los Angeles—most notably, the Charles Sessions Residence, the Residence at 1407 Carroll Avenue, the Morgan (Hale) Residence at Heritage Square, the Lewis Residence at 1425 Miramar, and the Fitzgerald Residence.

PARKINSON, JOHN (1861–1935) AND DONALD (1895-1945): The senior Parkinson was English and immigrated to Los Angeles in 1894 where he established a practice. In 1905 he joined Edwin Bergstrom in a partnership that was terminated in 1915. Together they produced the Los Angeles Athletic Club, the Alexandria Hotel, and the Pacific Mutual Building. In 1920, John Parkinson teamed with his son, Donald, to produce the Title Insurance Building, the Title Guarantee Building, and the legendary Bullock's Wilshire. Collaborations with other firms saw this father-and-son team involved with City Hall, Union Station, and the Stock Exchange Building.

ROEHRIG, FREDERICK L. (1857–1948): Roehrig worked in many styles: the Eddy Residence and Castle Green in Pasadena were in the Craftsman style. The Rindge Residence was built in the Châteauesque style, while the Durfee Residence was Tudor Revival.

SAARINEN, EERO (1910–1961): A Finnish-born, second-generation architect, Saarinen studied at the Academie de la Grande Chaumière in Paris and at Harvard. In 1948 he won the St. Louis Arch competition with his father, which brought international recognition. His best-known buildings include the TWA Terminal at Kennedy Airport in New York and the Dulles Airport in Washington, D.C. He also designed furniture, including a 1940 plywood chair with Charles Eames. Saarinen's only Los Angeles project was the Entenza Residence with Charles Eames.

SCHINDLER, RUDOLF (1887–1953): Schindler was an Austrian émigré, educated at both Vienna's Technical Institute and Academy of Arts. He apprenticed with Frank Lloyd Wright in both Chicago and California. He built an experimental home and studio duplex for himself on Kings Road in Los Angeles, which became a legendary gathering place for intellectuals in the 1920s. Schindler's most famous work is the Lovell Beach House. His Historic-Cultural Monuments in Los Angeles include the Buck and Tischler residences.

SORIANO, RAPHAEL (1907–1988): Soriano was born on the island of Rhodes. He was influenced by Mies's work but based his own designs on available building techniques and hand-crafted components. He built the first steel Case Study House. His house for architectural photographer Julius Schulman is a Historic-Cultural Monument.

WILLIAMS, PAUL REVERE (1894–1980): Orphaned at age three, and overcoming a childhood of poverty and discrimination, Williams was educated at the University of Southern California and the Beaux Arts Institute of New York. He was registered as an architect in 1915 and then apprenticed with Reginald Johnson and John Austin. Williams formed his own, very successful Period Revival practice in 1923. Fame and fortune ensued, as he became the "architect to the stars." Toward the end of his career, he was associated with more mainstream contemporary architecture. His own home is a Historic-Cultural Monument.

WRIGHT, FRANK LLOYD (1867–1959): Born in Wisconsin of Welsh parentage and educated at the University of Wisconsin (for two years), Wright left school to apprentice in the Chicago office of Louis Sullivan. He formed a practice that would span more than six decades and several architectural styles and periods. Wright is considered America's most important architect. His best-known works include the Guggenheim Museum, the "Fallingwater" house, and the Johnson Wax Building, but he was also known for residential works in the Shingle and Prairie styles, and later "modern" (Wrightian) styles. The Barnsdall, Storer, Freeman, and Ennis homes are Los Angeles Historic-Cultural Monuments. Other buildings in Southern California by Wright include the Stewart, Sturges, Oboler, Milliard, and Pearce residences; Anderton Court in Beverly Hills; and the Kundert Clinic in San Luis Obispo.

WRIGHT, LLOYD (1890–1978): Born in Oak Park, Illinois, the eldest son of architect Frank Lloyd Wright, the younger Wright studied landscape architecture in the Olmsted office. He relocated to Southern California, where he assisted his father. He began his own architectural practice in the 1920s with the Bollman houses. He is best known for the Hollywood Bowl, the Wayfarer's Chapel, and the Sowden house.

SELECTED BIBLIOGRAPHY

BOOKS:

Anger, Kenneth. *Hollywood Babylon*. New York: Dell, 1981.

Applebaum, Stanley. *The Chicago World's Fair of 1893*. New York: Dover, 1980.

Armor, John, and Wright, Peter. *Manzanar*. New York: Vintage, 1989.

Banham, Reyner. *Los Angeles, The Architecture of Four Ecologies*. London: Penguin, 1971.

Beck, Warren A., and Haase, Ynez D. *Historical Atlas of California*. Norman: University of Oklahoma Press, 1974.

Bixby-Smith, Sarah. *Adobe Days, A Book of California Memories*. Cedar Rapids, Iowa: Torch Press, 1925.

Blumenson, John J. *Identifying American Architecture, A Pictorial Guide to Styles and Terms, 1600-1945*. New York: W. W. Norton, 1977.

Boutelle, Sarah. *Julia Morgan, Architect*. New York: Abbeville Press, 1988.

Bradbury, Ray. *Los Angeles*. Los Angeles: Oxford University Press, 1984.

Breeze, Carla. *LA Deco*. New York: Rizzoli, 1991.

Burchard, John, and Bush-Brown, Albert. *The Architecture of America*. Boston: Little, Brown, 1961.

Cameron, David, and Owen, Tom, eds. *Historic-Cultural Monuments*. Los Angeles: City of Los Angeles Cultural Affairs Department, 1987.

Carmody, John M. *Los Angeles, A Guide to the City and Its Environs*. New York: Hastings House, 1941.

Carr, Harry. *Los Angeles, City of Dreams*. New York: Appleton, 1935.

Caughey, John and LaRee. *Los Angeles, Biography of a City*. Berkeley: University of California Press, 1977.

Dana, Richard Henry, Jr. *Two Years Before the Mast*. New York: New American Library, 1964.

Delehanty, Randolph. *In the Victorian Style*. San Francisco: Chronicle Books, 1991.

———. *Preserving the West*. New York: Pantheon, 1985.

DeMarco, Gordon. *A Short History of Los Angeles*. San Francisco: Lexikos, 1988.

Didion, Joan. *Slouching Towards Bethlehem*. New York: Washington Square Press, 1968.

Eisen, Jonathan, and Fine, David, with Eisen, Kim. *Unknown California*. New York: Macmillan, 1985.

Elder, Sandra, ed. *California Historical Landmarks*. Sacramento: California Department of Parks and Recreation, 1990.

Fleming, John; Honour, Hugh; and Pevsner, Nikolaus. *The Penguin Dictionary of Architecture*. London: Penguin, 1991 (fourth ed.).

Fogelson, Robert M. *The Fragmented Metropolis, Los Angeles, 1850-1930*. Berkeley: University of California Press, 1993 (first ed. 1967).

Gaines, Stephen. *Behind the Facade*. London: Ariel Books, 1985.

Gebhard, David, and Von Breton, Hariette. *Los Angeles in the Thirties, 1931-1941*. Los Angeles: Hennessey & Ingalls, 1989.

Gebhard, David, and Winter, Robert. *Architecture in Los Angeles, A Compleat Guide*. Salt Lake City: Peregrine Smith, 1985.

———. *A Guide to Architecture in Southern California*. Los Angeles County Museum of Art, 1965.

Gill, Brendan. *Many Masks, A Life of Frank Lloyd Wright*. New York: Putnam, 1987.

Gleye, Paul, with the Los Angeles Conservancy. *The Architecture of Los Angeles*. Los Angeles: Rosebud Books, 1981.

Halpern, John. *Los Angeles, Improbable City*. New York: Dutton, 1979.

Hamilton-Smith, Katherine (Introduction). *Curious Architecture*. Washington, D.C.: Preservation Press, 1991.

Hamlin, Talbot. *Architecture Through the Ages*. New York: Putnam, 1940.

Haneman, John Theodore. *Pictorial Encyclopedia of Historic Architectural Plans, Details and Elements*. New York: Dover, 1984.

Harris, Cyril M. *Illustrated Dictionary of Historic Architecture*. New York: Dover, 1977.

Hine, Robert V. *California's Utopianism, Contemplations of Eden*. San Francisco: Boyd & Fraser, 1981.

Hines, Thomas. *Burnham of Chicago, Architect and Planner*. Chicago: University of Chicago Press, 1974.

———. *Richard Neutra and the Search for Modern Architecture*. New York: Oxford University Press, 1982.

Hitchcock, Henry-Russell. *Architecture: Nineteenth and Twentieth Centuries*. Baltimore: Penguin, 1958.

Hoover, Mildred Brooke; Rensch, Hero Eugene; Rensch, Ethel Grace; and Abeloe, William N. *Historic Spots in California*. Stanford, California: Stanford University Press, 1990 (fourth ed., revised by Douglas E. Kyle).

Howard, Hugh. *How Old Is This House?* New York: Farrar, Straus & Giroux, 1989.

Huxtable, Ada Louise. *Goodbye History, Hello Hamburger*. Washington, D.C.: Preservation Press, 1986.

Jackson, Helen Hunt. *Ramona*. New York: New American Library, 1988 (first ed. 1884).

Jordan, Robert Furneaux. *Victorian Architecture*. Baltimore: Penguin, 1966.

Jordy, William H. *American Buildings and Their Architects, Progressive and Academic Ideals at the Turn of the Century*. New York: Anchor, 1976.

Kalman, Harold. *The Evaluation of Historic Buildings, A Manual*. Ottawa: Canadian Government Printing Office, 1978.

Kaplan, Samuel Hall. *LA Lost & Found*. New York: Crown, 1987.

Katz, Ephraim. *The Film Encyclopedia*. New York: Harper & Row, 1990.

Kidney, Walter C. *The Architecture of Choice: Eclecticism in America, 1880-1930*. New York: Braziller, 1974.

Kirker, Harold. *California's Architectural Frontier, Styles and Tradition in the Nineteenth Century*. Salt Lake City: Peregrine Smith, 1986 (reprint).

————. *Old Forms on a New Land, California Architecture in Perspective*. Niwot, Colorado: Roberts Rinehart, 1991.

Klein, Marylin W., and Fogle, David P. *A Clue to American Architecture*. Washington, D.C.: Starhill Press, 1986.

Knowland, Joseph. *California, A Landmark Story of Preservation and Marking of Early Day Shrines*. Oakland, California: Tribune Press, 1941.

Kostof, Spiro, ed. *The Architect, Chapters in the History of the Profession*. New York: Oxford University Press, 1977.

Krell, Dorothy, ed. *The California Missions, A Pictorial History*. Menlo Park, California: Sunset Publishing, 1991.

Lampugnani, Vittorio Magnago, ed. *Encyclopedia of 20th-Century Architecture*. New York: Abrams, 1986 (revised ed.).

Landau, Robert, and Pashdag, John. *Outrageous L.A.* San Francisco: Chronicle Books, 1984.

Lewis, Oscar. *Here Lived Californians*. New York: Rinehart, 1957.

Logan, William Bryant, and Ochshorn, Susan. *The Smithsonian Guide to Historic America—The Pacific States*. New York: Stewart, Taibori & Chang, 1989.

Longstreet, Stephen. *All Star Cast, An Anecdotal History of Los Angeles*. New York: Crowell, 1977.

Longstreth, Richard. *On the Edge of the World*. Cambridge, Massachusetts: MIT Press, 1989.

Los Angeles 2000 Committee (James P. Miscoll, Chairman). *Los Angeles 2000, A City for the Future*. Final Report of the Los Angeles 2000 Committee, 1988.

Maddex, Diane, ed. *All About Old Buildings, The Whole Preservation Catalog*. Washington, D.C.: Preservation Press, 1985.

————. *Landmark Yellow Pages*. Washington, D.C.: Preservation Press, 1990.

————. *With Heritage So Rich*. Washington, D.C.: Preservation Press, 1983.

Mallan, Chiki. *Guide to Catalina and California's Channel Islands*. Chico, California: Moon Publications, 1989.

McAlester, Virginia and Lee. *A Field Guide to American Houses*. New York: Knopf, 1991.

McClure, James D. *California Landmarks, A Photographic Guide to the State's Historic Spots*. Stanford, California: Stanford University Press, 1948.

McCoy, Esther. *Five California Architects*. Los Angeles: Hennessey & Ingalls, 1987.

————. *Richard Neutra*. New York: Braziller, 1960.

————. *The Second Generation*. Salt Lake City: Peregrine Smith, 1984.

————. *Vienna to Los Angeles: Two Journeys*. Santa Monica, California: Arts and Architecture Press, 1979.

McNeill, Morris, Inc. *The Los Angeles Cultural Master Plan*. Submitted to The City of Los Angeles Cultural Affairs Department, November, 1990.

McWilams, Carey. *Southern California, An Island on the Land*. Salt Lake City: Peregrine Smith, 1983.

Miller, John, ed. *Los Angeles Stories, Great Writers on the City*. San Francisco: Chronicle Books, 1991.

Moore, Charles; Becker, Peter; and Campbell, Regula. *Los Angeles, The City Observed*. New York: Random House, 1984.

Murtagh, William J. *Keeping Time, The History and Theory of Preservation in America*. New York: Sterling, 1990.

Naylor, David. *American Picture Palaces, The Architecture of Fantasy*. New York: Prentice Hall, 1981.

Neuenburg, Evelyn. *California Lure. . .The Golden State in Pictures*. Pasadena, California: California Lure Publishers, 1946.

Neutra, Richard. *Survival Through Design*. New York: Oxford University Press, 1954.

Newcomb, Rexford. *Franciscan Mission Architecture of California*. New York: Dover, 1973.

————. *Spanish-Colonial Architecture in the United States*. New York: Dover, 1990.

Newland, Joseph N., ed. *Johnson, Kaufmann, Coate, Partners in the California Style*. Claremont, California: Scripps College, Capra Press, 1992.

Newmark, Harris. *Sixty Years in Southern California, 1853-1913*. New York: Houghton Mifflin, 1930.

O'Donnell, Mayo Hayes (with photographs by Wynn Bullock). *Monterey's Adobe Heritage*. Monterey, California: Monterey Savings and Loan Association, 1965.

Parker, Robert Miles. *L.A.* New York: Harcourt Brace Jovanovich, 1984.

Pierson, William H., Jr. *American Buildings and Their Architects: The Colonial and Neo-Classical Styles*. New York: Doubleday, 1976.

————. *American Buildings and Their Architects, Technology and the Picturesque, the Corporate and the Early Gothic Styles*. New York: Doubleday, 1980.

Polyzoides, Stephanos; Sherwood, Roger; and Tice, James. *Courtyard Housing in Los Angeles*. New York: Princeton Architectural Press, 1992.

Popliers, John C.; Chambers, Allen; and Schwartz, Nancy B. *What Style Is It?* Washington, D.C.: Preservation Press, 1983.

Reece, Daphne. *Historic Houses of California, A Directory of Restored Historic Structures*. San Francisco: Chronicle Books, 1983.

Reid, David, ed. *Sex, Death and God in L.A.* New York: Random House, 1992.

Reiff, David. *Los Angeles: Capital of the Third World*. New York: Simon & Schuster, 1991.

Rifkind, Carole. *A Field Guide to American Architecture*. New York: New American Library, 1980.

Robinson, W. W. *Land in California*. Berkeley: University of California Press, 1948.

————. *Los Angeles, From the Days of the Pueblo*. San Francisco: California Historical Society, 1981.

Rolfe, Lionel. *Literary L.A.* San Francisco: Chronicle Books, 1981.

Rybczynski, Witold. *The Most Beautiful House in the World*. New York: Viking, 1989.

Schessler, Ken. *This Is Hollywood, An Unusual Guide*. Redlands, California: Ken Schlesser Publishing, 1991.

Service, Alastair. *Edwardian Architecture*. New York: Oxford University Press, 1977.

Shippy, Lee (with photographs by Max Yavno). *The Los Angeles Book*. Boston: Houghton Mifflin, 1950.

Sipe, Robert E., and Lee, Antoinette J. *The American Mosaic, Preserving a Nation's Heritage*. Washington, D.C.: United States Committee, International Council on Monuments and Sites, 1987.

Smith, Katherine. *Frank Lloyd Wright, Hollyhock House and Olive Hill*. New York: Rizzoli, 1992.

Starr, Kevin. *Americans and the California Dream, 1850-1915*. New York: Oxford University Press, 1973.

————. *Inventing the Dream, California Through the Progressive Era*. New York: Oxford University Press, 1985.

————. *Material Dreams, Southern California Through the 1920s*. New York: Oxford University Press, 1990.

Stern, Robert A. M. *Pride of Place, Building the American Dream*. Boston: Houghton Mifflin, 1986.

Stuhlmann, Gunther, ed. *The Diary of Anais Nin*. Vol. 7, 1966-1974. New York: Harcourt Brace Jovanovich, 1980.

Thomas Brothers. *Los Angeles County 1991*. Los Angeles: Thomas Brothers Maps, 1990.

Travis, Jack, ed. *African American Architects in Current Practice*. New York: Princeton Architectural Press, 1991.

Upton, Dell, ed. *America's Architectural Roots, Ethnic Groups that Built America*. Washington, D.C.: Preservation Press, 1986.

Vidal, Gore. *Hollywood, A Novel of America in the 1920s*. New York: Ballantine, 1990.

Walker, Derek. *Los Angeles, Architectural Design Profile, AD / USC Look at LA*. London: St. Martin's Press, 1981.

Weber, Eva. *American Art Deco*. New York: Crescent Books, 1992.

Weitz, Karen J. *California's Mission Revival*. Los Angeles: Hennessey & Ingalls, 1984.

Wheeler, Daniel, ed. *The Chateaux of France*. New York: Vendome, 1979.

Whiffen, Marcus. *American Architecture Since 1780: A Guide to the Styles*. Cambridge, Massachusetts: MIT Press, 1992 (revised ed.).

Williams, Henry Lionel and Ottalie. *A Guide to Old American Houses, 1700-1900*. New York: A. S. Barnes, 1962.

Wilson, Richard Guy. *A Monograph of the Works of McKim, Mead & White*. New York: The Architectural Book Publishing Company, 1990.

Winter, Robert. *The California Bungalow*. Los Angeles: Hennessey & Ingalls, 1980.

Withey, Henry F., et al. *Biographical Dictionary of American Architects (Deceased)*. Los Angeles: New Age Publishers, 1956.

Wolfe, Tom. *From Bauhaus to Our House*. New York: Farrar, Straus & Giroux, 1981.

Woodbridge, Sally B. *California Architecture*. San Francisco: Chronicle Books, 1988.

Woollett, William. *California's Golden Age*. Santa Barbara, California: Capra Press, 1989.

Wurman, Richard Saul. *Los Angeles Access*. New York: Access Press, 1991 (fifth ed.).

Young, Stanley (with photographs by Melba Levick). *The Missions of California*. San Francisco: Chronicle Books, 1988.

Zimmerman, Scott. *A Guide to Frank Lloyd Wright's California*. Salt Lake City: Gibbs-Smith, 1992.

EXHIBITION CATALOGUES

Anderson, Timothy J.; Moore, Eudorah M.; and Winter, Robert. *California Design, 1910*. Salt Lake City: Peregrine Smith, 1980.

Belloli, Jay. *Wallace Neff 1895-1982, The Romance of Regional Architecture*. San Marino, California: Huntington Library, 1989.

Gebhard, David, and Von Breton, Hariette. *Lloyd Wright, Architect, 20th Century Architecture in an Organic Exhibition*. Santa Barbara: University of California, 1971.

Karlstrom, Paul J., and Erlich, Susan. *Turning the Tide, Early Los Angeles Modernists 1920-1956*. Santa Barbara Museum of Art, 1990.

PERIODICALS

Anderson, Thomas R. "Los Angeles in the 30s and 40s." *Antiques and Fine Arts*. October 1989.

Calls, Harry. "A New Look at the Founding of Old Los Angeles," *California Historical Quarterly*. Winter 1976.

Chase, John. "Unvernacular Vernacular, Contemporary American Consumerist Architecture." *Design Quarterly*. No. 131, 1986.

———. "Where Mission Meets Modern." *Metropolitan Home*. August 1989.

Gordon, Paul. "Your House Is History!" *Buzz Magazine*. May 1993.

Henderson, Justin. "Living by Design." *Alaska Airlines Magazine*. September 1992.

Herr, Pamela, and Spence, Mary Lee. "By the Sundown Sea: The Los Angeles Letters of Jessie Benton Frémont, 1888-1902." *California History*. Winter 1992-93.

Hines, Thomas S. "Architecture: Reconsidering Lloyd Wright." *Architectural Digest*. May 1993.

Kahrl, William. "The Politics of California Water: Owens Valley and the Los Angeles Aqueduct, 1900-1927." *California Historical Quarterly*. Volume LV, No.1, Spring 1976.

Kirker, Harold. "California Architecture and Its Relation to Contemporary Trends in Europe and America." *California Historical Quarterly*. Volume LI, No. 4, Winter 1972.

———. "The Larkin House Revisited." *California History*. March 1986.

Maher, Thomas K. "A New Beginning in Los Angeles, Frank Lloyd Wright's Hollyhock House." *Antiques and Fine Art*. August 1989.

Reiff, David. "The Real L.A. Story." *Image Magazine of the* San Francisco Examiner. October 27, 1991, p. 14.

Rodriguez, Richard. "Into L. A." *This World (San Francisco Examiner)*. October 11, 1992, p. 8.

Sachner, Paul M. "Hollywood Comeback, Restoration of the El Capitan Theater." *Architectural Record*. January 1992.

Schindler, Pauline, "The Samuel House." *Architectural Record*. June 1930.

Snyder, John W. "Buildings and Bridges for the 20th Century." *California History*. Fall 1984.

Viladas, Pilar. "Wright in Hollywood." *House and Garden*. February 1990.

Weinstein, Robert A. "Santa Catalina: Island Jewel." *California Historical Quarterly*. Volume LI, No. 3, Fall 1972.

NEWSPAPERS

Los Angeles Times:

Corwin, Miles. "City to Consider Tougher Law on Historic Structures." December 3, 1991,
p. A1.

———. "Designing Without a Blueprint." January 11, 1992, p. A1.

———. "L.A.'s Faceless Landscape Due to Lax Planning, Report Says." January 1, 1992, p. A7.

Rasmussen, Cecilia. "L. A. Scene, The City Then and Now." June 15, 1992, p. B3

Ryon, Ruth. "Landmark Villa." January 4, 1993, p. B2.

———. "Zadora and Riklis Wrap up $10 Million of Work on Pickfair." January 22, 1993, p. B2.

Scheden, Laurie K. "Classic Flashbacks from Tinseltown's Boulevards." September 8, 1991, p. E12.

San Francisco Chronicle:

Associated Press. "History Society Buys Chinese Burial Shrine." January 23, 1993, p. A12.

———. "L.A. Subway Opens Its Doors Tomorrow." January 29, 1993, p. A3.

Evenson, Laura. "L.A. Area's Real Estate Takes Dive." December 21, 1992, p. A8.

Fleeman, Michael (Associated Press). "Star's Party Raises Million for Clinton." September 7, 1982, p. A1.

Garcia, Kenneth J. "After Years of Boom, Los Angeles Hits Skids." December 21, 1992, p. A1.

INDEX